LU XUN

SELECTED WORKS

VOLUME THREE

Translated by
YANG XIANYI *and* GLADYS YANG

FOREIGN LANGUAGES PRESS
BEIJING

First Edition 1957
Third Edition 1980
Third Printing 2003

Home Page:
http://www.flp.com.cn
E-mail Addresses:
info@flp.com.cn
sales@flp.com.cn

ISBN 7-119-03408-1

© Foreign Languages Press, Beijing, 2003

Published by Foreign Languages Press
24 Baiwanzhuang Road, Beijing 100037, China

Distributed by China International Book Trading Corporation
35 Chegongzhuang Xilu, Beijing 100044, China
P.O. Box 399, Beijing, China

Printed in the People's Republic of China

海嬰與魯迅

一歲另三十

Lu Xun with his son, Haiying

T'ai Hsü and his son Li-ying.

CONTENTS

ILLUSTRATIONS

EDITOR'S NOTE

The essays in this volume come from the following collections: *Three Leisures, Two Hearts, Mixed Dialects, False Liberty* and *Semi-Frivolous Talk.*

Three Leisures and *Two Hearts* were published in 1932. The former includes 34 essays written between 1927 and 1929 and a list compiled in 1932 of Lu Xun's writings and translations. The latter consists of 37 essays written during 1930 and 1931. *False Liberty*, published in 1933, has 43 essays written between January and May that year. *Mixed Dialects*, published in 1934, has 50 essays written in 1932 and 1933. *Semi-Frivolous Talk*, published in 1934, contains 64 essays written between June and November of 1933.

As indicated in the table of contents, all the essays in this volume were written in the six years between 1928 and 1933. This was during the earlier part of the Second Revolutionary Civil War (1927-36) in China. The Kuomintang had betrayed the revolutionary cause, surrendered to the imperialists and imposed a reign of terror throughout the land, imprisoning and massacring progressives and attacking the people's revolution by force of arms as well as in the cultural field. As a result, the country's position became one of increasing jeopardy. In 1931 the Japanese imperialists occupied vast territories in the Northeast. In 1932 they attacked Shanghai.

During this period the demands of the Chinese people were unequivocal. They called for an end to civil war so that the whole country might unite to resist the aggressors. But this the Kuomintang reactionaries refused to do, for they represented the interests of the compradore bourgeoisie and the feudal landlords. At the instigation of the imperialists they mobilized all the counter-revolutionary forces in China in an attempt to exterminate the Communists, while at the same time they knuckled under to the enemy and yielded to all Japan's demands. As such a regime lost popular support it became more and more desperate and resorted to repressive measures: freedom of speech and of the press was suppressed, bookshops were smashed, patriots and progressives were arrested or murdered. Since Lu Xun's name was on the black list and he could not publish his work freely, he wrote many of the essays in this collection under pseudonyms.

In addition to a policy of open terror, the Kuomintang government concocted various "theories" to disguise its betrayal of the national interests and to deceive the people. Their hirelings, the "westernized gentlemen" and "scholars" launched a concerted attack on progressive writers. Some spread rumours, others acted as spies. They donned various masks and disguises, denied the class character of literature or advocated "art for art's sake" in an attempt to deceive the younger generation and turn black into white. In this way they hoped to divert attention from the real issues at stake.

This meant that to tell the truth about the Kuomintang regime, expose the real nature of the seemingly dignified "scholars" and "professors" and refute their lies as well as those of their masters became urgent tasks for progressive cultural circles at that time. This is the historical background of the essays Lu Xun wrote during these years.

It is clear from these essays that Lu Xun always took the standpoint of the people to fight against the forces of reaction. He discloses the true nature of the Kuomintang policy: "We must settle troubles at home before driving out the invaders." He attacks the terrorization against patriots. Under his pen hypocrites assume their true form and are shown up as a pack of "homeless watchdogs of the capitalists." Lu Xun says:

> No writer living in a class society can transcend class, no one living in a time of wars can leave the battlefield and stand alone, and no one living today can write for the future — this is sheer fantasy. There are no such men in real life.

He tells the truth also about the so-called "third category," the writers of "nationalist literature" who shout and clamour "like mourners and musicians at a funeral to cover up the loss of our territory," but who have no concern for their country because they too are abject slaves of the imperialists.

Heated arguments between progressive writers also took place during this period. Lu Xun joined energetically in the debate on revolutionary literature with the Creation Society and the Sun Society, as we can read in this volume. Indeed, this controversy gradually led to a serious study of literary theory and did much to introduce true revolutionary principles of literature. By the time Lu Xun wrote "My Thoughts on the League of Left-Wing Writers," a united front had been formed among progressive writers.

The great advance in Lu Xun's ideas during this period is most striking. He explains this briefly in his preface to *Two Hearts* by saying:

> While I started by simply hating my own class which I knew so well, and felt no regret over its destruction, later on the facts taught me that the future belongs solely to the rising proletariat.

Because Lu Xun attacked all social injustice and waged an uncompromising battle against reactionary and backward ideas in the fields of politics and culture, these essays are extraordinarily profound and the range of subjects is extremely wide. As this volume contains a selection only of his writings from this period it cannot fully represent his many-sided activities. For instance, he wrote numerous articles during these years on translation, but since these are hard to render into another language we have included very few of them here.

1928

BEFUDDLED WOOLLINESS*

This year — by the old calendar as well as by the new — seems to be having a strangely stimulating effect on Shanghai writers. For both lunar and solar New Year have seen a spate of new periodicals, which have lavished all their attention on big, impressive topics, not caring how deadly dull the contents are. Even magazines more than one year old are thrashing about in desperation and undergoing sudden metamorphoses. Some of the writers are new, but many of them are old acquaintances, though a number seem like strangers because they have written nothing for a year or so. What were they doing all that time, and why have they taken up their pens again simultaneously? Well, that is a long story. Suffice it to say they did not have to write then, but now they have to — they are just the same as the old, inept literati. Consciously or subconsciously, they know this, and so they are announcing to their readers that they mean to "go abroad," "shut themselves up in their studies," or else "win over the masses." Great deeds are not accomplished at a stroke, but once men come back from abroad, leave their studies or win over the masses, that is something

---

* This essay was an answer to the attack on Lu Xun early in 1928 by the Creation Society, one of the literary groups founded after the May 4th Movement of 1919. The Society's literary trend was romantic, till its members were drawn close to the revolution. Then, owing to the extreme "leftism" and sectarianism of Cheng Fangwu and other leading members, they judged Lu Xun wrongly and carried out misguided attacks on him.

15

worth watching. The far-sighted, careful, timid and opportunistic will of course be well-advised to give them a "revolutionary salute" in advance. If you delay, it may be too late.

But all these journals, however different their style, have one common characteristic — woolliness. The reason for this woolliness, to my mind — although Feng Naichao has labelled me "befuddled"* — lies in those bureaucrats and warlords loved by some and hated by others. Those connected with or eager to be connected with them seem to smile cheerily all the time as they write, to show how friendly they are. But being far-sighted too, they sometimes dream of the terrible hammer and sickle and dare not flatter their present masters too openly. This accounts for their slight woolliness. Those who have lost their connections or never had any, and who are closer to the people, ought to be able to speak without any scruples. But however heroic their tone and however hard they try to impress their readers, very few of them are fools enough to forget who has the whip hand. So they leave things rather woolly too. That is why in the same place and at the same time we see writers' colours through would-be woolliness, and would-be true colours grown unavoidably woolly.

As a matter of fact, this woolliness is immaterial. Even in the most revolutionary countries, art and literature may appear rather woolly. Revolutionaries, on the other hand, are never afraid of self-criticism. They see clearly and dare speak plainly. The only exception is China where men who, aping others, consider Tolstoy a "vulgar moralist" and admit that in "the present situation" in China "the whole society is controlled by the forces of

---

* In the first issue (January 1928) of *Cultural Critic*, a journal of the Creation Society, Feng Naichao wrote, "Lu Xun often gazes out at the world with befuddled eyes from the top floor of a dark tavern."

darkness," show not a fraction of Tolstoy's courage to "unmask the tyranny of the government or the mockery of the courts." They know the limitations of humanitarianism, yet when "men are slaughtered like grass while no protest is made," they do not even utter a humanitarian protest. Unmasking and protesting are merely "words, words, words," not "direct action." Not that I want writers to take direct action. I know quite well that writing is all they are fit for.

Unfortunately they have left it a little late. The year before last the Creation Society called for share-capital, last year they engaged a lawyer, and only this year have they raised the banner of "revolutionary literature." Now that resurrected critic Cheng Fangwu has at last stopped defending the "palace of art" in order to "win over the masses" and to "guarantee the final victory" to revolutionary writers.* Such a volte-face may be necessary. As most men of letters are sensitive, feel deeply all the time and try to save themselves from falling, they clutch at any straw like a drowning man. This is shown by the rise and fall of expressionism, dadaism and so many other "isms" since the start of the twentieth century. This is a great age, an age of fluctuations and change. In most other parts of the world class antagonisms are now intense, and the masses of peasants and workers are coming into increasing prominence. If we want to save ourselves we should go over to them. Besides, "The petty-bourgeoisie has two souls." It may join the bourgeoisie or the proletariat.

This is only just beginning to be adumbrated in China. That is why it seems so strange to us, and why we write

---

* In the article "From a Literary Revolution to a Revolutionary Literature," *Creation Monthly* (another journal of the Creation Society), 1928, Vol. I, No. 9, Cheng Fangwu wrote, "Let us rid the masses of the pernicious influence of bourgeois ideology, win over the masses, and never cease to give them courage and uphold their self-confidence! . . . In this way we can guarantee the final victory."

on such enormous subjects as "From a Literary Revolution to a Revolutionary Literature." But in highly in-
dustrialized countries where there is a clear division between rich and poor, this is a common occurrence. Some
people go over to the workers because they see that the
future belongs to them, or because they would rather
help the weak than the strong, or for a combination of
these reasons. They are actuated by fear or by their
conscience. Cheng Fangwu, who tells us to overcome our
petty-bourgeois nature, seizes hold of the "masses" as
material to be "given" or "upheld." But his article leaves
one great question in my mind:

If you could not "guarantee the final victory" would
you still go over?

This is not even as good as Li Chuli's article in *Cultural Critic*, which also came into existence this year with
Cheng Fangwu's blessing. Li is all for proletarian
literature, but thinks it need not be written by the proletariat. Whatever your class origin and your surroundings, he says, all you need do is "use proletarian consciousness to produce a militant literature." This is much
franker and jollier. But when he sees the name of that
accursed *Tatler* school, which "merely tries to be interesting," he pauses to ask Mr. Gan Ren, "To which class does
Lu Xun belong?"

My class status has already been settled by Cheng
Fangwu:

> All they care for is "leisure, leisure, and yet more
> leisure." They represent the leisured bourgeoisie, or
> the unawakened petty-bourgeoisie. . . . Unless that
> confounded miasma over Beijing is blasted away with
> a hundred thousand ounces of T.N.T., they may go on
> with this way of life for ever.

I feel most precarious now that our critic, who has just
recorded the achievements of the Creation Society, in-

cluding its "negation of the negation,"* and is going to "win over the masses," already wants "a hundred thousand ounces of T.N.T.," and seems to mean to push me into the capitalist class (for " 'leisured' means 'money-ed' "). I was a little relieved when I read Li Chuli's statement:

> In my opinion, it does not matter whether a writer belongs to the first, second . . . hundredth or thou-sandth class — he can still join the literary movement of the proletariat. But we have to examine his motives first. . . .

In my case, though, they will still want to know my class. " 'Leisured' means 'moneyed.' " Without the money I could belong to the fourth class** and "join the literary movement of the proletariat." But by then, I know, they would want to examine my motives. Anyway, the main thing is to "acquire the class outlook of the proletariat." It is not enough this time just to "win over the masses." Since we shall never get this straightened out, we had better let Li Chuli "change the weapons of art into the art of weapons," while Cheng Fangwu sits in his semi-concession amassing "a hundred thousand ounces of T.N.T.," and I go on talking about what interests me.

I am interested by Cheng Fangwu's growl: "Leisure, leisure, and yet more leisure!" For I remember my stories being criticized as "cold, cold, and cold again." Though "cold" is not a very apt criticism, I am surprised that it made such a deep impression on this revolutionary

---

* Cheng Fangwu wrote in "From a Literary Revolution to a Revolutionary Literature," If we are to shoulder the responsibility of revolutionary intellectuals, we must once more negate our-selves (negation of the negation). We must endeavour to become class-conscious, to use, as far as possible, the language of the workers and peasants. . . ."

** I.e. the proletariat. The expression was derived from the concept of three estates in France at the time of the French Revolution.

critic that he came out with three "leisures" too. Had
there been four, I could not even have produced *Anecdotes of Chinese Fiction*. Had there been only two, I
should have been more active, and might have escaped
being *ao-fu-he-bian*ed. (This is the Creation school's
phonetic translation for "aufheben" — eliminate. I do
not know why they chose such a difficult phonetic version,
which must be harder for one of the fourth class to write
than the original.) Unfortunately there were exactly
three. But my earlier crime of not "striving to express
myself" must have been negated together with Cheng
Fangwu's "negation of the negation."

The Creation school "writes for the revolution." So
literature is still needed. In fact, it is the most important
thing today. For we are going to "change the weapons
of art into the art of weapons." Once we come to the
"art of weapons," we shall have changed from "the
weapon of criticism to the criticism by weapons." And
there is precedent in the world for this: "Waverers will
turn into supporters, and opponents into waverers."

But this immediately poses another big question: Why
can't we reach the "art weapons" straight away?

This is like "the talk of a sophist sent by the propertied
class." But so long as the proletariat has not freed itself from "bourgeois ideology" such problems are bound
to crop up. And this is not necessarily a nefarious plot
on the part of the bourgeoisie to withdraw or counter-
attack. As it is a bold, thoroughgoing proposal, it contains the seeds of doubt. The reply can only be:

Because the other side has the art of weapons. That
is why our side can only have the weapons of art.

We are reduced to using the weapons of art after breaking away from the illusion of non-resistance and suc-
cumbing to the new illusion that we can resist through
writing. But this is the only way for revolutionary artists
to keep up their courage — this is all they can do. If

they give up their art in an attempt to turn theory into practice, they will stop being revolutionary artists. So they have to sit in the proletarian camp, waiting for the "weapons of iron and fire" to appear. When these appear, they will have the "art of weapons." And if the iron-and-fire revolutionaries have "leisure" then to listen to accounts of their exploits, the writers will be soldiers just like the rest, and will win the final victory. It will still be difficult, though, to pass clear judgements on art and literature, because there are so many different strata in society. We have the historical evidence of advanced countries for this. To take two recent examples, *Cultural Critic* has grabbed Upton Sinclair, while *Creation Monthly* is carrying Vigny on its shoulders to "advance."

If by then they stop saying that "he who is not a revolutionary is a counter-revolutionary" and blaming the *Tatler* school for holding up the revolution, we shall still be allowed to earn half a loaf of bread a day as sweepers. Then in my leisure, after an eight-hour day, I shall sit in a dark room and go on copying out my *Anecdotes of Chinese Fiction* and discussing the literature of other countries, because I enjoy doing this. I am only afraid Cheng Fangwu and the rest may really become so many Lenins and "win over the masses." In that case they will probably go even further and promote me to the class of nobles or emperors so that I have to go into exile to the North Pole. Then it goes without saying that all my writings and translations will be banned.

Still, before long a great age will be here. Although the revolutionary writers and proletarian writers of the Creation school have been forced to play with "the weapons of art," the unrevolutionary militarists who have "the art of weapons" are beginning to play the same game too, producing these cheery periodicals.* Perhaps they

---

* Referring to journals sponsored by the Kuomintang.

are not too sure either of their "art of weapons." Into whose hands, then, has the highest art — "the art of weapons" — fallen today? Once we discover that, we shall know what China's immediate future is to be.

Shanghai
February 23, 1928

SITU QIAO'S* PAINTINGS

I first heard Situ Qiao's name four or five years ago in Beijing, where I learned that he cut his classes and had no teacher, but spent his whole time sketching on his own — old temples, bare hills, tumbledown huts, poor folk, beggars. . . .

Naturally these are the things most calculated to excite a traveller from the south. In that world of swirling yellow dust, where all is dust-coloured, human beings struggle with Nature. Dark red and emerald buildings, marble balustrades, gilded statues of Buddha, thick padded jackets, ruddy faces with networks of deep wrinkles . . . all go to show that men have not surrendered to Nature but are still battling on.

In art exhibitions at Beijing I saw the artist's expression of the Chinese soul with its defiance of Nature. I have in my possession his *Four Policemen and a Woman*. And I remember his *Jesus Christ,* with a woman's mouth kissing the crown of thorns.

When I met Situ Qiao this time in Shanghai, I asked him:

"Who is that woman?"

"An angel," was his reply.

This answer did not satisfy me.

For I had just discovered that the artist sometimes makes his own sense of beauty shine through the yellow dust of the northern scene — a scene made up of men fighting the elements — as well as the struggle. At least

---

* An artist from Guangdong Province.

he makes me aware of incipient Joy, for though blood
is gushing from the wounds in Christ's side, an angel —
or so the artist says — is kissing the crown of thorns.
Look at it as you will, this is a victory.

The later landscapes of luminous Jiangsu and Zhejiang, or of fiery Guangdong, show the artist in his true
element. If you compare these with his northern landscapes, you can tell how at home and delighted he felt
with his subject, as if he had rediscovered a long lost
friend. But I love his pictures of the yellow dust, for
from these I can see the pure-minded artist's horror at
the old battlefield where men contend with Nature, and
his participation in the battle.

The whole land of China must become one. If we escape being partitioned, I am sure this is the first step
young Chinese must take as they struggle to sweep away
the yellow dust.

Shanghai
The night of March 14, 1928

LITERATURE AND REVOLUTION*

April 4, 1928

Dear Mr. Dongfen,

Not being a critic I am no artist either, for nowadays to be any sort of specialist you have to be a critic too, or have a friend who is one. Without backing you are helpless, on the Shanghai Bund today at any rate. And not being an artist I have no special veneration for art, just as none but a quack doctor will give a boxing exhibition to cry up his wares. I regard art as merely a social phenomenon, a record of the life of the times. And if mankind advances, then whether you write on externals or on the inner life your works are bound to grow out-of-date or to perish. But recently the critics seem terrified of this prospect — they are set on immortality in the world of letters.

The outcrop of different "isms" is an unavoidable phenomenon too. Since revolutions are constantly taking place, naturally there is revolutionary literature. Quite a number of the world's peoples are awakening and, though many of them are still suffering, some already hold power. Naturally this gives rise to popular literature or, to put it more bluntly, literature of the fourth class.

I am not too clear, not too interested, either, regarding current trends in China's literary criticism. But from all I hear and see, different authorities seem to use a great

---

* Reply to a letter from Dong Qiufen, then a student of Beijing University.

variety of criteria: Anglo-American, German, Russian, Japanese and of course Chinese, or a combination of these. Some demand truth, others struggle. Some say literature should transcend its age, others pass sarcastic remarks behind people's backs. Yet others, who set themselves up as authoritative literary critics, are disgusted when anyone else encourages writing. What are they up to? This is most incomprehensible to me, for without writing what is there to criticize?

Let us leave aside other questions for the moment. The so-called revolutionary writers today profess themselves militants or transcendentalists. Actually, transcending the present is a form of escapism. And this is the path they are bound to take, consciously or otherwise, if they lack the courage to look reality in the face yet insist on styling themselves revolutionaries. If you live in this world, how can you get away from it? This is as much of a fraud as claiming that you can hoist yourself off this earth by pulling on your ear. If society remains static, literature cannot fly ahead on its own. If it flourishes in such a static society, this means it is tolerated by that society and has turned its back on revolution, the only result being a slightly larger magazine circulation or the chance for publication in the journals put out by big commercial firms.

To struggle is right, I believe. If people are oppressed, why shouldn't they struggle? But since this is what respectable gentlemen* dread, they condemn it as "radical," alleging that men the world over are meant to love each other and would do so were they not now corrupted by a gang of bad characters. The well-fed may quite likely love the starving, but the starving never love

---

* This refers to members of the Crescent Moon Society, a cultural and political association representing the compradore bourgeoisie.

the well-fed. In the days of Huang Chao* when men ate each other, the starving did not even love the starving; however, this was not due to trouble stirred up by the literature of struggle. I have never believed that literature has the power to move heaven and earth, but if people want to put it to other uses that is all right with me. It can be used for "propaganda" for example.

Upton Sinclair of America has said: All literature is propaganda. Our revolutionary writers treasure this saying and have printed it in large type, whereas the serious critics call Upton Sinclair a "shallow socialist." But I, being shallow myself, agree with him. All literature becomes propaganda once you show it to someone else. This applies to individualist works, too, as soon as you write them down. Indeed the only way to avoid propaganda is by never writing, never opening your mouth. This being so, literature can naturally be used as a tool of revolution.

But I think we should first try to achieve rich content and skilful technique, and not be in a hurry to set ourselves up as writers. The old trade-marks Dao Xiang Cun and Lu Gao Jian** have already lost their appeal, and I doubt whether a firm calling itself "The Dowager Empress Shoe Shop" could attract more customers than "The Empress Shoe Shop." Revolutionary writers bridle at the mere mention of "technique." To my mind, however, though all literature is propaganda, not all propaganda is literature; just as all flowers have colour (I count white as a colour), but not all coloured things are flowers. In addition to slogans, posters, proclamations, telegrams, textbooks and so forth, the revolution needs literature — just because it is literature.

But China's so-called revolutionary literature seems to be an exception again. The signboard has been hung up

---

* Leader of a peasant revolt at the end of the Tang Dynasty.
** Well-known delicatessens in Shanghai.

and our writers are busy patting each other on the back,
but they dare not look unflinchingly at today's tyranny
and darkness. Some works have been published, true,
but often more clumsily written than journalese. Or it
is left to the actors in a play to supply the stage-direc-
tions, such writing being regarded as "out-of-date."
Surely, then, the ideological content left must be most
revolutionary? Let me quote you the two superb last
lines of a play by Feng Naichao!*

Prostitute: I no longer dread the darkness.

Thief: Let us revolt!

Lu Xun

---

*Member of the Creation Society.

THE TABLET

The fearful thing about Chinese writers today is that they keep introducing new terms without defining those terms.

And everyone interprets them as he pleases. To write a good deal about yourself is expressionism. To write about others is realism. To write poems on a girl's leg is romanticism. To ban poems on a girl's leg is classicism. While —

A head drops down from the sky,
An ox on the head stands high,
Oh, my!
At sea green thunderbolts fly! . . .

is futurism . . . and so on.

And so disputes begin. This "ism" is good, that is bad . . . and so on.

Country folk tell a joke about two short-sighted fellows who wanted to see which had the better eyesight. Since neither could prove his claim, they agreed to go to look at a new votive tablet which was to be hung at the local temple that day. Each went secretly to the painter to find out what the inscription was to be. But each got hold of a slightly different version, and the man who knew only the big characters would not admit defeat, but accused the man who knew the small of lying. Since once again neither could prove his case, they had to appeal to a passer-by. After taking one look, however, the stranger told them:

"There's nothing there. The tablet hasn't been hung yet."

I think before competing as literary critics we must first hang up the tablet. For only the two sides involved know that they are actually arguing on nothing.

April 10, 1928

HEADS

The *Shen Bao* of March 25 had an article by Professor Liang Shiqiu on Rousseau, in which he declared that to quote Upton Sinclair's attack on Babbitt was "doing murder by another's hand" and "not necessarily the best method." His second reason for attacking Rousseau was that "Rousseau's immorality came to typify the standard conduct of most liberal writers, and therefore we can say that an attack on Rousseau's morals is an attack on the conduct of such men."

While this is not "doing murder by another's hand," it is "borrowing a head to display as a warning." Had not Rousseau "come to typify the standard conduct of most liberal writers," his head would never have been brought such a great distance to be displayed in China. So our "liberal writers" have injured their distant master, and made it impossible for him to rest quiet in his grave. He is punished today for his pernicious influence, not for his own fault — how sad!

The foregoing is not very "respectful," for all Professor Liang did was punish with his pen: he did not insist that Rousseau's head be displayed. I was the one to drag this in, because today's paper reported how after the Communist Guo Liang "paid the supreme penalty" in Hunan, his head was displayed right and left "all over Changsha and Yueyang." Unfortunately the Hunan authorities have not recorded Lenin's crimes against morality (or, to go further back, those of Marx, or — even further back — those of Hegel), and posted them up at the same time to prove his pernicious influence.   Apparently Hunan lacks critics.

I remember reading in the *Romance of the Three Kingdoms* how after the death of Yuan Shao someone wrote this poem lamenting him:

> *Bowing he left, carrying his sword,*
> *The most gallant man of his age.*
> *Ten thousand li the severed head was sent;*
> *You did wrong to kill Tian Feng.**

During my "three leisures," I have also written a lament to Rousseau:

> *Bareheaded he left, carrying his pen,*
> *The most wretched man of his age.*
> *Ten thousand li the severed head was sent;*
> *You did wrong to train the young.*

April 10, 1928

---

* Tian Feng served under Yuan Shao and warned him not to engage Cao Cao in battle. Yuan Shao ignored this advice and was defeated, whereupon in a rage he killed Tian Feng.

TWO LETTERS

I

Written from a bed of sickness
March 13, 1928

Dear Mr. Lu Xun,

Indescribably wasted in body and spirit — I could hardly be worse — I have propped up my feeble frame to utter one last cry to you, sir — an appeal for help, rather, and a warning!

You are well aware that you are preparing a feast of "shrimps steeped in wine"* for others. And I am one of the shrimps!

I started as a favourite son of the petty-bourgeoisie, a hot-house plant. Comfortably off, I could have lived quite at my ease. As long as I got my coveted "mortar-board" I should have been satisfied, for I had no other ambitions.

Then your *Call to Arms* was published, and the *Tatler* came out. (Unfortunately I had been too young to understand *New Youth*.) *On My Moustache, On Photographs* and your other essays each in turn stirred my heart. Though one of the youngest of the young, I became aware

---

* In a letter written to Mr. Youheng in 1927, Lu Xun referred to the live shrimps served in wine at Chinese banquets, saying that the more alive the shrimps the greater the feasters' enjoyment. He considered himself as one preparing such a dish, for by making young people more politically conscious he increased their sensitivity to pain.

33

of the superficiality and blindness of my companions. The call to arms: "Revolt! Revolt!" resounded through the streets, booming out more widely as the revolution gained ground. I was drawn by that call. And, of course, my disgust at the superficiality of youth made me want to find some aim in life. Who would have known that this time I was to experience the deceit, hypocrisy and treachery of men's nature? But sure enough, before long the warlords and politicians tore off their disguises to disclose their true crafty faces! And responding to the cry "Purge the Party!" my passionate, fiery heart was purged. I thought at the time I could find friends among the "staunch, straightforward" fourth class, and those "scholars withdrawn from the world." But ah! your worthy brother Mr. Qiming* spoke the truth when he said, "Though China has different classes, they share the same ideas. They all want to become officials or make money." I felt I was living in the days before Christ, and was always being bewildered by stupid words and actions — more stupid than those of wild beasts (maybe the champions of our national spirit think them essentially Chinese?). What could I do?

Sharp? There is nothing sharper than the arrows of disenchantment. I was disenchanted, and when the arrow of disenchantment pierced my heart, I began to spit blood. For some months now I have tossed helplessly in bed.

Men without hope should die — quite right. But I lack the courage for that, and I am still young — only just twenty-one. I have a sweetheart too. If I do not die, I must live in mental and physical agony every moment of the day. My sweetheart is already crushed by life, and I lost my own modest property through the revolution. So, unable to comfort each other, we can only sigh together!

---

* Zhou Zuoren.

To be insensate is happiness: that is why I am wretched. But you, sir, were the one to poison me. I was thoroughly befuddled by you. Now that you have brought me to this, sir, I beg you to point out the final stage of my road. Or failing that, benumb my faculties, for to be insensate is happiness. Fortunately you have studied medicine, and should easily be able to "give back my head!" I am going to repeat the cry of Liang Yuchun(?).*

Last of all, let me urge you, sir, to let well alone. Don't round up any more tasty morsels for the warlords, but spare other young men like me. If forced to write for a living, write more polemics. With your literary reputation, you may be sure of winning rank and riches. "Commissionerships" and "chairmanships" are yours for the taking.

Please give me some advice quickly! Do not stop halfway.

Answer in *Beixin*** or the *Tatler* — either will do. And if possible, don't publish this letter for others to laugh at.

Please excuse my scrawl — my illness has worn me out!

From a young man you have ruined,

Y —

II

April 10, 1928

Dear Mr. Y,

First of all I must apologize because, counter to your

---

* A young contemporary writer, who published an article in the *Tatler* entitled "'Give Back My Head' and Other Matters."
** A magazine edited by Lu Xun and others.

wishes, I am forced to publish your letter. You evidently want me to make a public answer, but if I suppress your original letter all I say will become like those poems without a title which no one can make head or tail of. And I see nothing ridiculous in your letter. Of course, a great many revolutionaries have been killed in China, while a great many others are still working for the revolution in spite of hardships; but there are also revolutionaries who live in comfort. . . . Naturally, you cannot be said to have been true to the end, since you are not dead, and you may feel you are letting the dead down but, all the living should be able to forgive you. All such men are simply dependent on luck themselves, or else on cunning and tricks. One look in the mirror should be enough to stop them posing as such heroes.

To begin with I did not have to write for a living. I first took up my pen to oblige a friend. But I must have had some resentment at heart, for I could not help writing with indignation, as if to incite the young. I can say with confidence, though, that for all we wrote when Duan Qirui was in power — in spite of rumours to the contrary — we received not one rouble from abroad, not one cent from wealthy patrons, not the least royalty from the booksellers. And because I had no wish to be a "man of letters," I never made connections with a gang of critics so that they might write me up. I never dreamed that more than ten thousand copies of my stories would be sold.

I admit that I do rather hope China will be reformed and undergo changes. Though I have been called a "poison pen" and an author with no way out — does a way out mean passing the palace examination? — I do not think I have run down everything. Because I have always thought low-class better than high-class people, and the young better than the old, I used not to spatter them with the blood on my pen. I know that the moment their own interests are affected they usually behave like the high-class and the old, but that is inevitable in this society. And they have so many opponents already, I saw no point in joining in casting stones. That is why I exposed one side only of the darkness — I did not set out to deceive my youthful readers.

That was my attitude while still in Beijing when, according to Cheng Fangwu, I was a petty-bourgeois not yet awakened. But when some careless remarks in my writing broke my rice bowl and made it necessary for me to leave, not waiting for the explosion of T.N.T., I drifted off to "the revolutionary base." After two months there I was aghast to find that all I had previously heard was false — the place was in the hands of soldiers and merchants. And then came the purge, the truth about which has seldom appeared in the papers, although some word has got round. Being truly hypersensitive, I felt this was indeed a "total massacre" and was most upset. I know this shows "superficial humanitarianism" which has been out of date for two or three years already, but as I have not yet got rid of my petty-bourgeois nature, I am always taking things to heart. Since it struck me at the time that I had probably helped to prepare the feast, I tried to clear myself briefly in my reply to Mr. Youheng.*

It is a fact that my old arguments were defeated, owing to my lack of foresight. The reason is probably that I spent so many years watching life "through a glass window with eyes befuddled by wine." But seldom can the world have known so many changes, and since I neither foresaw nor wrote of these you can see I am not too able a "poison pen." But neither did those revolutionary writers at the crossroads, among the people or in government offices, who were fifty years in advance of their day, foresee the events of that time; hence they did not wage any "theoretical struggle." Otherwise, many lives might have been saved. I mention revolutionary writers

---

* See Volume II of this selected works.

not to scoff after the event at their ignorance, but simply to point out that my failure to foresee future develop- ments proves the lack of stringency which gave rise to my mistakes. I have not discussed the question with others, however, nor decided — for reasons of my own — to deceive men.

But things turn out quite differently from what you intend. I suspect that some unfortunate young people who read my articles may have been goaded by them into joining the revolution, and this makes me very unhappy. But this is because I am not a born revolutionary, for a great revolutionary would think nothing of the loss of these few lives. In the first place, he himself would still be alive to continue giving leadership, for no revolution succeeds without leadership. Look at all the revolu- tionary writers who live in or near the foreign conces- sions in Shanghai. If a storm blows up, they have the foreign devils' barbed-wire defences to put between them- selves and the counter-revolutionary writers outside the concessions, and from behind this barbed wire they can hurl their T.N.T. — some hundred thousand ounces — to "aufheben" the whole leisured class in one great explo- sion.

Most of these revolutionary writers — a whole batch of them — came into being this year. As they are still busy singing each other's praises or opposing each other, I cannot make out whether they belong to the group which thinks the revolution a success or to the group which thinks it not yet accomplished. But apparently there is talk to the effect that it is because of my *Call to Arms* or *Wild Grass*, or because we are putting out the *Tatler* that the revolution has not yet been successful and young people have been put off it. They are more or less agreed here. This is the consensus of opinion of the revolutionary world of letters this year. And though I do not know whether to laugh or be angry, I am pleased in a way. For although I am guilty of delaying the revolution, I need not reproach myself for luring young people to their death. So I am in no way responsible for all the dead, wounded and wretched. I was actually shouldering a responsibility not my own. I made up my mind not to speak, teach or express any opinion, but to let my name perish from the earth to atone for my crimes. This year I felt more light-hearted and was thinking of becoming active once more, when I received your letter which has made my heart sink again.

Still, my heart is not as heavy as it was last year. For the last six months I have been collecting opinions and drawing on my own experience, and I know that revolutions depend on men, not on writing. You accuse me of poisoning you, yet all the critics here say quite categorically that my writing is "not revolutionary." If literature were able to move men, after reading my articles they should not want to have revolutionary literature. Now, though they have read my articles and decided that they are "not revolutionary," they still have not lost heart but want to be revolutionary writers. It is clear from this that writing has no influence on men — the only pity is that this refutes the high-sounding claims of revolutionary literature. But you and I, sir, have never met before, and I am sure you would not trump up a false charge against me. I will therefore approach the question from another angle. First, I think you too reckless. Those revolutionary writers were so terrified by my descriptions of darkness, and so fearful that there was no way out, that they felt compelled to harp on the final victory — your profit depends on your investment, just as in an insurance company. But you set no store by such things. All you want is to attack the darkness. That is one reason why you have suffered. Secondly, being too reckless, you are too serious. There are all sorts of revolutions. You have lost your property through revolution, but some acquire property through it. Others lose even their lives, while yet others get salaries and fees for writing, but lose the title of revolutionary. Of course these heroes are serious too; but if you have lost more than you gained, I think the root of your trouble is your extremism. Thirdly, you painted too rosy a picture of the future, so that the first setback made you lose heart completely. If you had not counted on certain victory, you would probably not have been so distressed by defeat.

Then am I not guilty at all? I am. At this very moment many respectable gentlemen and revolutionary writers, openly and covertly, are judging my crimes as a revolutionary or non-revolutionary, and a part of all the wounds I receive shall be a reparation to you for your "head."

A word of textual research here. "Give back my head!" according to the *Romance of the Three Kingdoms*, was said by Lord Guan Yu, not by Liang Yuchun.

Actually, the foregoing is empty talk. The moment I touch upon your personal problems it is exceedingly hard to do anything. These cannot be solved by such heroic language as "Forward! Kill! Youth!" And I do not like to tell the truth openly, because just now it is better not to practise exactly what you preach. But since you gave no address, I can only answer you in a few sentences here. First you must make a living, but to do that you must not be too particular. One moment, though. A good many not very bright fellows make the big mistake of thinking that the precept "the end justifies the means" is a Communist watchword. A great many people act in this way, but will not admit it. The Soviet commissioner of education Lunacharsky, in his book *Don Quixote Liberated*, makes a duke use these tactics, which shows how aristocratic and respectable they are. Secondly, you must take good care of your sweetheart. They say this is unrevolutionary, but never mind. So long as you write a few revolutionary articles urging revolutionary youths not to talk of love, you will be all right. Only if some powerful man or enemy puts you on trial may this be counted as one of your crimes, in which case you may regret having taken my advice. So first I must make this clear: once they put you on trial, even if you are innocent in this respect, they will pin something else on you. The way of the world is to make a man stand trial first, and collect evidence of his crimes — usually ten of them — afterwards.

I have written this, sir, to cover up a little for my mistakes. Because just for this I may be attacked even more. The revolutionary writers will be the first to abuse me tearfully as a "confounded nihilist!" Ah, the moment one is careless, one smears mud on the noses of new heroes. Let me seize this chance to excuse myself in advance. There is no need for all this excitement. This is not an "ism," only tactics. Even if it were an "ism," since I dared and was willing to write about it, I could not be too bad after all. When I am too bad, I shall store these things up, fill my hand with money, and live in a safe place while I urge others to sacrifice their lives.

I advise you too, sir, to enjoy yourself for a while. Take any job that will keep you. But I do not want you to remain at your "last gasp" for ever. Where changes are possible make them, whether big or small. And I promise to do as you direct me, not only to "let well alone" but also to "enjoy myself." This is not simply on account of your warning — such was my intention already. I mean to write more about what interests me, and to look for more leisure too. If I put my foot in it sometimes, that is a slip of the pen: my "motive" or "conscience" may not be like that.

As I have come to the bottom of the page, I will end my letter here. With kindest regards and best wishes for your health, and hoping that your sweetheart will not go hungry,

Lu Xun

THE SPELLS

The *Shen Bao* of April 6 carried this item of news:

During the last few days a groundless rumour has been circulating in Nanjing to the effect that work on Sun Yat-sen's mausoleum is about to be completed and the masons are collecting children's spirits to close the dragon's mouth. The people of Nanjing are frightening each other by spreading this rumour, and all the children are wearing a square of red cloth on their left shoulder, bearing a four-line spell to ward off danger. There seem to be three of these spells:

1

Whoever summons my spirit
Let him take my spirit's place;
If no one answers his call,
Let him fill the tomb himself.

2

The stone calls the stone monk,
Let it take his place itself;
Hurry home as fast as you can,
Or you'll be sealed up in the tomb.

3

> *You have built Sun Yat-sen's mausoleum —*
> *What has that to do with me?*
> *My spirit will not go when first you call,*
> *If you call again, you will have to go yourself.*

Any one of these three spells, short as they are, gives us in a nutshell ordinary citizens' views on their "revolutionary" government and their attitude to revolutionaries. Even writers skilled in expressing the horrors of our society could hardly write so concisely and profoundly.

> *If no one answers his call,*
> *Let him fill the tomb himself.*

Here we have the biography of many revolutionaries and a history of the Chinese revolution.

Some writers nowadays seem to insist that this is the "darkness before dawn." But since our citizens are like this, no matter whether it is dawn or dusk, revolutionaries will just have to go ahead with these citizens on their backs. We cannot discard them, and yet they are no asset. If things go on like this, even fifty or a hundred years from now we cannot be sure of finding a way out.

Revolutionary writers have recently shown a special dread of darkness and tried to cover it up, but our blunt citizens give the show away. And when low cunning clashes with crass indifference, revolutionary writers dare not look life in the face, but become superstitious old wives who welcome the magpie and are afraid of the crow. Intoxicating themselves with a few auspicious omens they have picked out, they think they have transcended their own age.

My congratulations! Let the heroes advance! The real age you spurn will respectfully see you off.

In fact, however, it still exists beside you. You have simply closed your eyes. Still, by closing your eyes you need not "fill the tomb," and that is your "final victory"!

April 10, 1928

WIPING OUT THE REDS — A
GREAT SPECTACLE

It was the *Shen Bao* of April 6 again that carried a "Letter from Changsha" describing the seizure of the provincial committee of the Communist Party by the Hunan authorities, who sentenced over thirty of them to death, and executed eight of them on March 29. This article is so well written that I am quoting it.

After the execution that day, because three of the prisoners belonged to the female sex — Ma Shuchun aged sixteen, Ma Zhichun aged fourteen, and Fu Feng-jun aged twenty-four — the whole city turned out to have a look. You could hardly move for the crowd. And the fact that the head of the Communist ring-leader Guo Liang was on display at Court Gate increased the number of spectators. Between Court Gate and the Octagonal Pavilion there was a traffic block. When the citizens near the South Gate had seen Guo Liang's head they went on to the Teachers' Association to see the female corpses. When the citizens near the North Gate had seen the female corpses at the Teachers' Association they went on to see Guo Liang's head at Court Gate. The whole city was in a ferment, and fresh impetus was given to the urge to wipe out the Communists. Not till dusk did the spectators begin to disperse.

Having copied this out, I realize I have blundered. I simply meant to make a few observations, but I see now that I shall probably be suspected of sneering (some say

I do nothing but sneer). Others will denounce me for spreading darkness, and call down destruction upon me so that I can carry all the darkness with me into the grave. Still, though I cannot keep quiet, I will confine my observations to "art for art's sake." How powerful that short report is! As I read it, I felt I could see the head impaled at Court Gate and the three headless female corpses at the Teachers' Association. They must have been stripped to the waist at least, too — or perhaps I am guessing wrongly because I am so corrupt. And then all those "citizens," one contingent heading south, another north, jostling and shouting . . . I could fill in the details too, the rapt anticipation on some faces, the satisfaction on others. I have never come across such powerful writing in all the "revolutionary" or "realist" literature I have read. The critic Rogachevski said, "Andreyev tries hard to frighten us, without success; while Chekhov, who does not try, can make us shiver." Yes, the couple of hundred words here are worth a whole heap of short stories, to say nothing of the fact that the account is true.

One moment, though. If I go on, I am afraid certain heroes will condemn me for spreading darkness and holding up the revolution. They have some reason for this. It is easy to fall under suspicion today, when the newspapers are constantly filled with accounts of the arrest or release of loyal comrades suspected of being Reds. If you are unfortunate and cannot clear yourself, that is just too bad. . . . Harping on this may lower strong men's morale, but revolutions have rarely been stopped by displaying heads. A revolution probably ends only when opportunists join the ranks and undermine it from within. I refer not merely to Bolshevism, but to revolutions of every conceivable "ism." Still, is it not precisely because men are in darkness and have no way out that they want to revolt? If you have to guarantee "a bright future" and a "way out" before they dare to join you, far from being revolutionaries they are not even opportunists. For not even opportunists can tell whether a venture will succeed or fail.

In conclusion, I want to expose a little more darkness by saying this: Our present-day (present-day, not transcendental!) Chinese actually do not care about political parties — all they want to see are "heads" and "female corpses." If these are available, no matter whose they are, our citizens will go to have a look. I have seen or heard of a good many cases of this in the short space of the last twenty years: the Boxer Rising, the suppression of revolts at the end of the Qing Dynasty, the happenings in 1913,* last year and this year.

April 10, 1928

---

* Referring to the warlord Yuan Shikai's massacre of the revolutionaries.

1929

SOME THOUGHTS ON OUR
NEW LITERATURE

A talk given to the Chinese Literature Society of
Yanjing University on May 22, 1929

For more than a year now I have spoken very seldom
to young people, because since the revolution there has
been very little scope for talking. You are either provocative or reactionary, neither of which does anyone
any good. After my return to Beijing this time, however, some old friends asked me to come here and say
a few words and, not being able to refuse them, here
I am. But owing to one thing and another, I never
decided what to say — not even what subject to speak on.

I meant to fix on a subject in the bus on the way here,
but the road is so bad that the bus kept bouncing a foot
off the ground, making it impossible to concentrate. That
is when it struck me that it is no use just adopting one
thing from abroad. If you have buses, you need good
roads too. Everything is bound to be influenced by its
surroundings, and this applies to literature as well — to
what in China is called the new literature, or revolutionary literature.

However patriotic we are, we probably have to admit
that our civilization is rather backward. Everything new
has come to us from abroad, and most of us are quite
bewildered by new powers. Beijing has not yet been
reduced to this, but in the International Settlement in
Shanghai, for example, you have foreigners in the centre,
surrounded by a cordon of interpreters, detectives, police,

"boys," and so on, who understand their languages and know the rules of foreign concessions. Outside this cordon are the common people.

When the common people come into contact with foreigners, they never know quite what is happening. If a foreigner says "Yes," his interpreter says, "He told me to box your ears." If the foreigner says "No," this is translated as "Have the fellow shot." To avoid such meaningless trouble you need more knowledge, for then you can break through this cordon.

It is the same in the world of letters. We know too little, and have too few materials to help us to learn. Liang Shiqiu has his Babbitt, Xu Zhimo has his Tagore, Hu Shi has his Dewey — oh yes, Xu Zhimo has Katherine Mansfield too, for he wept at her grave — and the Creation school has revolutionary literature, the literature now in vogue. But though a good deal of writing goes with this, there is not much studying done. Right up to today, there are still some subjects which are the private preserve of the few men who set the questions.

All literature is shaped by its surroundings and, though devotees of art like to claim that literature can sway the course of world affairs, the truth is that politics comes first, and art changes accordingly. If you fancy art can change your environment, you are talking like an idealist. Events are seldom what men of letters expect. That is why the so-called revolutionary writers before a great revolution are doomed. Only when the revolution is beginning to achieve results, and men have time to breathe freely again, will new revolutionary writers be produced. This is because when the old society is on the verge of collapse you will very often find writing which seems rather revolutionary, but is not actually true revolutionary literature. For example, a man may hate the old society, but all he has is hate — no vision of the future. He may clamour for social reforms, but if you ask what sort of society he wants, it is some unrealizable

Utopia. Or he may be tired of living, and long for some big change to stimulate his senses, just as someone gorged with food and wine eats hot pepper to whet his appetite. Then there are the old campaigners who have been spurned by the people, but who hang out a new signboard and rely on some new power to win a better status for themselves.

There have been cases in China of writers who look forward to revolution but fall silent once the revolution comes. The members of the South Club at the end of the Qing Dynasty are an example. That literary coterie agitated for revolution, lamented the sufferings of the Hans, raged at the tyranny of the Manchus and longed for a return to the "good old days." But after the establishment of the Republic they lapsed into utter silence. I fancy this was because their dream had been for "a restoration of ancient splendour" after the revolution — the high hats and broad belts of the old officials. As things turned out differently and they found the reality unpalatable, they felt no urge to write. Even clearer examples can be found in Russia. At the start of the October Revolution many revolutionary writers were overjoyed and welcomed the hurricane, eager to be tested by the storm. But later the poet Yesenin and the novelist Sopoly committed suicide, and recently they say the famous writer Ehrenburg is becoming rather reactionary. What is the reason for this? It is because what is sweeping down on them is not a hurricane, and what is testing them is not a storm, but a real, honest-to-goodness revolution. Their dreams have been shattered, so they cannot live on. This is not so good as the old belief that when you die your spirit goes to heaven and sits beside God eating cakes.* For they died before attaining their ideal.

---

* A reference to Heine's poem "Mir traumt': ich bin der liebe Gott" (I dreamt I was the Lord Himself) in *Die Heimkehr* (The Journey Home).

Of course China, they say, has already had a revolution. This may be so in the realm of politics, but not in the realm of art. Some say, "The literature of the petty-bourgeoisie is now raising its head." As a matter of fact, there is no such literature; this literature has not even a head to raise. Judging by what I said earlier — little as the revolutionaries like it — there has been no change or renaissance in literature, and it reflects neither revolution nor progress.

As for the more radical revolutionary literature advocated by the Creation Society — the literature of the proletariat — that is simply empty talk. Wang Duqing's poem, which has been banned here, there and everywhere, was written in the International Settlement in Shanghai whence he looked out towards revolutionary Guangzhou. But his

PONG, PONG, PONG!

in ever larger type merely shows the impression made on him by Shanghai film posters and advertisements for soya sauce. He is imitating Blok's *The Twelve*, but without Blok's force and talent. Quite a number of people recommend Guo Moruo's *Hand* as an excellent work. This tells how a revolutionary lost a hand after the revolution, but with that remaining to him could still hold his sweetheart's hand — a most convenient loss, surely! If you have to lose one of your four limbs, the most expendable certainly is a hand. A leg would be inconvenient, a head even more so. And if all you expect to lose is one hand, you do not need so much courage for the fray. It seems to me, though, a revolutionary should be prepared to sacrifice a great deal more than this. The *Hand* is the old, old tale about the trials of a poor scholar who ends, as usual, by passing the palace examination and marrying a beautiful girl.

But actually this is one reflection of conditions in China today. The cover of a work of revolutionary literature recently published in Shanghai shows a trident, taken from the cover of *Symbols of Misery*,* with the hammer from the Soviet flag stuck on its middle prong. This juxtaposition means you can neither thrust with the trident nor strike with the hammer, and merely shows the artist's stupidity — it could well serve as a badge for all these writers.

Of course, it is possible to transfer from one class to another. But the best thing is to say frankly what your views are, so that people will know whether you are friend or foe. Don't try to conceal the fact that your head is filled with old dregs by pointing dramatically at your nose and claiming, "I am the only true proletarian!" Folk are so hypersensitive today that the word "Russia" almost makes them give up the ghost, and soon they will not even allow lips to be red. They are scared of all sorts of publications. And our revolutionary writers, unwilling to introduce more theories or books from abroad, just point dramatically at themselves, till in the end they give us something like the "reprimands by imperial decree" of the late Qing Dynasty — no one has the least idea what they are about.

I shall probably have to explain the expression "reprimands by imperial decree" to you. This belonged to the days of the empire when, if an official committed a mistake, he was ordered to kneel outside some gate or other while the emperor sent a eunuch to give him a dressing-down. If you greased the eunuch's palm, he would stop very soon. If not, he would curse your whole family from your earliest ancestors down to your descendants. This was supposed to be the emperor speaking, but who could go and ask the emperor if he really meant all that? Last year, according to a Japanese magazine, Cheng Fangwu was elected by the peasants and workers of China to go and study drama in Germany. And we

---

* A book of literary criticism by Hakuson Kuriyagawa, translated by Lu Xun from the Japanese.

have no means of finding out if he really was elected that way or not.

That is why, as I always say, if we want to increase our understanding we must read more foreign books, to break through the cordon around us. This is not too hard for you. Though there are not many books in English on the new literature and not many English translations of it, the few that we have are fairly reliable. After reading more foreign theoretical works and literature, you will feel much clearer when you come to judge our new Chinese literature. Better still, you can introduce such works to China. It is no easier to translate than to turn out sloppy writing, but it makes a greater contribution to the development of our new literature, and is more useful to our people.

THE EVOLUTION OF ROUGHS

Neither Confucius nor Mo Zi was satisfied with the status quo. They both wanted reforms. But their first step was to win over their earthly masters, and the tool they used to control their masters was "Heaven."

The disciples of Confucius were scholars, while those of Mo Zi were gallants. "Scholars are gentle" — naturally they were quite safe. But gallants are simple souls, and the followers of Mo Zi sometimes fought "to the death." Later the really simple souls died off, leaving only the wily ones. The great champions of the Han Dynasty were already making up to nobles and powerful officials, so that at a pinch they could take refuge behind these patrons.

Sima Qian said, "Scholars flout the law by their writings, and gallant men break prohibitions by force of arms." They were not "rebels," mind you — they just stirred up a little trouble. And in any case they had powerful patrons like the five marquises* to back them.

Gradually these gallant men disappeared and their place was taken by brigands, who belonged, however, to the same category. Their watchword was "Carry out the will of Heaven." They opposed evil ministers, not the emperor, and robbed the people instead of generals and officials. When Li Kui fought on the execution ground, brandishing his axe, it was onlookers' heads that he chopped off. And *Outlaws of the Marshes* states quite ex-

---

* Five kinsmen of an empress of the Han Dynasty who were made marquises on the same day in 27 B.C.

plicitly that, because the outlaws were not against the emperor, when the government troops arrived they surrendered and set off to fight other brigands for the state — brigands who did not "carry out the will of Heaven." They were slaves after all.

When the Manchus came in and China was gradually subdued, even those with a "sense of gallantry" dared not think of being brigands, upbraiding evil ministers, or serving the emperor directly. Instead, they attached themselves as bodyguards to some good official or high commissioner, and caught robbers for him. This is clearly stated in *The Cases of Lord Shi,** and up to the present there have been endless examples like those in *The Cases of Lord Peng*** or *Seven Heroes and Five Just Men.**** These men have a blameless past, and have never committed a crime. Though they are under the high commissioner, at least they are over the people; so while they have to take orders from their master, they can lord it over all the others. With a greater degree of security, they are correspondingly more servile.

But just as robbers may be attacked by the government troops, those who pursue robbers may be attacked by them. Thus a gallant man who wants complete security finds neither of these courses safe enough. Then he becomes a rough. He beats up monks who are drinking, arrests men and women having a love affair, and bullies prostitutes and black-marketeers — in the interests of public morality. He cheats peasants who do not know the ways of the foreign concessions — because he despises ignorance. He jeers at women with short hair, and rages at social reformers — because he loves law and order. But he is backed by the traditional patrons, and since his opponents are not great and powerful he acts

---

* A popular Qing Dynasty novel about gallant men who served good officials.
** Ditto.
*** Ditto.

the tyrant among them. None of our modern novels has given us a good picture of this type. The nearest approach to it is Zhang Qiugu in *The Nine-tailed Turtle*,* who thinks he should bully the prostitute because she tries to fleece her clients — that is why he must punish her.

When standards drop even lower, such men will probably become the heroes of our literature. I am looking forward to the next work of our "revolutionary writer" Zhang Ziping.**

---

* Zhang Chunfan's novel about prostitutes, which appeared in 1910.

** Originally a member of the Creation Society, he degenerated into a writer of pornography and later worked for the Japanese. In an advertisement of his books, he called himself a revolutionary writer.

THE FUNCTION OF THE CRITICS
OF THE CRESCENT MOON SOCIETY*

The critics of the Crescent Moon Society dislike jeering, but they jeer at one kind of person — the writer of satire. The critics of the Crescent Moon Society disapprove of those who complain of the present order, but they have one complaint themselves — that such discontented individuals exist.

This must be a case of "paying a man in his own coin." They are compelled to help preserve law and order.

For instance, murder is bad. But though the man who kills a murderer is a murderer himself, who can say he is wrong? Beating people is bad too. But who can blame the runners who are ordered by the magistrate to spank a felon's bottom? No doubt it is on the same principle that the critics of the Crescent Moon Society, although they abuse others and are discontented themselves, are the only ones who can be exempted from these crimes.

But then it is the old story. Since the executioner and the runners have made their contribution to the preservation of order they must naturally be accorded some measure of respect, and may even be allowed to express a few opinions to impress the common folk with their authority. The official always turns a blind eye, so long as they do not greatly disturb public order.

---

* Founded in 1923, its members included Hu Shi, Xu Zhimo and Liang Shiqiu. Politically this society was anti-Communist and anti-popular; in literature it trumpeted the bourgeois theory of "human nature" and opposed proletarian literature.

After doing their utmost to preserve law and order, all the critics of the Crescent Moon Society want is "freedom of thought" — just freedom to think, not to realize their ideas.   And yet there are now measures for the preservation of order which do not even allow you to think.*   I fancy from now on there will be discontent on two scores.

---

* This refers to the "Emergency Measures for the Preservation of Order" introduced by the Kuomintang at that time, which prohibited freedom of thought.

THE HISTORY OF MY CONNECTION
WITH THE *TATLER*

I was connected with the *Tatler* for quite a time.

No doubt this is why the magazine of those "respectable gentlemen" dubbed me "*Tatler*'s commander-in-chief," and even ardent young progressives still speak of me as its "guide." Last year, when they had to abuse Lu Xun to save themselves, I received two copies of *Mountain Rain* belonging to the middle-of-the-roaders from an anonymous source. Looking through them, I found a short article saying that because Sun Fuyuan and Lu Xun were shabbily treated in Beijing by the *Morning News* they started the *Tatler*; but that now that Lu Xun was editor he appended wild comments to other contributors' manuscripts or distorted their real meaning, treating other writers very shabbily. Since Sun Fuyuan has excellent judgement, Lu Xun ought to defer to him in future. I believe we owe this effusion to Mr. Zhang Mengwen,* though he used a pseudonym. This is quite common today — what seems to be a whole crowd is only one or two people after all.

Of course, "commander-in-chief" and "guide" are not bad epithets, it is no disgrace to be shabbily treated by the *Morning News*, and for old people to be criticized by the young is progressive and admirable — so what am I worrying about? But "uncalled-for praise" is as irritating as "uncalled-for blame." If you have never com-

---

* An editor of *Mountain Rain*.

manded a single soldier, but someone praises you as "a second Napoleon," even though you hope to win fame as a warlord in future you cannot help feeling a little uncomfortable. The year before last I explained — apparently to very little effect — how far I was from being a "chief" — and now I would like to add that I was never shabbily treated by the *Morning News* and did not start the *Tatler* with Sun Fuyuan. The credit for starting the magazine is his entirely.

Fuyuan was editor of the *Morning News* supplement at the time, and he asked me to do some writing for it.

But as I did not write much, it was said that I had the status of a special contributor and received thirty to forty dollars a month regardless of how many articles I wrote. I believe the *Morning News* did have such superior writers, but I was never one of them. However, because of our teacher-student relation, if I may make so bold as to call it that for the moment, I fancy I received preferential treatment. In the first place, my contributions were published very quickly. In the second, I got two to three dollars for every thousand words, usually paid at the end of the month. In the third, I was sometimes even paid for random jottings. This happy state of affairs did not last very long, though, for Fuyuan's position was a most precarious one. A gentleman newly returned from studying in Europe and closely connected with the *Morning News* — unfortunately I forget his name — expressed great dissatisfaction with the supplement and made up his mind to reform it. In preparation for the fight he had started, on the advice of a "scholar," reading the works of Anatole France.

That was the time when France, Wells and Shaw were names to conjure with in China. You could use them to frighten young writers out of their wits, just as you can with Upton Sinclair this year. This being so, the situation was extremely critical. But I cannot say with any certainty how many days or months elapsed between the time when that gentleman back from abroad started reading Anatole France and the day when Fuyuan rushed in fury to my home.

"I've resigned! Confound him!"

These were his first words when he burst into my house that evening. It was only to be expected. There was no call for surprise. Of course I immediately asked the reason for his resignation, and was surprised to learn that I was involved. It seems the returned student had taken advantage of Fuyuan's absence to go to the type-setters and remove one of my manuscripts. The argument over this had forced Fuyuan to resign. The fate of my manuscript did not enrage me, for it was only three verses of doggerel entitled *My Lost Love* which I had written as a joke, ending each verse with "Let her go!" to parody the slush then in vogue. Later I added another verse and published it in the *Tatler*, while later still I included it in *Wild Grass*. Besides, I had used a new pseudonym, and it was only natural that I should be thrown out by the heads of a paper that never liked accepting the work of unknown writers.

I was very sorry, though, that Fuyuan should have resigned over my manuscript. A boulder seemed to be pressing down on my heart. Thus a few days later, when he proposed starting another journal himself, I was nat-urally glad to join him in a "call to arms." He and he alone, was the one to find contributors — sixteen of them as far as I remember — though later not all of them wrote for the magazine. Then advertisements were printed, posted up everywhere and distributed, and about a week later a tiny weekly appeared in Beijing, especially in the neighbourhood of the universities. That was the *Tatler*.

As for the name, I heard that it started when some people picked up a book at random, opened it at random, and chose the characters on which their fingers fell. Not having been there, I do not know what book they used,

Lu Xun delivers a speech in Beijing in 1929

or whether they picked this title the first time or after several attempts, eliminating those words which were unsuitable. At any rate, it is clear from this that the magazine had no definite aim or common programme. All sixteen contributors had different views. Professor Gu Jiegang, for instance, submitted articles on ancient history, counter to the *Tatler*'s preference for topical subjects. Moreover quite a few contributors, who had probably agreed at the start just to oblige Fuyuan, naturally withdrew to "a respectful distance" and then left after writing two or three times. Even Fuyuan himself, as far as I recollect, wrote only three articles altogether, in the last of which he announced that he meant to write much more for the *Tatler*. Since then, however, not a word have I seen from him. This meant the *Tatler* was left with no more than half a dozen steady contributors, all of whom unconsciously shared one common characteristic: they talked freely, without scruples, tried to expedite the birth of the new, and made strong attacks on all old things which might endanger the new. What kind of new things should be brought into being, though, they never explained very clearly; and whenever danger threatened, they deliberately used ambiguous language. That is why Professor Chen Yuan sneered at the *Tatler* for not daring to abuse the warlords openly and taunting famous writers instead. Still, taunting a pug-dog is more dangerous than taunting its master, as we knew. We used ambiguous language, because we hoped that when the pug sniffed out our treason and ran to report to its master, it would have to go into details and consume a good deal of energy, instead of receiving rewards straight off and having everything its own way.

Much hard work was needed to get the magazine going. I remember the two responsible at that time, apart from Fuyuan, were Xiaofeng and Chuandao — two fledglings with the down still on them — who ran to the printers, read the proofs, made bundles of the magazines and took them to the most crowded parts of town to sell. These young people and students taught their elders and teachers a lesson. One felt one was taking life too easily, simply doing a little thinking and writing, and should try to learn from them.

But I heard we were not much good as newsboys. We did best in the universities, especially Beijing University and its College of Arts — after that in the College of Science. The College of Law ignored us almost completely. In fact I think I am correct in saying that, with very few exceptions, the students of law, politics and economics in Beijing University were hardly influenced at all by the *Tatler*. I cannot tell what its effect was on the *Morning News*, but apparently they felt under heavy fire, for they went once to make peace with Fuyuan, and he was in ecstasies. Smiling triumphantly, he told me:

"Marvellous! Little did they know they were trampling on dynamite!"

It would not have mattered his saying this to anyone else. But I felt as if doused with cold water, suspecting that by "dynamite" he meant me. So all my thinking and writing would serve merely to blow me to smithereens on account of their petty quarrel!

"Confound it!" I thought. "I didn't know I had been buried in the ground."

So I started "wandering."

Mr. Tan Zhengbi once used the title of two of my books to make a clever comment on my writing. "Lu Xun starts with a 'call to arms,' " he said, "then takes to 'wandering.' " This might well be applied to my connection with the *Tatler*.

I did not spend long wandering, though, because I wanted to record my reactions to Nietzsche's *Zarathustra*, and if I could squeeze out an article I was willing to do so. I would make all the dynamite I could, however little that was. Thereupon I decided to go on contributing as usual, although I was upset for several days by this unexpected use that had been made of me.

The sales of the *Tatler* kept going up. At first it had been agreed that the contributors should share the printing costs, but after paying an initial ten dollars I was not asked for more, as enough was being made to cover costs — indeed later a profit was made. Then Xiaofeng received the honourable title of "boss." This promotion was not simply an act of kindness, but since Fuyuan had already become editor of the *Beijing Daily* supplement and Chuandao was still a mischievous boy, the few contributors had to grab tongue-tied, blinking Xiaofeng and confer this honour on him. He was also asked to give a dinner each month out of the profits. This method of "making up to a man from whom you expect a favour" proved successful, and thereafter a wooden placard bearing the words *Tatler* Society could sometimes be seen hanging outside the door of tea-houses or restaurants in the market. And if you stopped, you might hear Qian Xuantong's staccato, carrying voice. But as I was avoiding parties in those days, I have no idea what went on.

This is all there was to my connection with the *Tatler*. Sometimes I contributed more, sometimes less. But I went on writing for it until I left Beijing, by which time I was not sure who was editor.

Once in Xiamen (Amoy), I wrote very little for the *Tatler*. One reason was the great distance between us, which meant that no one was pressing me and therefore I felt less responsible. Another reason was that I was in a strange place among strangers, and most of the happenings there were old wives' tales — not worth writing about. Could I have written a *Robinson Crusoe's Life as a Teacher* or a *Dissertation on the Effect of Mosquito Bites* that might have been most interesting, but lacking the gifts for that, I simply sent in a few insignificant articles. At the end of the year I went to Guangzhou, and wrote very little there too. This was partly for the same reason as in Xiamen, partly because administrative duties kept me busy and I was not clear about conditions there. Later on I felt very strongly about certain things, but did not want to publish criticism of abuses under a rival regime.

Reluctance to praise the might of the powerful while threatened by their swords or to win their favour by jeering at their enemies seemed to be a common feature of the "Tatler clique." So although the Tatler escaped destruction at the hands of Duan Qirui and his pug-dogs, it was finally banned by General Zhang Zuolin* at the same time as its distributor — Beixin Publishing House — was closed. That was in 1927.

That year Xiaofeng came to see me in Shanghai, suggested printing the Tatler here, and asked me to act as editor. In view of our past connection I could not very well refuse, so I accepted. Only then did I find out how the magazine was edited. It was very simple: the editor had no authority to refuse articles by the other members: he had to accept them. All he could do was exercise a certain amount of discretion in the selection of articles from outsiders, and if necessary cut certain passages. This latter was all I had to do, and as a matter of fact nine out of ten of our members sent their manuscripts straight to Beixin Publishing House, which delivered them to the printers: I saw them only when printed and bound. The term "members" is ambiguous. Few of the early editorial board were left, and later members kept coming and going. As the Tatler liked to print the complaints of those who had run their heads against a wall, it had many contributors who had just started writing but could find no publisher, or who had quarrelled with their own cliques and used this chance to hit back. But once they had made a name, of course they calmed down. And naturally, owing to the changes in the situation, quite a few fell out with each other and withdrew. This is why

---

* A warlord in North China during the early days of the Republic.

the expression "members" is so vague. The practice the year before last was to treat anyone who sent in several manuscripts all of which were printed as someone to be trusted — just like an old member. But there were also writers introduced by old members who sent their articles direct to Beixin Publishing House, so that the editor never saw them until they were published.

The fortunes of the *Tatler* declined a good deal after I became editor. We received an official warning, were banned by the Zhejiang authorities, and were wildly attacked by the "revolutionary writers" of the Creation Society. I never understood the reason for the warning, though some people said it was because of a play. The ban was bewildering too, though it was said it was because we had an article exposing what went on behind the scenes in Fudan University, and at that time some high Kuomintang functionaries there were Fudan graduates. As for the attack on us by the Creation Society, it had historical roots. While they were still protecting the "palace of art" before becoming "revolutionary," they already considered certain members of the "*Tatler* clique" as thorns in their side. But that is a long story, which I must leave for another time.

The *Tatler* itself was actually going downhill. There were virtually no more criticisms of current events; even articles like this were rare, and then even more of the rump of the old guard dropped out. The reason for the first development, to my mind, was a lack of anything to say or a fear of speaking out — look at the warning and ban. As for the second, I think I was to blame. To take one example, after I was forced to publish a letter containing a very mild correction of some slips made by Mr. Liu Bannong in his "Capture of Lin Zexu," he never wrote another word for us. And after I refused a mimeographed article on Mr. Feng Yuxiang, recommended by Mr. Jiang Shaoyuan, he stopped writing for us too. Moreover, before long this mimeographed article appeared in *Contributions*, which Fuyuan was publishing, with a respectful account in small print of how I had turned it down.

Another obvious change was in the jumble of advertisements. You can generally tell the nature of a magazine from the type of advertisements carried. For instance, the *Modern Critic* brought out by "respectable gentlemen" has a long-term advertisement for the Jincheng Bank. *Autumn Plain*, brought out by overseas Chinese students from the South Seas, carries advertisements for Tiger Balm Medicine. And although many of the smaller papers dub themselves "revolutionary literature," so long as most of the advertisements are for restaurants or cures for venereal disease, you know who the authors and readers are. It is still the same old gang; only now they write about authors and authoresses instead of actors and singsong girls — either praising or abusing them, to make their mark in the field of letters. When the *Tatler* first came out the choice of advertisements was very strict, and if the members did not think well of a new book they would not print a notice of it. Since the magazine belonged to a few congenial spirits, the editor could carry out their wishes. They say the reason Beixin Publishing House published *Beixin Fortnightly* was because certain advertisements could not be printed in the *Tatler*. But once the magazine's headquarters moved to Shanghai, even doctors' names appeared in it, to say nothing of book notices. An advertisement for a stocking factory appeared too, and even one for pills to cure involuntary emissions. True, no one can guarantee that the readers of the *Tatler* do not suffer from involuntary emissions, the more so since this is no crime; but for remedial measures one should read the *Shen Bao* or, to be on the safe side, the *Medical Journal*. I received several accusing letters because of this, and in the *Tatler* itself we printed an article sent in condemning us.

Before this, though, I had done all I could. When the stocking factory appeared, I challenged Xiaofeng to his face. His answer was: "The man who sends advertisements must have made a mistake." When the involuntary emissions appeared, I wrote a letter to which I received no answer. After that, however, these advertisements stopped. I fancy Xiaofeng was making a compromise, because at that time Beixin Publishing House was not only responsible for circulation, but was paying some writers directly; hence the *Tatler* was no longer the magazine of a few congenial spirits.

When I was richer by half a year's experience, I proposed to Xiaofeng that we discontinue publication; but he did not agree. Then I resigned from the editorship. When Xiaofeng asked me to find a successor, I recommended Rou Shi.*

But somehow or other, when Rou Shi had been editor for six months and finished the first half of Volume V, he resigned too.

This is all that happened during the four years of my connection with the *Tatler*. If you compare the earlier numbers with the latter, you will see what a great change took place. The most striking difference was that the magazine virtually stopped touching on current events and printed more long articles, because this made it easier to fill space and avoid disaster. Although this force which destroyed the old and disclosed the old things hidden in the new is still hated by both the old-fashioned and those who think themselves modern, this force belongs to the past.

December 22, 1929

---

* See "Written for the Sake of Forgetting" on p. 234 below.

1930

1950

"HARD TRANSLATION" AND THE
"CLASS CHARACTER OF
LITERATURE"

I

I hear members of the *Crescent Moon* clique say their sales are going up. Very likely. Even I, few as my connections are, have seen the combined issue of numbers six and seven of Volume II in the hands of two young people. Glancing through it, I found most of it devoted to short stories and essays on "freedom of speech." But near the end was an article by Mr. Liang Shiqiu entitled "On Mr. Lu Xun's 'Hard Translation,'" which he considers "next door to literal translation." And "this fashion for literal translation should not be encouraged," he says. He quotes three passages I have translated, as well as my note at the end of *Art and Criticism:**

Owing to my inadequacy as a translator and the limitations of the Chinese language, upon reading through my translation I find it obscure and uneven, and in many places very hard to understand. Yet if I were to cut the redundant phrases, it would lose its original flavour. As far as I am concerned, I must either go on producing these hard translations, or produce

---

*Lu Xun's translation, published in 1929, of Lunacharsky's essays on art.

none at all. I can only hope readers will be willing to make the necessary mental effort to read it.

He carefully marks this passage with circles,* drawing double circles by "hard translation," and then "solemnly" pronounces this "criticism": "We made 'a mental effort to read it,' but to no purpose. What difference is there between 'hard translation' and 'literal translation'?"

Though the *Crescent Moon* denies that it is organized, and its essays seem to show a hatred for proletarian "organizations" and "cliques," the fact is it is organized. All the essays on politics in this number, at any rate, support each other. As for art, this article was printed in the wake of another by the same critic entitled "Has Literature a Class Character?" In this we read:

> Most unfortunately, though, I cannot understand a single one of these books. . . . What I find most difficult is the language . . . it is harder than reading some occult formula. . . . So far not a single Chinese has explained to us in language that Chinese can understand just what the theory of proletarian literature is.

These words are marked with circles too, but I have taken the liberty of leaving them out to save the printers trouble. The thing is that Mr. Liang looks upon himself as the representative of all Chinese. So if he cannot understand these books no Chinese can understand them, and they ought to disappear from China — that is why he points out that "this fashion should not be encouraged."

I cannot represent all other translators of "occult formulae," but speaking for myself I doubt if the matter is so simple. In the first place, Mr. Liang considers he made "a mental effort to read it." But did he really? Is he capable of one? This is one question. A characteristic of the *Crescent Moon* clique is the way it prides itself on

---

* Equivalent to underlining for emphasis.

being hard, when in fact it is as soft as cotton. In the second place, though Mr. Liang offers to represent all China, is he really the best Chinese? This is another question. Answers to these questions can be found in his article "Has Literature a Class Character?" There is no need to translate "proletariat" phonetically when one can translate its meaning, yet this critic declares:

> If we look up the dictionary, this word has a most undignified connotation, for according to the big *Webster Dictionary*, "proletariat" means: "A citizen of the lowest class who served the state not with property, but only by having children . . ." (in Roman times at least!).

There is actually no need to argue about "dignity," for surely no one with the least common sense would mistake the present day for Roman times, or imagine the modern proletariat is like the old Romans. Suppose we translated "chemistry" phonetically, would readers confuse it with the alchemy of ancient Egypt? I would not dream of studying the etymology of Mr. Liang's name in considering his essays, or marvelling that a "one-plank bridge"* should be able to write. Even "looking up the dictionary" (the big *Webster Dictionary!*) would still be "to no purpose." I doubt if this is true of all Chinese.

II

What interests me most, however, is the passage already quoted from Mr. Liang's article, where twice he uses the expression "we" — so suggestive of a group or a clique. Though an author wields his pen in solitude, there must naturally be many others who share his views. He is therefore quite right to use "we" — this

---

* The character *liang* means "bridge."

sounds stronger, and the author need not shoulder the whole responsibility. But "before all can think in one way," at a time when "there should be freedom of speech," there is a "snag" here of the kind Mr. Liang criticizes in capitalist society. Yes, indeed, the existence of "we" means there must also be "they." So though "we" of the Crescent Moon Society believe that "this fashion for literal translation should not be encouraged," there are others who do not feel that they have read "to no purpose." They keep alive my hard translation which is rather different from literal translation.

I am one of the Crescent Moon Society's "they," because my translations fall completely short of Mr. Liang's requirements.

His essay "On Hard Translation" starts by declaring distorted translations better than literal ones.

> It is impossible for a translation to be a complete misrepresentation. . . . Maybe unfaithful renderings give a wrong idea of the original, but they give the reader something even though they are mistaken. Even if the wrongness does damage, it is still pleasant to read.

The last two sentences might well be marked with double circles, if I went in for that sort of thing. But instead of translating in order to give people "pleasure," I often try to make them uncomfortable, or even exasperated, furious and bitter. The only reading material to "give pleasure" is that written by the translators and authors of the Crescent Moon Society! Mr. Xu Zhimo's poems, the short stories of Shen Congwen and Ling Shuhua, Mr. Chen Yuan's idle thoughts, Mr. Liang Shiqiu's criticism, Mr. Pan Guangdan's eugenics, and Mr. Babbitt's humanism.

Mr. Liang goes on to say, "Reading books like this is like reading a map — you have to trace your way through the syntax with your finger." To my mind this is nonsense — absolute drivel. I agree that "reading books like this" is like reading a map if you have to trace your way through the syntax. But though reading maps is not such a "pleasure" as looking at pictures of "Lady Yang Emerging from Her Bath" or "The Three Friends of Winter,"* and you may have to use your finger (actually I suspect this applies only to Mr. Liang, whereas those who are used to maps use merely their eyes), still a map is not a literal representation. Thus if the same effort is needed for "hard translation," it too must differ slightly from literal translation. Those who know the alphabet and consider themselves the new scholars may still be ignorant of chemical formulae. Those who can use the abacus and consider themselves mathematicians may not be able to make head or tail of sums on paper. In the world today, studies in one field do not make you omniscient.

Then Mr. Liang gives as examples three passages from my translation, though quite clearly: "Lifted out of context, they cannot be too intelligible." And in "Has Literature a Class Character?" he uses a similar dodge, basing his judgement of the whole on two translated poems. "Perhaps no great proletarian literature has appeared yet," he says. "In that case I am willing to go on waiting." Tricks like these do give "pleasure," it is true, but let me quote a passage from this number of the *Crescent Moon* — original writing! — from the eighth page of "Moving House."

"Does a chicken have ears?"
"I have never seen a chicken with ears."
"Then how can it hear me call it?"
She was thinking how Fourth Aunt had told her two days before that ears were for hearing and eyes for seeing.
"Is this egg a yellow chick or a black one?"
When Fourth Aunt did not answer, Zhi'er stood up

---

* Plum, pine and bamboo.

and stroked one egg.

"You can't tell yet. Wait till the chick is hatched."
"Wan'er says chicks turn into hens. Will these chicks turn into hens too?"

"If you feed them properly. This chick wasn't so big as this when we bought it, was it?"

Enough. The language is intelligible, and there is no need to trace your way through the syntax with one finger, but I am not willing "to go on waiting." No "pleasure" is involved in this passage. Indeed there is very little difference between this and not writing at all.

Finally Mr. Liang raises a problem:

Chinese is unlike other languages — that is what makes translation difficult. If the grammar, syntax and vocabulary of two languages were identical, we should have no trouble in translating. . . . With intelligibility as our prime criterion, there is no harm in changing the order of sentences, because "making a mental effort" is no fun, and it is doubtful whether "hard translation" can preserve "the essential style of the original." Certainly, if "hard translation" could preserve the essential style of the original that would be a miracle, and we could not accuse the Chinese language of having "limitations."

I am not quite such a fool as to look for a foreign language which is like Chinese, or hope that "the grammar, syntax and vocabulary of the two languages will be identical." But I believe it is relatively easy to translate from languages which have a complex grammar. It is relatively easy, too, to translate from a language akin to your own, although that still requires some trouble. Can we say that it is no trouble to translate Dutch into German or Russian into Polish? Japanese is very different from all European languages, yet it is gradually acquiring new methods of expression, so that it is easier to translate now than classical Japanese without losing the flavour of the original. To begin with, of course, you have to "trace your way through the syntax," which is far from "fun" for certain people. But once you are used to this, you assimilate these expressions into your own language. Chinese grammar is even more deficient than that of classical Japanese, but it has known changes too. For instance, the languages used in Sima Qian's *Historical Records* and the *Han History** are different from that of the *Book of History,*** and our modern vernacular is different again. There have been additions and inventions, as in the Tang Dynasty translations of Buddhist scriptures and the Yuan Dynasty translations of the emperor's edicts. At the time, much of that "grammar, syntax and vocabulary" was new-fangled; but once men got used to it they could understand it without tracing the words with their fingers. And now that we are dealing with "foreign languages" we may need many new forms of construction — which, to put it strongly, have to be made by "hard translation." In my experience, you can retain the flavour of the original better by this method than by rearranging your sentences; but modern Chinese has its limitations because it is still waiting for new constructions. There is nothing "miraculous" about this. Of course, for some people it is no "fun" to have to "trace with a finger" or "make a mental effort." But I had no intention of giving these gentlemen "pleasure" or "fun." If some readers can learn from my translations, it is quite immaterial to me whether Mr. Liang Shiqiu and his likes enjoy them or not.

But though Mr. Liang feels no need to seek help from proletarian literary theory, he is still confused on many points. For instance, he says, "The works Mr. Lu Xun translated a few years ago, such as Hakuson Kuriyagawa's *Symbols of Misery,* were not unintelligible. But

---

* The *Historical Records* and the *Han History* were written during the Han Dynasty.
** A collection of records dating from the earliest ages.

recently his style seems to have changed." Anyone with
a grain of common sense knows that "Chinese is unlike
other languages," but the "style" and "syntax" vary
according to the individual writer in every language.
Sentences may be complex or simple, the vocabulary may
be popular or specialized; you will never find all the
writers in one language equally easy to understand. I
translated *Symbols of Misery* according to the same principles I am following today — sentence by sentence,
sometimes even word by word. If Mr. Liang Shiqiu
actually found it intelligible that is because the original
was easy to understand, and because Mr. Liang Shiqiu
is one of China's modern critics; also because he was
fairly accustomed to the new constructions I used. A
scholar in a tiny village who reads nothing but ancient
Chinese would find it more difficult than an "occult
formula."

III

But these translations of proletarian literary criticism
— "more difficult than an occult formula" — have made
quite an impression on Mr. Liang. It may sound odd
that he should be influenced by something he cannot
understand, yet such is the case. In "Has Literature a
Class Character?" this critic writes, "In my present criticism of so-called proletarian literary theory, I can judge
only by the few pieces I understand." In other words,
his knowledge of this theory is far from comprehensive.

But we (I include all translators of "occult formulae,"
hence the plural) are only partly responsible for this
crime. The critic is also to blame for his own stupidity
or laziness. I do not know about "this Lunacharsky and
Plekhanov," but there are English translations of three
essays by "Bogdanov and the rest of them," and half of
Trotsky's *Literature and Revolution.* Since there is no

"Mr. Lu Xun" in England, the translation should be extremely intelligible. And since Mr. Liang has so courageously expressed his readiness to "go on waiting" for the production of great proletarian literature, why did he not wait a little to read some of the theory before passing judgement on it? A fool does not look for a thing because he does not know of its existence, while a lazy man does not look although he knows. By just sitting there quietly he may find some "pleasure." But if he opens his mouth it is easy for cold air to go down his throat.

Take that noble essay "Has Literature a Class Character?" for example, which concludes that literature does not. I think the best attempts at wiping out class character are Mr. Wu Zhihui's learned work "Marx and Parx" and that other gentleman's "Ain't No Such Thing as Class." So let all little birds stop cheeping, and the world will be at peace. But Mr. Liang, poisoned by this Marxism, admits that there is a capitalist system in many places, and that under this system you find proletarians. However, "the proletarians had no class consciousness to begin with. It was a few excessively kind-hearted and radical-minded leaders who taught them to be conscious of themselves as a class," to make them unite more quickly and arouse their fighting spirit. Right, but I think their teachers must have been actuated not by excessive sympathy but by the wish to change the world. Besides, "something which does not exist" can hardly have consciousness or be aroused. If this happens, that shows that it exists after all. And something that exists cannot be kept hidden long, just as, to begin with, Galileo with his claim that the earth rotates and Darwin with his theory of evolution were either nearly burned by the religious or fiercely attacked by the conservative, yet today nobody finds anything strange in their teaching, because the earth really does rotate and living things are evolving. To acknowledge that a thing exists and then conceal its existence requires extraordinary skill.

But Mr. Liang has his own method of doing away with conflict, for he believes with Rousseau: "Property is the foundation of civilization." "Therefore to attack the capitalist system is the same as attacking civilization," he claims. "If a worker who is any good works hard all his life, he should acquire a decent property. This is the proper way to struggle in life." In my opinion, although Rousseau lived a hundred and fifty years ago, he could hardly have thought that all the culture of the past and future must be based on property. (Had he said economic relationships were its base, he would of course have been right.) Greece and India have had great civilizations, but their most glorious ages were not in bourgeois society, as he should have known. If he did not know, that was his mistake. As for the "proper" way in which proletarians should painstakingly climb up into the propertied class, this is what rich old gentlemen in China used to teach poor workers when they were in a good mood. Indeed there are many workers today who want by "hard and honest" labour to climb one rung in the social ladder. But this is before anyone has taught them "to be conscious of themselves as a class." Once they learn this, they will no longer be content to climb up one by one, for truly as Mr. Liang says:

> As a class, they want to be organized. As one group, they will not simply follow the beaten track but spring up to seize political and economic power, to become the ruling class.

But are there any working men left who still want to "work hard and honestly all their lives, till they acquire a decent property"? Of course there are, but they should rank as "not yet moneyed property-owners." Mr. Liang's advice will be so violently rejected by working men that he will be reduced to exchanging compliments with old gentlemen.

What does the future hold, then? Mr. Liang sees no cause for alarm. For "these revolutionary times cannot last, and by a natural process of evolution the law of the survival of the fittest will be confirmed again, when the most able and intelligent occupy the best positions, and the workers remain workers." But, as no doubt the proletariat realizes also: "The barbarous forces will sooner or later be vanquished by the forces of civilization," and they will "build a so-called proletarian culture . . . including art and science."

And now we come to our main subject — literary criticism.

IV

First Mr. Liang considers that the main mistake of proletarian literary theory is that it "attaches the fetters of class to literature," because though a capitalist and a worker are different they also share common features. Their "human nature" — there are circles beside these words — "is the same." For instance, both know joy and anger, both know love (here we speak of "love itself, not of modes of loving"). "Literature is the art which expresses this most basic human nature." These remarks are contradictory and meaningless. If property is the base of culture and the most "deserving" of the poor try their hardest to get on in the world, social climbing must be the main aim of human life and rich men the crowning glory of mankind. It is enough, then, for literature to portray the bourgeoisie only — why this "excessive sympathy"? Why include the working class which is doomed to extinction? In any case, how do you portray "human nature" itself? For instance, all chemical substances, whether elements or compounds, have chemical affinities; all physical matter has a certain degree of hardness, but to reveal these qualities you must use two

substances. There is no magic method of revealing the
chemical affinity or degree of hardness "themselves" —
you have to use matter. And then the phenomena vary
according to the matter. Literature without human
characters cannot show men's "nature" either. But once
you use human characters, especially in a class society,
you cannot get round their inherent class character. This
is not a question of superimposing class "fetters" — it is
something inevitable. Of course, it is human nature to
know joy and anger, but the poor are never worried because they lose money on the stock exchange, and an
oil magnate cannot know the trials of an old woman collecting cinders in Beijing. Victims of famine will hardly
grow orchids like rich old gentlemen, nor will Jiao Da
in the Jia family fall in love with Miss Lin.* Certainly
"Oh, Steam whistle! Oh, Lenin!" is not proletarian
literature, but neither does writing like "All things! All
men!" "When joy comes, all men rejoice!" show "human
nature" itself. If we consider the literature which
portrays the lowest common denominator of human
nature as the highest, then descriptions of the most basic
animal functions — eating, breathing, moving and pro-
creation — must be even better. Better still would be
those which dispense with movement and just describe
biological nature. If you say we must describe human
nature because we are men, then workers must produce
proletarian literature because they are workers.

Next Mr. Liang says that a writer's class has no effect
on his writing. Tolstoy belonged to the nobility, yet he
sympathized with the poor, though he did not advocate
class struggle. Marx was certainly not a member of the
proletariat, and Dr. Johnson, who remained poor to the
end of his days, talked and behaved more like a
noble than the nobles themselves. So to judge a work

---

* The heroine of *A Dream of Red Mansions*. Jiao Da was a
servant.

of literature you must read it, instead of letting yourself be influenced by the author's social position and class.

These examples quite fail to prove that literature has no class character. It was precisely because Tolstoy was a noble who had not lost all his old propensities that he merely sympathized with the poor without advocating class struggle. Marx certainly did not come from the proletariat, but since he wrote no works of literature we cannot assume that had he done so he would certainly have described love itself, not modes of loving. As for Dr. Johnson, who was poor to the end of his days yet talked and behaved more like royalty than a prince of the blood, I cannot account for his attitude because I know too little about English literature and about his life. Perhaps his idea was to "work hard and honestly all his life, till he acquired a decent property," and then climb up into the nobility. But doomed to extinction, he did not even acquire the property. He could only pose for his own "pleasure."

Next Mr. Liang says, "Great works are invariably the property of a minority. The majority will always be stupid, always averse to literature." But taste or the lack of it has nothing to do with class, because "the appreciation of literature is an inborn gift." Exactly: so even among the proletariat, there may be men with this "gift." As far as I can see, a man with this gift may be too poor to go to school and unable to read a single word, but he will appreciate the *Crescent Moon Monthly,* thus proving that "human nature" and art as such have no class character. Since Mr. Liang knows, however, that there are not many proletarians blessed with this inborn gift, he has chosen some other art (?) for them: "Popular operas for instance, films, popular stories and so on," because "most workers and peasants need amusement and a little artistic entertainment sometimes." Looked at this way, it does seem as if literature varies from class to class, but this is determined by men's taste, the development of which has nothing to do with money but is just an "inborn gift." So writers should write freely. They should not pen essays in praise of royal or noble patrons, nor let themselves be intimidated by the working class. Quite right. But in none of the proletarian literary theory we have seen has it been said that writers should not be backed by royal or noble patrons, nor let themselves be intimidated by the working class, to pen essays in praise of either. All it'claims is that literature has a class character, and that though authors in a class society consider themselves "free" and above classes, they are bound to be controlled unconsciously by the ideas of their class; hence what they write cannot be the culture of some other class. As a case in point take this article by Mr. Liang, aimed at doing away with the class character of literature and blazing the truth abroad. We can see at a glance that this view of property as the base of culture and of the poor as scum doomed to extinction is the "weapon" — I mean the "reasoning" — of the bourgeoisie. Literary critics of the proletariat believe that those who advance the theory of literature for "all mankind," "transcending classes," are helping the propertied class — and here we have clear evidence of it. As for those like Mr. Cheng Fangwu who say, "They are bound to triumph, so let us go to guide and comfort them," after saying "go" they see "them" off — "them" being the proletarian writers other than themselves. Quite obviously, he shares Mr. Liang's mistake of twisting the literary theory of the proletariat to suit himself.

Then what Mr. Liang hates most is the way proletarian literary critics consider art as a weapon in the struggle — as propaganda. He "does not disapprove of anyone using writing to attain some ulterior end," but he "cannot agree that this propaganda is literature." To my mind, he is simply worried about nothing. Judging by what I have read of those theories, it merely says that all art is bound to be partisan — no one claims that propaganda alone is literature. It is true that during the last couple of years a great many poems and stories interlarded with slogans have been passed off as proletarian literature in China. But it was because there was nothing working-class about either their content or form that they had to use slogans to show their "modernity." They are not really proletarian literature either. This year, to defend "revolutionary literature," that well-known "proletarian literary critic" Mr. Qian Xingcun quoted Lunacharsky in the periodical *The Pioneer*, under the impression that because Lunacharsky advocated writing the masses could understand it showed that no one should object to slogans. But to my mind, consciously or unconsciously, he has distorted the truth just as much as Mr. Liang Shiqiu. When Lunacharsky spoke of writing the masses could understand, he had in mind the sort of pamphlets Tolstoy printed and distributed to his peasants, using songs and jokes in language that workers and peasants could easily comprehend. We see this too from the fact that Demyan Byedny, who received the Red Flag badge for his poetry, has no slogans in his poems.

Last of all, Mr. Liang wants to test the goods themselves. Indeed, this is the most realistic approach; but it is not fair simply to display two translated poems to the public. The *Crescent Moon* once carried an article entitled "The Difficulties of Translation," and these difficulties apply most of all to poems. Judging by my own reading, China has produced no works during the last eleven years to compare with Lunacharsky's *Liberation of Don Quixote*, Fadeyev's *The Nineteen* or Gladkov's *Cement*. I assert this of groups like the Crescent Moon Society which, skulking in the twilight of bourgeois culture, are defending bourgeois writers so zealously. I cannot instance any really successful works by self-professed proletarian writers either. But Mr. Qian Xingcun is a good apologist. He explains that a rising class is naturally childish and naive in its writing, and none but the unfriendly "bourgeois" would demand good works from them straightaway. This is sound as far as workers and peasants are concerned: the request is as unreasonable as demanding to know why a man who has long gone cold and hungry is not as fat as a millionaire. But none of China's present writers have just laid down hoe or axe. By far the greater number of them are intellectuals, and some of them have long been well-known authors. Are we to believe that when they overcome their petty-bourgeois outlook even their old skill in writing vanishes too? Impossible! The old Russian writers, Alexei Tolstoy, V. Veresayev and Prishvin, are still producing good work. Our Chinese writers' bad habit of using slogans unsupported by facts arises not from their view of "art as a weapon in the class struggle" but because they "use the class struggle as a weapon in art." Under the banner of "proletarian literature" many mountebanks have gathered. If you look at last year's book notices, practically all are described as revolutionary works. Then the critics use their apologies to "liquidate" opposition. Since they put literature under the wing of the "class struggle," the writers need make no effort themselves, and their works have little in common either with literature or revolution.

But of course present conditions in China cannot disprove the fact of the rise of proletarian literature. Mr. Liang knows this too, which is why he admits at the end:

> If proletarian intellectuals insist on calling their propaganda proletarian literature, we must consider it a new form of writing, a new achievement in literature. There is no need for them to shout "Down with bourgeois literature!" to capture the world of letters, because this is big enough to make room for the new."

This reminds me of the slogan: "Let China and Japan

be friends, and prosper together side by side!"* In the eyes of the half-fledged proletariat, it is tantamount to cheating. I am afraid there are still proletarian writers who agree with him, but these are the "proletarians" whom Mr. Liang describes as "deserving," who want to climb into the bourgeoisie. What they write sounds like the complaints of poor scholars before passing the palace examination; but from the start, during their climb and after, they produce no proletarian literature. Proletarian literature is one part of the workers' struggle to liberate their own class and all other classes. They want the whole place, not one corner. Let us compare them with our literary critics. If we place two arm-chairs in the "humanistic Palace of Art" (to borrow a phrase from Mr. Cheng Fangwu), and ask Mr. Liang Shiqiu and Mr. Qian Xingcun to sit there side by side, one holding the *Crescent Moon* in his right hand, the other the *Sun*** in his left, they will truly be an example of well-matched "labour and capital."

V

At this point, let me revert to my "hard translation."

It seems that another question should be asked here: If proletarian literature lays such stress on propaganda, and propaganda must be intelligible to the masses, why do you make these "hard" and obscure translations of theoretical "occult formulae"? Surely your labour is wasted?

My answer is: I translate for myself, for a few who consider themselves proletarian critics, and for some

---

* A slogan raised by the Japanese imperialists to deceive the Chinese people.

** The Sun Society, founded in 1927 in Shanghai, advocated revolutionary writing. In 1928 and 1929, under the influence of the "Leftist" adventurist line then prevailing, the Sun Society carried out misguided attacks on Lu Xun.

readers who want to understand these theories and are
not out for "pleasure" or afraid of difficulties.

For the last two years there has been an enormous
number of attacks on me. You can find the name Lu
Xun in virtually every magazine, and a glance will show
that most of the authors write like revolutionary men
of letters. After reading a few, however, I began to find
them empty and meaningless. The scalpel fails to
pierce the skin; the bullet fails to inflict a mortal wound.
For instance, my class has not been determined yet. One
moment they call me a petty-bourgeois, the next a bourgeois; sometimes they promote me to "spawn of feudalism," which is some kind of ape (see "A Letter from
Tokyo" in *Creation Monthly*). Once they took exception
to the colour of my teeth. In a society like this the
spawn of feudalism is all too likely to show off, but no
"materialist view of history" has ever explained why it
should resemble an ape, or why yellow teeth should
injure the proletarian revolution. So to my mind theoretical reference works on these subjects are all too few,
which accounts for the general confusion. Today we
cannot avoid dissecting and devouring our enemies; but
if we had books on anatomy and cookery and were guided
by them, we should be clearer about the structure of the
body and produce something tastier. Revolutionaries are
often compared to the legendary Prometheus, because in
spite of the torture to which Zeus exposed him he had so
much love and fortitude that he never regretted stealing
fire for mankind. But I stole fire from abroad to cook
my own flesh, in the hope that if the taste proved
agreeable those who tasted it would benefit more, and
my sacrifice would not prove in vain. I was actuated by
sheer individualism, mingled with the ostentatiousness
of a petty-bourgeois, and the "vindictiveness" shown
when I slowly picked up a scalpel and plunged it into the
heart of those who have dissected me. "They want re-
venge!" says Mr. Liang. In fact, "they" are not the only

ones. This applies to many of the "spawn of feudalism" too. Still, I too wanted to be of some use to society, for then onlookers could at least see my fire and light. So I started with *The Policy on Art*,* because that contains the views of many schools.

Mr. Zheng Boqi keeps a bookshop now, and has printed the plays of Hauptmann and Lady Gregory. In the days when he was still a revolutionary writer and editor of *Art and Life*, he scoffed at me in its pages for translating this, saying I was unwilling to be left behind but unfortunately others had got ahead of me. If you can bob up again by translating one book, it is really too easy to be a revolutionary writer — that was never my intention. One of the minor papers described my translating Plekhanov's *Theory of Art* as a "surrender." Yes, there have been many cases of surrender. But at that time Generalissimo Cheng Fangwu had crawled out of the hot springs in Japan and taken rooms in a hotel in Paris, so to whom could I turn? This year opinions have changed. In both *The Pioneer* and *Modern Stories* we are told there is "a change of direction." In some Japanese magazines I read these words applied in a complimentary sense to Teppei Kataoka of the former new impressionist school.** In fact, this confused talk is part of our old trouble — we are taken in by names and refuse to think for ourselves. To translate one book on working-class literature is not enough to show one's direction, and mistranslated it may even cause harm. I translate for those proletarian critics who pass unduly hasty judgements, because they should not be afraid of trouble but should be willing to study these theories seriously.

And I can say with confidence that I never deliberately

---

* A collection of resolutions of the C.P.S.U. retranslated from the Japanese.

** Teppei Kataoka, who founded this school in 1924, joined the progressive camp in 1926.

distort the meaning of any work. When it touches critics I despise on the raw, I laugh. When it touches me on the raw, I put up with it. But I absolutely refuse to make additions or cuts, hence I have always believed in "hard translation." In the long run better translators are bound to appear, who will neither distort the meaning nor give "hard" or "literal" translations; and of course when that happens my translations will be weeded out. All I am trying to do is fill the gap between "having none" and "having better" translations.

But there is still a great deal of paper in the world, and each literary coterie is small. They have grandiose aims but little strength and cannot use all that paper. So when the critics in each group whose function it is to attack their foes, help their friends, and make a clean sweep of heresies see anyone else wasting paper, they sigh bitterly, shake their heads and stamp with rage. The *Shen Bao* in Shanghai was so outraged that it described those who translate works of social science as "curs and cats." When Mr. G. C. Jiang, whose "status among China's new writers is known to all," went to Tokyo for medical treatment he met Koreto Kurahara, who told him they had some appalling translations in Japan, much more difficult to read than the original. . . . Mr. Jiang retorted with a smile:

> Translating in China is even more of a farce. Recently many of our books have been translated from the Japanese, so if the Japanese make mistakes, cuts or alterations in translating a European writer, you can imagine how the book will have changed by the time the Japanese is translated into Chinese! *(The Pioneer.)*

This shows dissatisfaction with translation, especially with translation at two removes. But while Mr. Liang names books and points out their faults, Mr. Jiang just gives a smile and makes a clean sweep — this is much more thoroughgoing. I personally am greatly indebted to Kurahara, who has translated many novels and books on the theory of art directly from the Russian. I wish China had one or two translators from the Russian of his integrity to introduce good books systematically, instead of thinking they have done their duty as revolutionary writers by calling others "bad eggs"!

But Mr. Liang Shiqiu does not translate such works, nor does the great man who describes others as "curs and cats." Mr. Jiang who has studied Russian is highly qualified for the task, but unfortunately since his illness he has only produced *A Week*, two translations of which have already appeared in Japan. There used to be much talk in China of Darwin and Nietzsche, until during the World War they came in for a great dressing-down; but there is still only one Chinese translation of Darwin and only half of Nietzsche has been translated. Since the scholars and men of letters who have studied English and German either have no time or think translating beneath them, I am afraid all we can do is to let others laugh at or abuse us for the time being, but go on translating from the Japanese, or making a literal translation from the original with the help of a Japanese version. I mean to go on doing this myself, and hope others will do the same, to fill in the emptiness in our lofty discussions, because we cannot consider it "a farce" like Mr. Jiang, nor should we be "willing to wait" like Mr. Liang.

VI

Earlier on I wrote, "One characteristic of the Crescent Moon Society is the way it prides itself on being hard, when actually it is as soft as cotton." I must amplify this statement now to wind up this article.

When the *Crescent Moon* first appeared, it was all for "a serious attitude," yet it abuses those who abuse it and jeers at those who jeer at it. There is nothing wrong in this. It is simply paying them back in their own coin; and though this also shows "vindictiveness," it is not of a personal nature. The notice from the combined issue of Numbers 6 and 7 in Volume II says, "We all remain 'tolerant' — except that we cannot tolerate 'intolerance' — we all appreciate seasoned, rational ideas." There is nothing wrong with these two last sentences either. "An eye for an eye and a tooth for a tooth" is consistent with the principles first stated. But once you take this road you are bound to come across people who "resist violence with violence" and this cannot be tolerated by the "seasoned ideas" so dear to the gentlemen of the Crescent Moon Society.

Now the Crescent Moon Society's freedom of speech has been curtailed. Judging by their old rule, they ought to suppress the suppressors, but instead they have reacted with an article in the *Crescent Moon* entitled: "A Letter to Those Who Restrict the Freedom of the Press." First they quote the other side's party principles, then foreign laws, and finally examples from Eastern and Western history, to show that all who suppress freedom finally perish themselves — a warning to the other side.

So in the last analysis, the "serious attitude" of the Crescent Moon Society and its method of demanding "an eye for an eye" are only used towards foes of equal or lesser strength. If someone stronger gives them a black eye, they make an exception for him, and simply cover their face with their hands to shout:

"Look out for your own eye!"

CUSTOM AND REFORM

Those who have ossified mentally and physically invariably oppose the slightest reform. At first glance they seem afraid of inconvenience, while in fact they are afraid of losing out; yet they often produce most high-sounding justifications.

The ban on the lunar calendar this year was a small matter, having no bearing on affairs of state, but of course the shopkeepers* set up a howl of dismay. Not only that, even Shanghai hooligans and clerks in business firms heaved many bitter sighs and declared that this was too bad for the peasants on their farms and for those waiting for the tides at sea. This actually made them remember the peasants and sailors they had so long forgotten — an instance, surely, of universal love.

On the twenty-third of the twelfth month by the lunar calendar, crackers started exploding everywhere.

"You are still celebrating the lunar New Year this year," I said to a shop assistant. "Will you have to celebrate the solar one next year?"

"Next year is next year," he answered. "We shall see."

He did not believe they would have to celebrate the solar New Year next year. Yet the lunar calendar has in fact been cut out of the calendar, leaving only the twenty-four festivals. At the same time, however, an advertisement has appeared in the papers for a "Com-

---

* It was customary for shopkeepers to collect payment at the end of the lunar year.

97

bined Lunar and Solar Calendar for the Next Hundred and Twenty Years." Fine! They have prepared a lunar calendar for our grandsons and great-grandsons for the next hundred and twenty years!

Although Mr. Liang Shiqiu and his friends have such a dislike for the majority, its strength is enormous and decisive. Unless would-be reformers understand the people thoroughly and find a way to tempt them along the right path, noble arguments and lofty ideas, romantic or classical literature will be unable to touch them and will simply be read by a few men in their studies for their private satisfaction. Even a "good men's government,"* if it issued orders for reform, would be dragged back by them before long to the old path.

A true revolutionary can see further than other men, as in the case of Mr. Lenin, who looks on tradition and custom as part of "culture," and believes that to change them will be very hard. But to my mind unless these are changed the revolution can last no longer than a sand-castle. Wide support was given to the revolution to drive the Manchus out of China because its watchword "Restore the old!" — or "Back to the past!" — appealed to conservatives. But they were most dissatisfied when the usual prosperity which follows a change of dynasty failed to materialize — they had lost their queues for nothing.

After that, relatively new reforms failed one after the other. An ounce of reform went with ten pounds of reaction, just as this time the banning of the lunar calendar was accompanied by the appearance of a combined lunar and solar calendar for the next hundred and twenty years.

Many people must welcome this combined calendar, because it is based on tradition and custom, and there-

---

* In 1922 Hu Shi advocated a government of "good men," by which he meant bourgeois liberals.

fore will be backed by tradition and custom. The same applies in other fields. Unless you go out among the masses to study, analyse and judge their traditions and customs, setting up standards for keeping or doing away with them, and finding a way of making a careful selection, any reform whatsoever will be crushed under the dead weight of tradition, or will simply float on the surface for a while.

This is no longer the time to hug books in the library and hold abstract discussions on religion, law, literature and art. . . . If we want to discuss these things, we must first understand tradition and custom, and have the courage and integrity to look darkness in the face. For unless we see clearly, we cannot make reforms. Mere shouting about the brightness of the future is actually a deception to fool our lazy selves and our lazy hearers.

UNREVOLUTIONARY EAGERNESS
FOR REVOLUTION

Some say that all the fighters in a great revolutionary army must have absolutely correct and clear ideas before it can be a real revolutionary army — otherwise it is not worth a straw. At first sight this seems most reasonable and thoroughgoing, but in fact it is an impossible demand and mere empty talk, a sugared pill to poison the revolution.

This is just as impossible as to teach the whole country "universal love" under the imperialists, so that the people beam and bow with clasped hands and "the whole world is at peace." Under the enemies of the revolution it is equally impossible to convert all our countrymen by words or deeds to think correctly. The only idea held in common by fighters of a new revolutionary force is opposition to the status quo. Their final aims are very different indeed. Some revolt for society, others for a clique, a woman, themselves, or as a means of committing suicide. But still the revolutionary army advances. For in this campaign the enemy can be killed just as well by an individualist's bullet as by a collectivist's bullet. And no matter which type of soldier is killed or wounded, the loss to the army's fighting strength is the same. Of course, because of the difference in ultimate aims, during the struggle men may drop out, run away, grow decadent, or turn renegade. But so long as they keep advancing, as time goes by their force will grow less mixed and better trained.

When I wrote a preface for Ye Yongzhen's *Only Ten Years*, I thought this was what happened when a man did what he could for society. The hero of this novel did go to the front and stand sentry (though no one had ever taught him to fire a gun). He was therefore much more practical than those scholars who hug their knees and wail, or write of their indignation. To insist that all fighters should hold correct views and be as firm as steel is not only a Utopian dream, but also an unreasonable demand.

But later I read an even sharper, more radical criticism in the *Shen Bao* expressing deep dissatisfaction because the hero joined up for selfish motives. Since the *Shen Bao* is all for peace and dead against revolution, at first sight this seems most incongruous. But let me explain how a seemingly radical revolutionary — actually a most unrevolutionary or anti-revolutionary individualist commentator — can make such a criticism fit such a paper.

One type is the decadent. Lacking definite ideals or ability, he drifts about in search of momentary entertainment, till very soon he wearies of settled pleasures and has to keep looking for new excitement — he can only enjoy the most intense sensation. Revolution is a new excitement for him. It is the same with a glutton whose palate is jaded and whose appetite is spoilt, who must eat enough pepper or paprika to perspire before he can swallow half a bowl of rice. He wants out-and-out, absolutely revolutionary writing. And as soon as any faults of the age are revealed, he frowns and thinks it not worth a straw. He does not mind your departing from the truth, as long as it gives him pleasure. Everyone knows of Baudelaire, the decadent French poet who welcomed revolution but who hated the revolution when it threatened to interfere with his decadent life. So revolutionaries on paper — the most out-and-out, fervid revolutionaries before a revolution — tear off the masks they themselves are unconscious of wearing, when the revolution approaches. Such precedents should be mentioned to "revolutionary writers" like Cheng Fangwu who, after the first little setback, if they have any status (or money) scuttle east to Tokyo or west to Paris.

Another type is hard to classify. The main thing about them is that they have no convictions, hence they always consider others in the wrong and themselves in the right. In the last analysis, these are those most satisfied with the status quo. When speaking as critics, they seize hold of anything at random to silence the other side. To refute the theory of mutual aid they speak of the struggle for existence, and vice versa. To oppose talk of peace they advocate the class struggle, and to discredit this they uphold universal love. When arguing with an idealist they take a materialist stand, but to refute a materialist they turn idealist. In a word, by using English rulers to measure Russian *versts* and French rulers to measure inches, they discover there is no one up to the mark. Since no one else is up to the mark, they can go on considering themselves the sole exponents of the golden mean, and remain complacent for ever. According to them, anything with a defect is not good enough. But since the world today cannot be a hundred per cent right, to be on the safe side one had better lie doggo. Yet to lie doggo is also a big mistake. In short, life in this world is exceedingly difficult, but to be a revolutionary is naturally even more so.

Although the *Shen Bao* criticizes the hero of *Only Ten Years* for not being an out-and-out revolutionary, it also makes cutting gibes at translators of works on social science. Its soul therefore belongs to the second category, with a dash of the decadents' world-weariness which makes it want paprika to whet its appetite.

THOUGHTS ON THE LEAGUE OF
LEFT-WING WRITERS*

A talk given at the inaugural meeting of the League
of Left-Wing Writers on March 2, 1930

I need not speak about subjects already dealt with in
detail by others. In my view, it is very easy for "Left-
wing" writers today to turn into "Right-wing" writers.
First of all, if you simply shut yourself up behind glass
windows to write or study instead of keeping in touch
with actual social conflicts, it is easy for you to be extremely radical or "Left." But the moment you come up
against reality all your ideas are shattered. Behind closed
doors it is very easy to spout radical ideas, but equally
easy to turn "Rightist." This is what is meant in the
West by "salon-socialists." A salon is a sitting-room,
and it is most artistic and refined to sit discussing socialism — with no idea of bringing it into being. Socialists
like this are quite unreliable. Indeed today, with the
exception of Mussolini who is not a literary man, it is
rare to find writers or artists without any socialist ideas at
all, who say workers and peasants ought to be enslaved,
killed and exploited. (Of course, we cannot say there
are none whatsoever, as witness the literati of China's
Crescent Moon clique and D'Annunzio, the favourite of
the aforesaid Mussolini.)

---

* The League of Left-Wing Writers was founded in Shanghai
on March 2, 1930 and dissolved at the beginning of 1936. Lu Xun
was one of its founders and chief leader. This talk became the
fighting programme of Left-wing writers.

Secondly, it is also easy to become "Right-wing" if you do not understand the actual nature of revolution. Revolution is a bitter thing, mixed with filth and blood, not as lovely or perfect as poets think. It is eminently down-to-earth, entailing many humble, tiresome tasks, not as romantic as the poets think. Of course there is destruction in a revolution, but construction is even more necessary to it; and while destruction is straightforward, construction is troublesome. So it is easy for all who have romantic dreams about revolution to become disillusioned on closer acquaintance, or when a revolution is actually carried out. The Russian poet Yesenin is said to have welcomed the October Revolution at first with all his heart, shouting, "Long live the revolution in heaven and on earth! . . . I am a Bolshevik!" But afterwards, when the reality proved completely different from what he had imagined, he grew disillusioned and decadent. And they say this disillusionment was one of the reasons for his subsequent suicide. Pilnyak and Ehrenburg are other cases in point. And we find similar instances during our 1911 Revolution. Writers like those of the South Society started as most revolutionary; but they cherished the illusion that once the Manchus were driven out there would be a complete return to the "good old days," and they could all wear wide sleeves, high hats and broad girdles, and tread with majestic strides. To their surprise, though, after the Manchu emperor was driven out and the Republic set up it was all quite different. So they were disillusioned and some of them even opposed the new movement. Unless we understand the true nature of revolution, it will be easy for us to do the same.

Another mistaken view is this notion that poets or writers are superior beings, and their work nobler than any other work. For example, Heine thought since poets were the noblest beings and God was infinitely just, when poets died they went up to sit by God who offered them light refreshments. Today, of course, no one believes that about God offering refreshments, but some still believe that the poets and writers who support the labouring people's revolution today will be richly rewarded by the working class when the revolution is accomplished, enjoying special treatment, riding in special cars, and eating special food. The workers may even offer them bread and butter, saying, "Help yourself, you are our poets!" This is another illusion: it simply could not happen. Probably things will be harder after the revolution than they are now. There may not even be black bread, let alone bread and butter, as happened for a year or two after the Russian revolution. If we fail to understand this, it is easy for us to become "Right-wing." The fact is that no workers, unless they are the type described as "deserving" by Mr. Liang Shiqiu, feel any special respect for intellectuals. Look at Metik, an intellectual in Fadeyev's *The Nineteen* which I translated, who was often laughed at by the miners. Needless to say, intellectuals have their own tasks which we should not belittle; but it is certainly not the duty of the working class to give poets or writers any preferential treatment.

Now let me mention a few points to which we must pay attention.

First, in the struggle against the old society and old forces, it is necessary to be firm, enduring and to pay attention to strength. The roots of the old society go deep, and we cannot shake it unless our new movement is even stronger. Besides, the old society has good means of making our new forces compromise, although it will never compromise itself. There have been many new movements in China, yet each has succumbed to the old, largely because they lacked definite, general aims, their demands were too modest, and they were too easily satisfied. Take the movement for the vernacular, which was desperately opposed at the start by the forces of the old society. Before long they sanctioned writing in the vernacular, granted it a wretched sort of status and allowed

essays written in the vernacular to appear in odd corners
of newspapers, because from their point of view they
could permit this new thing to exist as it was perfectly
harmless, and the new for its part was content now that
the vernacular had the right to live. It has been much
the same with the proletarian literary movement of the
last couple of years. The old society has sanctioned
working-class writing because it is no menace — in fact
some of the diehards have tried their hand at it themselves and used it as an ornament, for putting a workman's coarse bowl beside the old porcelain and antiques
in the sitting-room seems so exotic. And once proletarian
writers had their small corner in the world of letters and
were able to sell their manuscripts, they stopped strug-
gling, and the critics sang paeans of triumph, "Proletarian
literature has conquered!" But apart from the success
of a few individuals, what has proletarian literature itself
achieved? It should be an intrinsic part of the proletarian struggle for liberation, growing apace with the
social strength of the working class. The fact that proletarian literature has a high position in the world of
letters while the social status of the proletariat is so low
only goes to show that the writers of proletarian literature
have become divorced from the proletariat and gone over
to the old society.

Secondly, I think we should broaden our battlefront.
Last year and the year before we did have some battles
in literature, but on too limited a scale. Instead of dealing with the old literature and old ideas, our new writers
started scrapping with each other in one corner, allowing
the old school to watch in comfort from the side.

Thirdly, we ought to bring up a host of new fighters,
for today we are really short-handed. We have several
magazines, and quite a few books are published; but because they all have the same few writers, the contents
are bound to be thin. Nobody specializes, each dabbles
in everything — translation, story-writing, criticism, even

poetry. Of course the result is poor. But the reason for
this is the dearth of writers. If we had more, translators
could concentrate on translating, writers on writing,
critics on criticism; then when we engaged the enemy
our forces would be strong enough to overcome them
easily. Let me give an illustration of this in passing.
The year before last when the Creation Society and the
Sun Society attacked me, they were actually so weak that
even I lost interest later on and there seemed no point
in making a counter-attack, for I realized they were
using "empty city tactics."* The enemy devoted their
strength to raising a din instead of drilling troops. And
though there were many articles abusing me, you could
tell at once that they were written under pseudonyms —
all the abuse boiled down to the same few remarks. I
was waiting to be attacked by someone who had mastered
the Marxist method of criticism, but no such man appeared. I have always thought it important to train a
younger generation of fighters, and have formed several
literary groups in my time, though none of them amount-
ed to much. But we must pay more attention to this in
future.

While we urgently need to create a host of new fighters,
those of us now on the literary front must also be "tenacious." By tenacious I mean we should not be like those
Qing Dynasty scholars who used the *bagu*, or eight-
legged, essays as "a brick to knock on the door." These
essays were the means by which scholars passed the
examinations and became officials in the Qing Dynasty.
Once you passed the examinations on the strength of this
"presentation, amplification, argument and conclusion"**
you could then throw it aside and never use it again for
the rest of your life. That is why it was called a "brick,"

---

* Zhuge Liang, the famous strategist of the Three Kingdoms
Period, is said to have invited the enemy into an undefended
city. The enemy, fearing a trap, dared not go in.
** The four chief parts in this form of essay.

for it was used only to knock on the door, and once the door was opened it could be thrown aside instead of being carried around. Similar methods are still being used today. We notice that after men have published one or two volumes of verse or short stories they often disappear for ever. Where do they go? After winning a greater or lesser amount of fame by publishing a couple of books, they become professors or find some other job. Since their name is made and they need not write any more, they disappear for ever. This is why China has so little to show in literature and science. But we need some works, for they would come in useful. (Lunacharsky even proposed preserving Russia's peasant art because foreigners would buy what the peasants make, and the money would come in useful. I believe if we had some contribution to make in literature and science, it might even help us in our political movement to free ourselves from the imperialists.) But to achieve anything in literature, we must be "tenacious."

Last of all, I think it essential for a united front that we have a common aim. I seem to remember hearing someone say, "The reactionaries already have their united front, but we have not yet united." In fact, theirs is not a deliberate united front, but because they have a common aim and act consistently they seem to us to have one. And the fact that we cannot unite shows that we are divided in our aims — some of us are working for small groups or indeed only for themselves. If all of us wanted to serve the masses of workers and peasants, our front will naturally be united.

THE CRITICS WE NEED

Judging by what we can see (no definite figures are available here), since last year the self-professed "revolutionary" novelists have had fewer readers, and the publishing world is paying more attention to works on social science. We must admit that this is a good trend. At first, young readers were bewitched by those advertisement-style reviews which sounded like charms into believing that there was a future for them if they read "revolutionary" literature — both they and society would be saved. So they seized whatever they could and gobbled it up, not knowing that most of it was not nutriment but sour wine in new bottles or rotten meat in red paper packages. And this made them so uncomfortable that they felt like vomiting.

After this bitter experience, it is naturally an appropriate step forward for them to turn for a cure to basic, down-to-earth social science.

Owing largely to this demand, however, translated works of social science are pouring out thick and fast, and the relatively better ones rub shoulders on the bookstalls with the worst, so that readers beginning to look for accurate information are bewildered. Yet the new critics say nothing, and fellows bearing some semblance to critics seize this chance to condemn all these translations at one stroke as "cats and curs."

All we need at this stage are a few solid, intelligent critics who really understand social science as well as literary criticism.

China has long had critics. Practically every literary

group has its own set of literati. At least it has a poet,
a novelist, and a critic whose function it is to proclaim
the glories and achievements of the group. All these
groups announce that they are out for reform and mean
to storm the old strongholds; but on the way, at the foot
of the old strongholds, they start squabbling among
themselves till they have no energy left. Since all they
do is "squabble," none of them is badly hurt — they are
simply out of breath. And each as he pants imagines
he is the victor and starts chanting triumphant paeans.
Thus there is no need for guards on the old strongholds
— they can just stand there with folded arms, looking
down on the comedy played out by these new foes. They
keep silent, but they are the victors.

Though we have had no masterpieces during the last
year or two, in my opinion some fairly good books have
come out, such as Li Shouzhang's *Travellers*, Tai Jingnong's *Son of the Soil*, the first half of Ye Yongzhen's
Only Ten Years, Rou Shi's *February* and *Death of the
Old Era*, Wei Jinzhi's *Autobiography in Seven Letters*,
and Liu Yimeng's *Unemployment*. Unfortunately our
famous critic Liang Shiqiu is too busy echoing Professor
Chen Yuan to pay any attention to these; Cheng Fangwu
after mourning the departed glories of the Creation
Society suddenly turned into Shi Housheng, then vanished like a shooting star; and Qian Xingcun of late, in his
Pioneer, has been quoting Koreto Kurahara paragraph
after paragraph in a squabble with Mao Dun. Amid such
hectic or leisurely combats, all writers outside these
literary groups are "dismissed" or allowed to perish in
silence.

The reading public's new interest in social science is
a good, healthy trend, which will impel literature and
art along the right path, beside benefiting other fields of
activities. But what with the welter of books and the
jeers of the onlookers, it may very easily perish. That

is why what we need above all now is: a few solid, intelligent critics who really understand social science as well
as literary criticism.

GOVERNMENT-BY-GENTLEMEN-ISM

In the "Miscellany" of a recent number of the *Crescent Moon,* Mr. Liang Shiqiu also approves of "dissatisfaction with the present situation." He considers, however, that "the responsibility of intellectuals today (especially those generally known as 'pioneers,' 'authorities' or 'progressives') is not just to publish a few sneering, jeering essays to express their dissatisfaction, but to go a step further and search in all sincerity for a prescription to cure the 'present situation.'"

Why is this? Because when you are ill you need medicine. "The Three People's Principles* are one remedy," says Mr. Liang, "communism is another, nationalism another, anarchism another, government-by-gentlemen-ism another." But if you "dismiss all these remedies as worthless and laugh them out of court. . . . What mentality does that show?"

It would certainly show a deplorable mentality. But in point of fact I have never seen essays like this by one single author who believes, for instance, that the Three People's Principles are counter to English and American ideas of freedom, that Communists have accepted Russian roubles, that nationalism is too narrow, anarchism too vague. . . . So Mr. Liang in his "Miscellany" has exaggerated the crime of the essayists he knows.

As a matter of fact, it is quite legitimate to point out faults in reasoning or the evils any "ism" may give rise

---

* The famous principles enunciated by Dr. Sun Yat-sen as the guiding policy of the Kuomintang.

to even if you have no alternative "ism" yourself. It is like crying out if you are crushed — you need not clench your teeth in silence until you have thought of some better "ism." Though of course if you have one that looks more impressive.

But I think the "government-by-gentlemen-ism" which Mr. Liang so modestly puts at the end should more modestly be set aside altogether. For from the Three People's Principles to anarchism are names of different remedies, heating or cooling, like gypsum or cinnamon — their efficacy is another matter. Only the "remedy" of "government-by-gentlemen-ism" is not the name of a medicine but more like the advertisement "A Good Cure" or the wordy "recommendation" of a proud, well-known physician. True, no one can say you should use bad drugs to cure a disease, but it does not take a doctor to shake his head over prescriptions like this. Anyone can "dismiss them as worthless."

And if the doctor then loses his temper and shouts, "You laugh at my government-by-gentlemen-ism. All right — suggest something else!" that is such a ridiculous aspect of the "present situation" that even without relying on any "ism" you may start having random thoughts. Indeed, the inexhaustibility of random thoughts is due to the fact that too many such situations exist today.

April 17, 1930

HOMELESS, SENSELESS WATCHDOG
OF THE CAPITALISTS

Since being dubbed a "watchdog of the capitalists" by *The Pioneer*, Mr. Liang Shiqiu has written an article announcing that he is not angry. First he quotes the definition on page 672 of Number 2 of *The Pioneer*, and says, "I feel rather like a proletarian." Then to define a "watchdog" he writes "all watchdogs try to please their masters for the sake of a little reward." And so he raises these questions:

> *The Pioneer* says I am a watchdog of the capitalists. Which capitalist, may I ask? Or is it of all capitalists? I do not know who my master is. If I knew, I would certainly take him a few magazines to show my loyalty, and he might even reward me with some gold sovereigns or roubles. . . . As it is, I toil on to make a bare subsistence. For where can I learn the skill needed to collect sovereigns from the capitalists' counting-house, or roubles from the C— Party?

This is a portrait to the life of a "watchdog of the capitalists." Though watchdogs may be kept by a single capitalist, they actually belong to the whole class, which is why they behave so well to all rich men they meet and bark so madly at the poor. It is precisely because they do not know who their master is that they behave well to all the rich — sure sign that they belong to the class as a whole. If no one keeps them and they are half-starved, they grow wild; but still they behave well to all rich men they meet and bark madly at all the poor, only by then they are even less clear who their masters are.

Judging by Professor Liang's description of his hardships, rather like those of a "proletarian" (whom he formerly described as "doomed to extinction"), and as he does not know who his master is, he must belong to the second category. So for the sake of clarity we should add the epithet "homeless" to this "watchdog of the capitalists."

But still this title is incomplete. After all, Mr. Liang is a learned professor, not one of the common herd. Instead of asking "Has literature a class character?" in his "Answer to Lu Xun" he skilfully inserts the slogan written on a telegraph pole: "Armed Support for the Soviet Union!" and a reference to the glass smashed in a newspaper office while in the passage quoted earlier — "roubles from the C— Party" — readers guess at once that the Communist Party is meant. This shows that all who believe in "the class character of literature" and offend Professor Liang, support the Soviet Union or accept their roubles. The same sort of trick was used when Duan Qirui's guards shot the students, and the *Morning News* said the students had lost their lives for the sake of a few roubles; or when my name appeared in the League of Freedom,* and the *Revolution Daily* reported that I "had been bought by glittering gold roubles." Professor Liang may think it a form of "criticism" if he ferrets out a "bandit" (an academic bandit) for his masters, but this profession is lower even than a henchman's.

I remember how it was all the rage, during the cooperation between the Kuomintang and the Communist Party, to praise the Soviet Union in speeches and writing. Now times have changed, the newspapers denounce the slogans on telegraph poles and the C— Party, and the

---

* A revolutionary organization set up in Shanghai in February 1930, with Communist support and leadership, to win freedom of speech and of the press. Lu Xun was one of its sponsors.

police are very busy making arrests. So to dub your opponent a supporter of the Soviet Union or a member of the C— Party is naturally all the rage today, and may even bring you a "little reward" from your master. But it is unfair to accuse Professor Liang of being out for a reward or gold sovereigns. That could never be. All he wants is to use these things to strengthen his hand, and to make good the deficiencies of his "literary criticism." So looking at it from the angle of "literary criticism," in front of "watchdog" we should add another adjective: "senseless."

April 19, 1930

1931

THE REVOLUTIONARY LITERATURE OF THE CHINESE PROLETARIAT AND THE BLOOD OF THE PIONEERS

The revolutionary literature of the Chinese proletariat, coming into being as today passes over into tomorrow, is growing amid slander and persecution. Now at last in the utter darkness its first chapter has been written with our comrades' blood.*

Throughout history our toiling masses have been so bitterly oppressed and exploited that even the boon of a schooling was denied them. They could only suffer slaughter and destruction in silence. And our ideographic script is so difficult that they have no chance to learn to read themselves. Once our young intellectuals realized their duty as pioneers they were the first to raise a battle-cry, a cry which terrified the rulers as much as the cries of revolt of the toiling masses themselves. Then hack-writers rallied to the attack, spread rumours or acted as informers. And the fact that they always operated in secret and under false names simply proves them creatures of darkness.

Since the rulers knew their hack-writers were no match for the revolutionary literature of the proletariat, they started banning books and periodicals, closing bookshops, issuing repressive publishing laws, and black-listing

---

* On January 17, 1931 Rou Shi, Bai Mang, and three other young members of the League of Left-Wing Writers were arrested by the Kuomintang authorities. On February 7, they were secretly murdered at night in Shanghai.

authors. And now they have resorted to the lowest tactics of all, arresting and imprisoning Left-wing writers and putting them to death in secret — to this day they have not made these "executions" public. While this proves them creatures of darkness on the verge of extinction, it also testifies to the strength of the camp of revolutionary literature of the Chinese proletariat. For as their obituaries show, the age, courage and, above all, the literary achievements of our martyred comrades were enough to stop the frenzied yapping of the whole pack of curs.

But now these comrades of ours have been murdered. This naturally represents a certain loss to the revolutionary literature of the working class and a great grief to us. Yet our proletarian literature will continue to grow, because it belongs to the broad masses of revolutionary toilers; and as long as the people exist and gain in strength, so long will this revolutionary literature grow. Our comrades' blood testifies that the revolutionary literature of the working class is subjected to the same oppression and terror as the toiling masses, that it is fighting the same battles and shares the same destiny, that it is the literature of the revolutionary toilers.

Now according to the warlords, even old ladies of sixty have been poisoned by "noxious writing," and the police in the foreign concessions are periodically searching even primary-school children. Apart from the guns given them by the imperialists and apart from a few toadies, the die-hards have nothing left, nothing but enemies. Old folk and children alike are all against them, not to mention the youth. And these enemies of theirs are all on our side.

As with bitter grief in our hearts we commemorate our fallen comrades today, we must impress on our memories that the first page in the history of the revolutionary literature of China's proletariat has been written with our comrades' blood.   It is a lasting exposure of the enemy's contemptible savagery, an inspiration to us never to cease our struggle.

THE PRESENT CONDITION OF ART IN DARKEST CHINA

Written for the American magazine *New Masses**

Actually the only literary movement in China today is the revolutionary literary movement of the proletariat. Though it is like a tender shoot in the desert, apart from it China has no modern literature at all. The so-called writers attached to the ruling class have become too corrupt even to produce "art for art's sake" or "decadent" works. Their only way of attacking left-wing writers nowadays is to slander, persecute, arrest and murder them. Hence the left-wing writers' only opponents are thugs, spies, watchdogs and murderers.

This has been clearly shown by the happenings of the last two years.

The year before last, when Plekhanov's and Lunacharsky's books on literary theory were first introduced to China, the disciple of Professor Irving Babbitt** felt the indignation of a sensitive "scholar," for he did not believe the proletariat had any art. If a proletarian wants to create or appreciate art, he must first work hard to save enough money to crawl up into the bourgeoisie — he should not burst noisily into the garden in his rags. This gentleman also spread the rumour that those who advocate proletarian literature in China have accepted Russian roubles. This device was not entirely unsuc-

---

* Lu Xun wrote this at the request of Agnes Smedley.
** Liang Shiqiu.

cessful, for many Shanghai reporters keep making up stories like this, sometimes even giving the number of the roubles. But intelligent readers do not believe them, for the guns actually sent in by the imperialists to massacre our workers speak much more clearly than these reports.

Though the officers of the ruling class are slower in the uptake than scholars, they tightened their grip from day to day last year. They banned magazines and books, not merely those in the least revolutionary but even those with red characters on the cover, or those written by Russian writers. A. Serafimovich, Vsevolod Ivanov and N. Ognev are naturally forbidden and so are even some of the stories of Chekhov and Leonid Andreyev. This means the bookshops are reduced to selling arithmetic textbooks and children's stories like dialogues between Mr. Cat and Miss Rose, expatiating on the pleasures of spring. As the translated tales of Helena zur Mühlen have been banned too, the only thing left is to praise spring for all you are worth. But now a general is angry, and says this making animals talk and calling them "Mr." shows a contempt for human beings.

But since a simple ban does not go to the root of the problem, this year five left-wing writers disappeared. When their families made inquiries, they discovered they were being held by the secret police and could not be seen. A fortnight later when they inquired again, they heard they had been "liberated" — a witty way of saying "killed" — but not a word of this appeared in the Shanghai papers, Chinese or foreign. Then the bookshops which print or sell new books have been closed, sometimes as many as five in one day. Now they are opening up again one by one, and we do not know what has happened, but judging by their advertisements they are busy producing bilingual texts with Chinese on one page and English on the other, of such authors as Robert Louis Stevenson and Oscar Wilde.

The ruling class has taken positive steps too, however,

in relation to literature. For one thing, after driving away the original booksellers and their assistants, they secretly installed an obedient crew. But this proved a failure at once, as all the watchdogs there gave the place the sinister atmosphere of a yamen, and since there is nothing so hated and feared by the Chinese as a yamen naturally no one goes there. Only a few watchdogs with time to spare like to trot in occasionally. That being so, business is not very brisk. Then again, they write articles and publish magazines to take the place of the banned left-wing publications. They have produced about ten of these to date. But this has proved a failure too. The biggest drawback is the fact that the sponsors of this "literature" are a member of the Shanghai Municipal Council and an inspector in the secret police, who are much more famous as "liberators" than as authors. If they were to write a *Methods of Murder* or *The Art of Detection*, they might find quite a few readers; but instead they will try to paint pictures and write poetry. This is as if Mr. Henry Ford in America stopped talking about cars and took up singing — people would be very surprised indeed.

Because no one goes to these official bookshops or reads their magazines, they try to save the situation by forcing well-known authors who are not declared leftists to write for them, to boost their circulation. Only one or two muddle-heads have been taken in. The majority have so far written nothing for them — and one has been scared into running away altogether.

Today their most treasured writers are some who called themselves left-wing when the left-wing movement in literature started, when it was supported by the revolutionary youth and did not suffer any persecution, but who have now crawled under the rulers' swords and turned to snap at left-wing writers. They treasure these men because having once been left-wing some of their magazines still appear partly red, only the pictures of peasants and workers have been replaced by Aubrey Beardsley's drawings of diseased-looking characters.

Under these conditions, readers who like the old-fashioned stories about bandits and the modern stories about sex feel quite at home. But more progressive young people have nothing to read. To satisfy their hunger for a time, they are reduced to reading books with very little content but a great deal of empty talk — for these are not banned. For they know it is better to drink from an empty cup rather than buy the poisonous official books which make you want to vomit. At least you do yourself no harm. But the majority of our revolutionary youth, notwithstanding everything, are still enthusiastically demanding, supporting and carrying forward our left-wing art and literature.

So apart from the official magazines and those published by their flunkeys, other journals have to try as best they can to include a few relatively progressive articles; for they know they cannot go on indefinitely selling empty cups. The left-wing literature is supported by the masses of revolutionary readers — the future belongs to them.

So this left-wing literature is still growing. But of course it is like a tender shoot crushed under a heavy boulder, which makes it grow crookedly. The pity is that none of our left-wing writers are of worker or peasant origin. One reason is that peasants and workers have always been too oppressed and ground down to have a chance to get any education. Another is that the Chinese ideographs — no longer recognizable for what they represent — make it impossible for workers and peasants to express themselves freely in writing even after ten years of study. This gives pleasure to those "writers" with swords. They think if you know enough to write an article you must be a petty-bourgeois at least, and a petty-bourgeois should hang on to his little property: if he shows any leaning towards the working class that must be "hypocrisy." Only those petty-bourgeois writers who attack proletarian literature are "sincere." Since "sincerity" is better than "hypocrisy," their slander, persecution, arrest and murder of left-wing writers is their best art.

But this "best art" of the sword shows in fact that the left-wing writers suffer from the same oppression and terror as the workers and share the same destiny. If left-wing writers and artists today share the same sufferings as the workers, in future they will surely rise up together. Simply killing men is not art after all, hence these thugs have admitted their own bankruptcy.

A GLANCE AT SHANGHAI
LITERATURE

A talk given to the Social Science Study Group
on August 12, 1931

Shanghai literature began with the *Shen Bao*. This paper started sixty years ago, but I know nothing of those times. I can merely cast my mind back to thirty years ago, when the *Shen Bao* still used Chinese bamboo paper printed on one side only, and most of its contributors were "talented scholars" from elsewhere.

The educated men of those days could be divided roughly into two categories: orthodox scholars and talented scholars. The orthodox scholars confined their reading to the Four Books and Five Classics, wrote *bagu* essays, and were extremely correct. The talented scholars read novels like *A Dream of Red Mansions* too, and wrote poems in different classical metres which were not required for the examinations. That is, they read *A Dream of Red Mansions* openly, while whether or not the orthodox scholars read it in secret I have no means of knowing. Once there were foreign concessions in Shanghai — sometimes called "Western settlements" or "barbarian settlements" — talented scholars started flocking here, because such men are broad-minded enough to go anywhere. Since orthodox scholars rather look down on things foreign and are set on winning rank and fame through the proper channels, they never rush about lightly. Confucius said, "If the Way makes no progress,

I shall get upon a raft and float out to sea."* Talented
scholars are rather partial to this viewpoint, which is
why they think the way of orthodox scholars "folly."

These talented scholars were delicate, sensitive souls,
enraged by a cock's crow and upset by moonlight. Once
in Shanghai, they met prostitutes. When they went
whoring they could surround themselves with ten or
twenty girls, much as in *A Dream of Red Mansions*, till
they fancied themselves the young hero of that novel.
Since they were talented scholars, the prostitutes of
course were beautiful girls — and so were born the books
about scholars and beauties. The general thesis was that
only scholars could sympathize with fallen beauties, and
only beauties could appreciate ill-fated scholars; but after
many, many trials they would marry happily or become
immortals.

These men helped the *Shen Bao* to publish certain
essays and articles of the Ming and Qing dynasties,
formed literary groups, and wrote lantern riddles; and
as they used anthologies of these as gifts, they had a wide
circulation. They published long works too, like *The
Scholars, Zheng He's Travels* and *Pleasant Stories*. These
small volumes are still to be found on secondhand book-
stalls, with the announcement on the title page: "Published by the *Shen Bao* Press, Shanghai."

These books about beauties and scholars remained in
vogue for many years, till by degrees talented scholars
began to change. They discovered that it was money
alone, not "a passion for talent" that made beauties turn
prostitute. But how could a beauty covet a scholar's
money? Then the talented scholars devised clever means
to deal with the prostitutes, so that far from being
cheated themselves they could take advantage of the
girls; and stories describing their tactics were highly
popular as textbooks for whoring. The hero of such

---

*A quotation from *The Analects*.

books was no longer a scholar-cum-simpleton, but a brave gallant who got the better of drabs — a scholar-cum-hooligan.

Prior to this had appeared the *Dianshizhai Pictorial* edited by Wu Youru, with pictures of men and immortals, domestic and foreign news. But since Wu was rather hazy about foreign affairs, he depicted a battleship as a cargo boat with cannon on the deck, and "a duel" as two uniformed soldiers fighting with swords in a sitting-room till all the vases were broken. Still, his "Bawd Beats a Strumpet" and "Hooligan Assaults a Girl" were excellent drawings, doubtless because he had seen so many cases in real life. Even today in Shanghai, we can see many faces just like those he painted. This pictorial was extremely influential in its time, selling in every province and considered required reading for all who wished to understand "current events" — the equivalent of our present-day "new learning." Some years ago it was reprinted under the title *Wu Youru's Album*, and the extent of its influence was fantastic. We need not mention illustrations in novels; even textbook illustrations often have children with caps askew, slant eyes, fleshy jowls and the look of hooligans.

Among our new hooligan artists is Ye Lingfeng. Mr. Ye has plagiarized the drawings of Aubrey Beardsley, who believed in "art for art's sake" and owed much to the Ukiyoe school of painting in Japan. Though Ukiyoe was a popular art, most of the artists belonging to this school drew plump prostitutes and actors with slant-set, erotic eyes. But Beardsley's figures are thin because he belonged to the decadent school, and since most decadents are cadaverous, they dislike robust women who give them a sense of inferiority. Now that our Mr. Ye's new slant-eyed drawings are crossing with Wu Youru's old slant-eyed drawings, they should be popular for quite a few years. Mr. Ye does not draw hooligans only, however. At one time he also drew proletarians, though his workmen were slant-eyed too and held out huge fists. I personally think proletarians should be drawn realistically, just as they are — there is no need to make their fists bigger than their heads.

Modern Chinese films are still much influenced by the scholar-cum-hooligan, and their heroes — supposed to be "good characters" — are all slick types like the sleek young Shanghai fellows who are adepts in "sowing wild oats," "finding pickings" or "getting girls into trouble." These films give you the impression that to be a hero or good fellow you must be a hooligan.

But the novel of the scholar-cum-hooligan gradually died out. For one thing, I think, they harped too long on the same old theme — the prostitute wanted money but the scholar tricked her — and you could not write on that for ever. Another reason was that only natives of Shanghai or Zhejiang could understand the Suzhou dialect in which those books were written.

Then another novel of the scholar and beautiful girl type appeared which was all the rage for a time. That was the translation of Rider Haggard's *Joan Haste*. Only the first half appeared, though. According to the translator, he bought it on a secondhand bookstall and found it excellent, but unfortunately could not get the second volume. Sure enough, this story touched the sensitive hearts of scholars and beauties, and was very widely read. Later on it even touched the heart of Mr. Lin Qinnan,* who translated the whole book, using the same title. But he was violently abused by the first translator for bringing it out in full, thereby detracting from Joan's worth and upsetting the readers. And only then did we learn that the reason for publishing only one half before was not because the second half was missing, but because in it Joan had an illegitimate child. In fact,

* One of the earliest translators of Western novels who lived during the early days of the Republic.

they would not print a medium-sized novel like this in two volumes abroad. But this gives us a good idea of Chinese views on marriage at that time.

Next new scholar-and-beauty novels circulated, but the beauty was a girl of good family who shared the scholar's pleasures and would not leave him. Under the willows and blossoming trees they were like two butterflies or love birds; but because their parents were cruel or fate unkind, they sometimes came to an unhappy end instead of living happily ever after — and we must admit that this was a great advance. When not long ago the magazine *Innuendo* appeared, edited by Mi. Tian-xu-wo-sheng, who also manufactures tooth powder which can be used as face powder, that was the heyday of this "scholar-and-beauty" writing. Later, though *Innuendo* was banned, its influence remained as strong as ever until *New Youth* grew powerful enough to attack it. Then the appearance of a new form of writing — translations of Ibsen's plays and Hu Shi's *Marriage** — made an end of that school whose basic theme was marriage.

After that appeared the new talented men's Creation Society. They laid emphasis on individual genius, believed in art for art's sake and the value of the individual, worshipped original writing and detested translation — especially translation at secondhand. These men opposed the Shanghai Literary Research Society. Their very first announcement declared that some people — meaning this society — were "monopolizing" the literary arena. In fact, the reverse was true. The Literary Research Society believed in art for life, encouraged translation as well as writing, and did what it could to introduce the literature of oppressed peoples. Because these belonged to small countries and no one in China understood their languages, they nearly all had to be translated at secondhand. Moreover because the society expressed its sup-

---

* A play published in *New Youth* in March 1919.

port for *New Youth*, there was old and new enmity, and
it was attacked on three sides. First the Creation Society, which believed in art for art's sake, naturally ran
down the officious Literary Research Society which believed in art for men's sake, considering it "vulgar" as
well as incompetent, and even writing long articles ex-
pressly to point out one mistake in translation. Secondly
there were the gentlemen-scholars who studied in America, who thought art the prerogative of ladies and gentlemen. Apart from ladies and gentlemen they considered all other characters must be men of letters,
scholars, artists, professors or débutantes — they must
speak English — so as to show the dignity of the élite.
At that time Mr. Wu Mi* wrote an article saying he could
not understand why some people liked to write only
about the lower orders. The third side was the scholar-
and-beauty school already mentioned. I do not know
what means they used to get the publishers to dismiss
the member of the Literary Research Society who edited
Story Monthly and to bring out *Story World* to print
their articles. This journal only stopped coming out last
year.

On the face of it, the Creation Society seemed to have
won this battle. Many of their writings appealed to the
taste of those who used to style themselves scholars, and
with help from the publishers their strength increased.
Once this happened, big firms like the Commercial Press
started publishing translations by its members — I refer
to the works of Guo Moruo and Zhang Ziping. After that,
as far as I can remember, the Creation Society stopped
writing articles on the translation mistakes they had
discovered in Commercial Press publications. Here I
seem to detect traces of the scholar-cum-hooligan. But
"new Shanghai" is no match for "old Shanghai." While

---

* A professor of Western literature who held conservative
views.

chanting songs of triumph, members of the society suddenly realized that they were providing commodities for their publishers and that all their efforts, from the bosses' point of view, were no better than the blinking dummy which serves merely as an advertisement in an oculist's window. When they wanted to publish independently the publisher sued them, and after they won independence, though they said all their books would be re-edited and printed elsewhere, their old boss went on using the old types, printing, selling and slashing prices every year in honour of some anniversary or other.

Able neither to go on providing commodities nor living independently, naturally their only path was to Guangzhou, "the cradle of revolution" where the prospects seemed a little brighter. Hence the appearance in Guangzhou of the expression "revolutionary literature" — unaccompanied by any works — while in Shanghai not even this expression was used.

Only the year before last did this "revolutionary literature" begin to flourish here, sponsored by some veterans of the Creation Society newly back from the "cradle of revolution" and a few newcomers. It flourished naturally owing to the situation, because ordinary people and young folk wanted it. When the Northern Expedition set out from Guangzhou, most young enthusiasts rushed into action, and there was no definite revolutionary movement in literature. But when the sudden change in the political situation and the setback to the revolution caused a clear differentiation between classes, and to "purge the party' the Kuomintang killed so many Communists and revolutionaries, the young people who survived found themselves in oppressive surroundings again. Then revolutionary writers became extremely active in Shanghai. So the upsurge of revolutionary literature here looks different on the face of it from that in other countries, being due not to a high tide of revolution but to a setback. Some of these writers, it is true, were old literati

who put down their batons to take to their old trades
again. Some were youngsters who had to write for a
living because they were squeezed out of real jobs. But
as revolutionary literature had a genuine mass foundation, among the new recruits were some who were firm
and clear-headed. As I see it, however, lack of planning
caused many mistakes in the revolutionary literary
movement. For instance, no detailed analysis of Chinese
society was made, and methods suited only for use under
Soviet political power were mechanically applied. Again,
many of these writers, notably Mr. Cheng Fangwu,
created the impression that revolution is a fearful thing
and behaved in an extremely leftist, threatening manner,
as if to show that once the revolution came all non-
revolutionaries must die, making everyone afraid of
revolution. In fact, revolution is not to make men die
but live. This "I'll give you a taste of the terrors of the
revolution" for the personal satisfaction of the teller also
showed the bad influence of the scholar-cum-hooligan
school.

Quick to kindle, quick to calm down, and even quick
to grow decadent, men of letters can always find reasons
and precedents from the classics to justify their shifts
of allegiance. For instance, if they need help they quote
Kropotkin's doctrine of mutual aid, while when they
want to fight they use Darwin's theory of the survival
of the fittest. All those from ancient times till now who
hold no definite views and have no guiding principle for
the changes they advocate, but make use of the arguments of different schools, deserve to be called hooligans.
Take a Shanghai hooligan. If he sees a man and woman
from the country walking together, he calls out, "Hey!
You're immoral — you've broken the law!" Here he uses
Chinese law. If a peasant makes water by the roadside,
he shouts, "Hey! That's not allowed. You've broken
the law, and deserve to be locked up!" Here he is using
foreign law. But in the end the law can go by the

board — if you grease his palm he will let the matter drop.

There is quite a difference in China between last year's revolutionary writers and the ones of the year before. Of course this is due to the changed circumstances, yet some "revolutionary writers" have the root of disease in themselves. "Revolution" and "literature" seem distinct and yet connected, like two boats close together. One boat is "revolution," the other "literature," and the writer stands with one foot on each. When conditions are fairly good, he puts more weight on the revolutionary boat, and is clearly a revolutionary; but when the revolution is being crushed, he shifts his weight to the boat of literature, and becomes a simple man of letters. So the men who were so radical two years ago in clamouring for a clean sweep of all non-revolutionary literature last year recalled how Lenin liked to read the works of Goncharov, and decided non-revolutionary writing could be highly significant too. Even that out-and-out revolutionary writer Mr. Ye Lingfeng, who gave that out-and-out description of revolutionaries who used my *Call to Arms* as toilet paper, is now tagging along, Heaven knows why, behind the so-called writers of "nationalist literature."*

Mr. Xiang Peiliang is a similar case. When the star of revolution was in the ascendant, he was very revolutionary. It was he who said young people should not merely clamour but show their teeth like wolves. This was not a bad idea, but we should be careful, because wolves are the ancestors of dogs, and once tamed by men they become dogs themselves. Today Mr. Xiang Peiliang is all for human art, and opposes class art; he divides men into good and bad, and considers art as a weapon in the "struggle between good and evil." Dogs divide

---

* A slogan raised in June 1930 by some hacks of the Kuomintang to cover up its capitulation to the Japanese invaders.

men into two kinds too: the good are the masters who
feed them, while all poor people and beggars are bad
in their eyes, to be either barked at or bitten. But this
is not a bad idea either, because it shows they still have
some wildness in their nature. If they were to turn into
pug-dogs, which work hard for their masters for all their
air of detachment, they would be like those famous men
who say they are not concerned with mundane affairs
but believe in art for art's sake — all they are fit for is
to adorn some university classroom.

Such petty-bourgeois intellectuals keep turning somersaults like this. Even when they become revolutionary
writers and write revolutionary works, they are liable
to distort the revolution. And since this does damage
to the cause, their shifts in allegiance need not upset us
at all. When the revolutionary literary movement was
going strong many petty-bourgeois writers suddenly came
over to us, describing their volte-face as a mutation. But
we know that a mutation means that when all necessary
conditions but one exist, the appearance of the last condition will lead A to turn into B. For water to freeze,
for instance, the temperature must be zero and there
must be some movement of air. Without the latter, water
will not freeze even if the temperature drops to zero; but
with it, it will suddenly turn into ice. Though such
mutations look sudden, in reality they are not. And until
all the necessary conditions exist, even if you claim to
have changed, that will not be true. This is why some of
those petty-bourgeois revolutionary writers who pro-
fessed to have changed overnight changed back again so
quickly.

The establishment of the League of Left-Wing Writers
in Shanghai last year was an important event. As the
theories of Plekhanov, Lunacharsky and others had been
introduced by then, they enabled us to study them and
become firmer and stronger. But precisely because of
this, we were oppressed and persecuted in a way scarcely

ever known in the world. And this being so, those so-
called revolutionary writers who had thought Left-wing
writing was going to be all the fashion and authors would
be offered bread and butter by the workers immediately
changed again — some recanted, while others turned to
attack the League of Left-Wing Writers to show how
much wiser they were this year. Though the League did
not take the initiative in this, it still served as a sort of
house-cleaning; for those authors, whether they change
back or not, are incapable of good writing.

But can the Left-wing writers who remain write good
proletarian literature? I think it is very hard. For all
our Left-wing writers today are still educated people —
intellectuals — hence it is difficult for them to write the
truth about the revolution. H. Kuriyakawa of Japan
once posed the question: "Must an author write solely
about his own experience?" His answer was: "No, because he can study other people's experience. To describe
a thief he need not steal himself; to describe illicit love
he need not have an affair." But to my mind, an author
can understand all these things because, living in the old
society, he is acquainted with the things and people in
it. He cannot do this, though, in connection with the
working class and characters with which he has had no
contact, or he will paint a wrong picture. So revolutionary writers must at least share in the life of the
revolution or keep their fingers closely on its pulse. (The
Left-Wing League's recent slogan to "Proletarianize the
writers!" shows a very correct understanding of this.)

In a society like China today, the best we can hope for
is the appearance of works showing the revolt of the
petty-bourgeoisie against their own class, or works of
exposure. For a writer who has grown up in this dying
class has a deep understanding of and hatred for it, and
so he can deal a most powerful, mortal blow. Of course
some seemingly revolutionary writers do not really desire the overthrow of their class or of the bourgeoisie,

but are angry or disappointed because they cannot carry
out reforms to maintain their position any longer. From
the working-class point of view, this is simply "brothers
at loggerheads" fighting inside the enemy's camp. These
books are like bubbles on the revolutionary tide. I see
no need to call works like this proletarian literature, nor
need such authors — with an eye to future fame — style
themselves proletarian writers.

Even those writers who merely attack the old society
may do harm to the revolution unless they see abuses
clearly and understand the root of the trouble. The pity
is that so many of our present authors — including revolutionary writers and critics — are incapable of this, or
dare not look society in the face to find out its real nature,
the enemy's nature in particular. Let me give an example at random. An article on modern Chinese literature
in the old *Lenin Youth* said that Chinese writers could
be divided into three camps. First it described the
Creation Society at great length as the literary group of
the proletariat; then it dealt briefly with the *Tatler* group
representing the petty-bourgeoisie; and thirdly it dealt
even more briefly — in less than one page — with the
Crescent Moon Society representing the bourgeoisie.
Apparently that young critic had the least to say about
those he hated most. In other words he had not studied
them.

Of course it is less comfortable, amusing and profitable
to read books by our opponents than by our friends; but
to my mind a fighter who wants to understand the revolution and the enemy should make the closest analysis
of the foe confronting him. The same applies to literature. Not only must we know the facts about revolution; we need a thorough knowledge of the enemy and
all aspects of the situation today before we can foresee
the future of the revolution. The sole hope of development for our literature lies in understanding the old and
seeing the new, in comprehending the past and deducing

the future. I believe it is possible for writers in present-day conditions to do this, if they will make the effort.

Today, as I mentioned earlier, literature and art are
being oppressed and persecuted as seldom before, and a
general dearth is the result. Literature voicing any protest or attacking old abuses is being suppressed just as
often as revolutionary work or work criticizing present
conditions. This shows that so far the revolution of the
ruling class has been nothing more than a tussle for an
old chair. When they try to knock it over the chair looks
odious, but once in their hands it turns into a treasure,
and they realize how much they have in common with
the old. Twenty years ago everyone called the first
emperor of Ming a national revolutionary, when in fact
this was not true. As soon as he ascended the throne
he addressed the Mongol court as "the great Yuan court"
and killed more Han people than ever the Mongols had.
When a slave becomes a master, he insists on being addressed as "sir" and generally gives himself greater, more
ridiculous airs than his former master. It is the same
with some Shanghai workers who have made a little
money and started a small factory — they treat their
workers worse than anyone else.

In an old collection of anecdotes — I forget its title —
I read that during the Ming Dynasty a military officer
called in a story-teller who told the tale of Tan Daoji,
a general of the Jin Dynasty. At the end the officer
ordered the story-teller to be beaten, and when questioned said, "If he tells me about Tan Daoji, he's bound
to go and tell Tan Daoji about me." Our rulers today are
as neurotic as that officer — afraid of everything. So
they have introduced improved hooligans into the
publishing world, who cannot be recognized as hooligans
yet use the most vicious tactics: advertisements, libel and
blackmail. Some men of letters have actually put themselves under the protection of hooligans for profit or
safety's sake. So revolutionary writers should be on

their guard not only against open enemies but also against the turncoat spies on their own side. This is much more difficult than the simple battle of books, and hence its effect on art and literature.

Though piles of so-called literary magazines are still published in Shanghai, they actually have no content. To steer clear of trouble, those printed by publishers out for a profit choose the most innocuous articles they can on such subjects as "Revolution is necessary — but it must not be too radical." The unique thing about them is that you may read them from beginning to end, but will find nothing in them. As for the government-owned magazines and those published to please the authorities, the contributors are a mixed lot whose one aim is to make money. They themselves think nothing of their writing and do not believe their own arguments in such articles as "English Literature of the Victorian Age" or "Why Sinclair Lewis Received the Nobel Prize." That is why I say all the literary magazines in Shanghai have no content. Revolutionary writing is being suppressed, and the magazines sponsored by those doing the suppressing contain no literature either. Do the oppressors really have no literature then? They have, but not here. It is contained in telegrams, decrees, news items, "nationalist literature," court sentences and the like. A few days ago, for instance, the *Shen Bao* carried a story of a woman who accused her husband of buggering her and beating her black and blue. The court replied that there was no law forbidding a husband to bugger his wife, and although she was bruised from her beating that did not count as a physical injury, so her charge could not be accepted. Now the man is suing his wife for making a "false charge." I know nothing of the law, but I have studied a little physiology. When the skin is black and blue, though the lungs, liver and kidney are not necessarily impaired, physical injury is done to the place bruised. This is common enough in China today —

nothing out of the ordinary — yet I think this gives us a better picture of society than the average novel or long poem.

In addition to the foregoing, I should have analysed what passes by the name of nationalist literature and the adventure stories which have been popular so long. But as there is no time left, I must wait for another occasion. This is all I shall say today.

THE TASK AND FATE OF "NATIONALIST LITERATURE"

I

It is the policy of colonialists to protect and rear hoodlums. In the eyes of the imperialists, they are the most indispensable slaves and stooges to carry out the task demanded of colonial peoples, namely, relying on one hand on the military might of the imperialists and on the other on the traditional might of their own country, to root out "trouble-makers" and "bad elements" who will not bow to their fate. So hoodlums are the pets — the lap-dogs, rather — of foreign potentates in colonial countries. Though their position ranks lower than that of their masters, it is none the less higher than that of other slaves. Shanghai is of course no exception to this rule. The police are hand in glove with the gangs; and a peddler, even though he has a little capital of his own, is hard put to it to keep a foothold unless he finds some hoodlum to be his creditor and pays him high interest. Last year there even appeared "writers" in literary circles who kowtowed to the leaders of a certain gang.

This, however, was simply a most blatant example. The fact is that even if they have not joined any gang, many so-called "writers and artists" have always functioned as lap-dogs. Though they raise such different slogans as "art for art's sake," "the national essence," "nationalism" or "art for humanity," these are merely like the different weapons in the hands of the police — muskets, carbines, rifles or mausers — having only one ultimate aim which is to kill all those "counter-revolutionaries" who oppose imperialism and the government, or those people who are simply rather discontented.

Among such lap-dog writers, the biggest hullabaloo is made by the writers of so-called "nationalist literature."* But they fall far short of the illustrious merits of detectives, police and executioners, the reason being that they can only bark, not bite outright. Moreover they usually lack the drive of the hoodlums, being simply floating corpses drifting this way and that. But this is precisely the special feature of "nationalist literature" and the reason why they retain their position as "pets."

Let us take a look at one of their periodicals, in which all kinds of characters who formerly held all kinds of different views now seem to have come together. Is it the giant hand of "nationalism" that has kneaded them into one? No. These floating corpses which for so long bobbed up and down past the Shanghai Bund, and were originally scattered far and wide, driven by the wind and waves have drifted together to form a conglomeration. And, because each one is putrid, they now give off a stronger stench.

These "barks" and "stench" are distinguished by their ability to carry a fair distance, and this benefits the imperialists. It is what is known as "clearing the way for the king," and that is why this floating corpse literature will always coexist with hoodlum politics.

II

But what are the wind and waves mentioned above? Just a small storm stirred up by the rising of the pro-

---

*See footnote on p. 135 above.

letariat. Some former so-called writers and artists may
have been semi-consciously or subconsciously aware of
their own decadence, so to deceive themselves as well as
others they took cover under such fine phrases as "standing aloof" of "letting oneself go" (in modern terms,
"decadence"). They painted nude women, still life or
death; wrote of flowers and the moon, the Holy Land,
insomnia, wine and women. As the collapse of the old
society became more evident and class struggle more
acute, they saw that the proletariat, their mortal enemy,
was going to create a new culture by sweeping away all
the filth of the past, and realized that they themselves
were part of this filth and would share the same fate as
their rulers. Thereupon, inevitably, they gathered under
the banner of "nationalist literature" raised by submissive
compatriots under the control of the imperialists, to put
up a last struggle together with their masters.

So although they are a mishmash of floating corpses,
they share a common aim: like their masters, they use
all means to crush the proletariat in order to prolong their
feeble existence. Still, they are only a mishmash, usually
retaining some vestiges of their original hair and hide,
which is why since issuing their manifesto they have
not produced any clear-cut work, while the manifesto
itself is a mishmash concocted at random by a small
bunch of mishmash, not worth taking seriously.

However, *Vanguard Monthly*, No. 5 has given us a
lucid piece of writing which the editor describes as "a
true description of the punitive campaign against Yan
Xishan and Feng Yuxiang* by a participant." Stories
about warfare are nothing remarkable, but what is odd
is the psychology of the author — this "young soldier" —
on the battlefield. As a self-portrait of a "writer of nationalist literature," it is well worth quoting:

---

* This compaign against these warlords was launched by Chiang
Kai-shek in May 1930.

Each night as I stood beneath those glittering stars, carbine in hand, I heard the chirping of insects, while around me swarmed countless mosquitoes. All this brought to my mind the life of the French "Foreign Legionaries" shedding their blood as they fought against the Arabs in the African desert. (Huang Zhenxia: "*Along the Longhai Railway Line.*")

So as seen by this "young soldier" and "writer of nationalist literature," the fighting among Chinese warlords is not internecine strife among nationals of one country, but a war of foreigners against other foreigners, involving two countries and nations. Once night falls on the battlefield, he has the exalted sensation that his skin has turned white, his nose grown higher, and he has become a Latin soldier in barbarous Africa. No wonder then that he regards all the common people around as enemies who should one by one be killed off. From the nationalist point of view, a Frenchman need have no pity on Arabs in Africa. In a larger sense, this description alone explains why Chinese warlords bacame the imperialists' hatchet-men to massacre the Chinese people, because they identified themselves with the French Foreign Legion. In a lesser sense, this makes it clear that the Chinese "writers of nationalist literature" basically associate themselves with those foreign masters; if they speak of "nationalism" to fool their readers, this is because they sometimes feel as if they belonged to the Latin or Teutonic races.

III

Since Mr. Huang Zhenxia spoke so frankly, he must have expressed his true feelings; but judging by the knowledge shown in his story there was still something somewhat counterfeit, as he was aware but deliberately

would not admit. This was his mealy-mouthed substitu-
tion of "French Foreign Legionaries" for "French Annamese troops,"* which makes this rather a far cry from
a "true description" and invites the criticism made
earlier.

However, the writer is intelligent. He has heard a
great deal from his "friend Fu Yanchang"** and "in many
places was, frankly speaking, influenced by him."
Moreover after studying Chinese and foreign history and
legends, he followed this up with a dramatic poem more
closely akin to the subject of "nationalism" for this time
he did not bring in the French — it was *Blood of the
Yellow Race* (*Vanguard Monthly*, No. 7).

This dramatic poem deals with the Western Expedition of the Yellow race, its hero being General Batu,
grandson of Genghis Khan, a genuine specimen of the
Yellow race. He set out to conquer Europe but his actual
objective was Russia, this being the author's target; his
united force was composed of Hans, Tartars, Nuchens
and Khitans, this being the author's design; they advanced from victory to victory but, unhappily, later on these
four races failed to understand the importance of "friendship" and the "strength which lies in unity" and fell
upon each other, enabling the warriors of the White races
to gain the upper hand — this was the author's moral,
his cause for grief.

Let us look at the overwhelming might and ferocity of
this force of the Yellow race.

> *Fearful, the oil oozing from burning corpses,*
> *The horror of putrid bodies strewing the ground;*
> *The God of Death seizes white girls in frenzied*
> *embrace,*
> *Beauties are turned into fearsome skeletons;*
> *Cannibals struggle like beasts in ancient palaces;*

---

* The French hired Annamese mercenaries to invade Africa.
** One of the chief exponents of "nationalist literature."

> *A foul stench wafts from coffins a thousand years*
> *   old;*
> *There is sorrow on the faces of the Crusaders;*
> *Iron hooves trample broken bones,*
> *Camels utter wild howls;*
> *God has fled; vengeful devils have raised the scourge*
> *   of fire.*
> *The Yellow Peril is here! The Yellow Peril!*
> *Asian warriors' bloody maws are devouring men.*

This "Yellow Peril" trumpeted by Germany's Kaiser Wilhelm in order to advocate "Deutschland, Deutschland, über alles" and the "Asian warriors' bloody maws" were aspersions cast by our poet at Russia, the first country where now the proletariat rules, to destroy this proletarian model, for such is the aim of "nationalist literature." However, since it is after all "nationalist literature" written by submissive subjects in a colonial country, the hero chosen by our poet was not the Han Zhao Gou* but the Mongol Batu, and those whose "bloody maws were devouring men" were not Chinese but "Asian warriors," while what he hoped for was not friendship based on equality among different nationalities but "friendship" under the rule of Batu. This is the blatant characteristic of so-called "nationalist literature," but it is also a cause for grief for the author, the "young soldier."

IV

Batu is dead, and the only one of the Yellow races in Asia today that can be compared with the Mongols of that period is Japan. Though Japanese warriors also hate Russia, they have no love for Chinese warriors either. Though they talk so loudly of the "intimate re-

---

* (1107-1187), the first emperor of the Southern Song Dynasty.

lationship between Japan and China" which seems to accord with "friendship," the facts do not bear this out. This is certainly sad from the viewpoint of "writers of nationalist literature," so it is only natural and in no way surprising if they use it as an analogy.

Indeed, the poet's sad premonition appears to have come true, and something much worse has happened. Just as they are about to "raise the scourge of fire" to destroy Russia, as Batu did in the end, the Koreans are massacring Chinese,* and the Japanese opening their "bloody maws to devour men" have gobbled up our northeastern provinces. Is this because they have not been sufficiently influenced by Mr. Fu Yanchang to understand the "strength of unity," so that they consider the warriors of China just like the Arabs in Africa!

V

This is really a heavy blow. Before the writer who is a "soldier" has shouted his battle-cry, we now see the anger and despair of lesser warriors published in the press under the banner of "nationalism." This is also natural and in no way surprising. Illusions and reality are prone to come into conflict. When they had illusions, these were tinged with sadness, thus now faced with reality they are bound to despair. And so those lesser warriors want to fight.

> Fight! Make the final decision
> To wipe out all our foes;
> See the enemy's bombardment;
> Press on to build a Great Wall with our bodies.
> Thunder rumbles overhead,

---

* At the instigation of the Japanese on the eve of their invasion of China, in 1931 the Koreans attacked overseas Chinese living there.

Waves roar underfoot,
Hot blood sets our hearts afire
As we race towards the front.
    (Su Feng, *Battle Song*, published in the
        Minguo Daily)

Go, go to the battlefield,
Our blood is boiling,
Our bodies have turned berserk,
Our hot blood will clog the invaders' guns,
Our limbs block the muzzles of their artillery.
Go, go to the battlefield,
Relying on our courage,
On our pure spirit of love,
To drive out our foes,
No, to kill all our foes.
    (Gan Yuqing, *Go, Go to the Battlefield*, published
        in *Shen Bao*)

Compatriots, awake,
Away with the hearts of weaklings,
Away with the brains of weaklings.
See, see
The spurting blood of our compatriots,
The sliced off flesh of our compatriots,
The hung up corpses of our compatriots!
    (Shao Guanhua, *Compatriots Awake*, Ibid.)

One thing clearly apparent in these poems is the
writers' knowledge that, having no arms, we can only
replace them with "bodies," "the pure spirit of love" and
"corpses." This is the same sorrow expressed by the
author of *Blood of the Yellow Race*, and explains his call
for "friendship" after following General Batu. Arms
have to be bought from the master, and all proletarians
are enemies; therefore if the master shows no appreciation and wants to deal out punishment, the only way
out actually is to die.

We are a group of new recruits
With firm determination,
Seething hot blood,
Come to wipe out the savage invaders.
Fellow countrymen, dear fellow countrymen,
Rise up quickly, ready to fight,
Rise up to give battle,
To die in battle is our only way out.
          (Sha Shan, *The Students' Corps,* Ibid.)

Heaven is shrieking,
Earth is quaking,
Men are charging, beasts are roaring,
The whole universe is clamouring.
Friends,
We are ready to have our heads cut off by the foe.
          (Ji Zhijin, *Great Death,* Ibid.)

Some are for going all out, others are singing of heroic
death. There is no harm in such writing, but were they
really to act in this way that would show too much
ignorance of the subtlety of "nationalist literature." And,
indeed, they have already done their duty as "writers of
nationalist literature."

VI

The poet Huang Zhenxia, author of *Blood of the Yellow
Race* published under a big-character caption by
Vanguard Monthly, has told us about the ideal General
Batu. This poet, influenced by Mr. Fu Yanchang, has
looked up historical records Chinese and foreign and
knows that "Eastern Europe in the Middle Ages was the
meeting point of three conflicting beliefs,"* so surely
he should know that China at the end of the Song

---

* A quotation from his foreword to *Blood of the Yellow Race.*

Dynasty was ravaged and plundered by the Mongols. When General Batu's grandfather Genghis Khan invaded China, his troops wherever they went raped and carried off women and burned down houses. When they reached Qufu in Shandong and saw an image of Confucius, the Mongol soldiers swore at it, "Aren't you that fellow who said, 'Even when the barbarians have a king, they cannot compare with the Chinese without a king'?" With that they loosed off an arrow at its face. This was related with tears in the anecdotes of some Song scholar, just like the tearful writings we see so often nowadays in the press. The poet Huang's wonderful description of Russia, "The God of Death is seizing white girls in frenzied embrace . . ." actually applied to China in that period; but didn't they go off arm in arm on the Western Expedition when it came to the time of Genghis' grandson? Now the Japanese troops' "Eastern Expedition" to our northeastern provinces is the first step to the "Western Expedition" dreamed of by our "writers of nationalist literature," and the "Asian warriors" have just begun to open "their bloody maws to devour men." Only first they must take a bite out of China. Because Genghis Khan in his day, before his onslaught on Russia, had first to turn the Chinese into slaves and drive them to fight his wars; he did not use "friendship" or send invitation cards. Hence the Mukden Incident* not only does not conflict with "nationalist literature," but has actually helped make its writers' dreams come true. If people do not understand this and insist on going to lose their heads to decrease the number of "Asian warriors," that would really be a pity.

Does this mean, then, that "nationalist literature" can dispense with all those lamentations and invocations to death? No. They should and must play that tune, other-

---

* This was the attack launched on China by the Japanese in Shenyang on September 18, 1931.

wise all such tricks as the principle of non-resistance, appeasement and the relinquishment of territory will appear too obvious in the silence. Bitter lamentations, roars of rage and shaking fists are needed to confuse people with their clamour, so that they are moved to tears or give vent to anger on hearing tragic and heroic songs; for in this way the "Eastern Expedition" which is the first step to the "Western Expedition" will pass unnoticed. In a funeral procession there is anguished sobbing as well as martial music, the idea being to use this din to cover up the "death" of the one sent to his grave, so that all will quickly forget it. The present works of "nationalist literature," whether militant or mournful, serve the same purpose.

But from now on the writers of "nationalist literature" will draw closer to grief because the problem, now more imminent, is whether in future their master will avoid General Batu's mistake and go on trusting and giving preferential treatment to his loyal and brave slaves, or rather "warriors." This is really a most grave and fearful problem, the crucial problem of whether or not master and slaves can co-exist and share prosperity.

History tells us: Impossible. This can never happen, as even the writers of "nationalist literature" themselves are aware. They can only function as mourners in a funeral procession, for ever nursing their grief for their master. Not until the storm of proletarian revolution breaks and sweeps the whole country clean, will they be able to extricate themselves from this stagnant, degraded and corrupt fate.

HARD TO KNOW, HARD TO DO

It has always been the custom for Chinese emperors in time of security or trouble to make up to men of letters. When they are secure they put on a show of "laying down arms to cultivate the arts of peace." When in trouble they consult them, because they really believe that scholars know how to "pacify the empire." Frankly speaking, this is like the remark in *A Dream of Red Mansions*: "In case of serious illness, one turns to all sorts of doctors in desperation."

When "Emperor Pu Yi" was bored by sitting still after his abdication, Dr. Hu Shi played a similar role.

Funnily enough, after his interview the first question people asked was how they had addressed each other.

"He called me Mister," said Dr. Hu Shi.* "I called him Your Majesty."

Apparently they did not discuss great affairs of state, for all His Majesty did later was write a little doggerel. But still he was bored, and he ended by being driven out of his golden palace.** He is due to resume power now, for they say he will be emperor of the three northeastern provinces. And in Shanghai today we read that "Chiang has sent for Hu Shi and Ding Wenjiang. . . ."

---

* From Hu Shi's article "Pu Yi and Hu Shi" published in 1922.
** In 1924 when Feng Yuxiang's troops occupied Beijing, Pu Yi was driven out of the palace and moved to the foreign concessions in Tianjin. After the Japanese invasion of the Northeast in 1931, he was used as a puppet. In November that year the Japanese escorted him to the Northeast. In 1932 they set up Manchukuo, and in 1934 gave him the title of Emperor Kang De.

"A dispatch from Nanjing reports that Ding Wen-jiang and Hu Shi have gone to the capital to visit Chiang. He sent for them to make inquiries about affairs of state. . . ." (The *Shen Bao* of October 14.)

This time no one asks how they addressed each other. Why not? This time they know: "I called him Chairman!"

Because Professor Liu Wendian, president of Anhui University, failed to call Chiang "Chairman," he was locked up for quite a few days and it was with the greatest difficulty that he succeeded in getting out on bail. But of course being fellow-provincials and old colleagues, Dr. Hu Shi knew Liu's adventure. So: "I called him Chairman."

No one asks about the nature of those inquiries either. Why not? Because this is known too — they concerned "affairs of state." And "affairs of state" are less troublesome than arguments about "the dictatorship of the Kuomintang" or "English-style freedom,"* and those about "hard to know, easy to do," or "easy to know, hard to do."** So the doctor came out again.

Dr. Luo Longji of the Crescent Moon Society says:

> There should be a radical change in the government . . . which must take in talented men from all over the country who represent all shades of political opinion. . . . We can sacrifice our political views. In fact this should be done. (*The Shenyang Incident.*)

A government composed of talented men of all shades of political opinion who will also sacrifice their political views — this is surely a most mysterious sort of "gov-

---

* In "What Political System Do We Want?" published in *Crescent Moon*, Vol. II, No. 12.
** Hard to know, easy to do" was a saying of Sun Yat-sen. In October 1929, *Crescent Moon* carried an article by Hu Shi entitled "Hard to Know and Hard to Do" in which he criticized Sun Yat-sen's view and advocated a "government of experts." He hoped to join the Kuomintang government.

ernment." But the man who believes in "hard to know, easy to do" has now consulted the man who advocates "hard to know, hard to do." So there seems to be something in the air.

THE NEW DON QUIXOTES OF
THE CHINESE REPUBLIC

Towards the end of the sixteenth century the Spanish author Cervantes wrote a long novel *Don Quixote*, describing how Mr. Quixote, fuddled by reading too many romances, determined to imitate the knight errants of old. In a shabby coat of mail he roamed the country on a sorry nag, accompanied by his serving-man, eager to kill wicked ogres and rescue those in distress. But because the age of chivalry was over, he simply succeeded in making a fool of himself and getting plenty of knocks into the bargain. In the end he landed in serious trouble, was badly wounded and slunk home to die. And only on his deathbed did he realize that he was just an ordinary fellow, not a great knight at all.

This allusion was very much used in China last year, and the worthies who received the title "quixotic" were rather put out by it. The fact is a fool like Quixote is a Spanish fool — you will not find his counterpart in China where we set such store by the Doctrine of the Mean. When Spaniards court a girl, they serenade her every day; when they feel religious, they burn heretics at the stake; when they make a revolution, they pull down churches and kick out their king. Our Chinese scholars, however, always accuse the women of seducing them, trace all religions to one common source and protect temple property, and allow Pu Yi to remain as emperor in the palace for years after the revolution.

I remember reading once in the paper about some shop

assistants who were so carried away by stories of swords-
men that they suddenly decided to go to Wudang Mountain to learn the art. That was thoroughly quixotic. But
as there has been no sequel to their story, we do not know
whether they accomplished wonders or went home again
by and by. According to the Doctrine of the Mean, going
home would appear more appropriate.

The next Chinese Quixotes to appear were the Young
Reinforcements League.* They were not soldiers but
insisted on going to the front. The government wanted
to appeal to the League of Nations, but they insisted on
taking action themselves. The authorities forbade them,
but still they went. China has a few railway lines, but
they were willing to go on foot. It is cold in the north,
but they would not wear padded clothes. In fighting
the question of weapons is all-important, but all they
emphasized was their morale. This and much more was
thoroughly quixotic. Still these were Chinese Quixotes,
so where Quixote was one they were a league, and where
Quixote was jeered at and marvelled at they were sent
off amid cheers. Whereas he lived deep in the mountains they came to the town of Zhenru. And while he
tilted at a windmill, their trials included collecting combs
in Changzhou and visiting beautiful girls. (See "Free
Talk" in the *Shen Bao* for December.) Alas, what a difference between them!

True, there are too many stories, ancient and modern,
Chinese and foreign, in which we find references to
"coffin carrying," "finger cutting," "weeping before the
Qin court"** and "swearing to Heaven." So of course

----

* A group organized in Shanghai to support Ma Zhanshan,
deputy chairman of Heilongjiang who continued to resist after
the Japanese invasion of the Northeast.

** These are classical allusions. Troops carried coffins to show
their determination to fight to the death. Finger cutting also
signified resolution. When the army of Wu took the capital of
Chu in the fifth century B.C., Shen Baoxu wept in the court of
Qin for seven days and seven nights, till the Duke of Qin gave
Chu military aid.

men cannot help being influenced and acting as pall-
bearers, cutting off fingers, weeping at Sun Yat-sen's
tomb, and vowing to set out. But when Dr. Hu Shi
preached a cultural revolution during the May 4th Movement, he already proposed: "Down with the classics!"
So in our actions today we can ignore these precedents.

In all war literature, whether in older books like
Remarque's *All Quiet on the Western Front* and Ludwig
Renn's *The War* or in newer ones like Serafimovich's
Iron Stream and Fadeyev's *The Nineteen*, there has never
been a Youth League like this. That is why there was
some real fighting.

ON "SHOCKING OUR FRIENDLY NEIGHBOURS"

Everyone with the least sense knows that the students sent in their recent petitions because Japan has occupied Liaoning and Jilin, yet the Nanjing government is looking on helplessly and has merely appealed to the League of Nations, though the League is on Japan's side. Stick to your study, they say. Yes, students ought to study, but how can they study with a quiet mind while the big shots are giving away our territory? We see in the papers that the Northeastern University has been disbanded, as well as Feng Yong University, and that Japanese troops shoot anyone who looks like a student. Laying down satchels in order to send in petitions is surely pathetic enough. Yet on December 18 the Kuomintang government dispatched a telegram to all local military and civil authorities accusing the students of "disturbing the peace by wrecking organizations, obstructing traffic, assaulting members of the Central Committee, seizing automobiles, attacking passers-by and government employees, and taking the law into their own hands." It was pointed out that this was bound to "shock our friendly neighbours. If it goes on, the country will be ruined!"

Fine "friendly neighbours" these! They were not shocked when the troops of imperialist Japan seized Liaoning and Jilin and shelled government offices. They were not shocked when these soldiers cut railways, blew up passenger trains, arrested officials and shot people.

They were not shocked by the years of civil war and
record floods, the children sold through dire poverty, the
display of decapitated heads, the secret assassinations,
the confessions extracted by electric shock under Kuomintang rule. But when students sounded a note of
protest — then they were shocked!

Fine "friendly neighbours" of the Kuomintang government! The bastards!

Even if the accusations made are true, these are things
that happen in every "friendly country." The prisons
they use to maintain their "law and order" have ripped
off their "cultured" masks. What nerve to speak of being
shocked!

But as soon as our "friendly neighbours" are shocked,
our government trembles. "If this goes on, the country
will be ruined!" Apparently losing the three northeastern
provinces makes Kuomintang China more like a
country than before. Nobody uttered a word when they
were lost, except for the few students who sent in petitions, and the Kuomintang won the praise of our
"friendly neighbours" for making China more like a
country than before — long may it last!

The short telegram makes quite clear the nature of
our government and of our "friendly neighbours." Our
"friendly neighbours" want us to make no sound when
they hack off our flesh. If we trespass in the least they
butcher us. And the Kuomintang wants us to respect
the wishes of our "friendly neighbours," otherwise telegrams will be sent to all military and civil authorities:
"Urgent measures must be taken. No one must shift
the responsibility on the pretext that he could not stop
the trouble."

Our "friendly neighbours" know there is no stopping
Japanese soldiers, but surely students can be stopped?
What use are you "military and civil authorities" making of your eighteen-million-dollar military allocation
and four-million-dollar administrative fund each month?

Just one day after writing this, I read this telegram from Nanjing in the *Shen Bao* of the twenty-first:

Zhang Yikuan of the Examination Yuan was reported to have been carried off and badly hurt by students the day before yesterday. According to Zhang himself, however, owing to a mistake on the part of his driver he was taken with the crowd to the Central University, but he extricated himself and reached home in safety. A secretary of the Executive Yuan who was dragged to the Central University also left straight away — he did not disappear.

And in the column headed "The Academic World," reliable figures are given for the number of casualties among the students of a few Shanghai schools who went to Nanjing to present petitions.

Two died and thirty were wounded from the China Public School. There were two casualties from Fudan University, ten from Fudan Middle School. One student of The East Asia Middle School (a girl) disappeared. One from Shanghai Middle School disappeared and three were injured. One was killed and five injured from The Vincent School. . . .

Obviously the students were not "disturbing the peace" as alleged by the government telegram, but the authorities suppressed them just the same, and slandered and butchered them just the same. Our "friendly neighbours" will not be shocked in future. They can come with an easy mind to divide the loot.

A REPLY TO THE MAGAZINE
THE DIPPER

— What is the secret of good writing?

December 27, 1931

Dear Sir,

You should have addressed your question to American writers or Chinese professors in Shanghai, whose heads are full of "rules of writing" and "the art of writing fiction." Though I have written a score or so of short stories I have never had any set views on the subject, in much the same way as I can speak Chinese but could never write *An Introduction to Chinese Grammar*. But since you did me the honour of consulting me, here are a few tips from my experience:

1. Take an interest in everything and see as much as you can. Don't write as soon as you have seen a little.

2. Don't force yourself to write when not in the mood.

3. Don't choose definite models for your characters, but create them out of all that you have seen.

4. Read your story through at least twice after finishing it, and ruthlessly cut all words, phrases and sections that are not essential. It is better to compress the material for a story into a sketch than to stretch the material for a sketch into a story.

5.   Read foreign stories, especially those of Eastern and Northern Europe, as well as Japanese works.
6.   Never make up adjectives or phrases that no one else can understand.
7.   Never believe any talk about "rules of writing."
8.   Never trust Chinese "literary critics," but read the works of reliable foreign critics.

That is all I can say on this subject.
I send you my greetings!

Lu Xun

1932

PREFACE TO LIN KEDUO'S
EYE-WITNESS ACCOUNT OF
*THE SOVIET UNION**

About ten years ago, when I went to a foreign hospital for some treatment, in the German weekly *Die Woche* in the waiting-room I saw a cartoon on the October Revolution. It showed judges, teachers, even doctors and nurses, grasping revolvers and glaring. That was the first cartoon I had seen on the October Revolution, but my only feeling was one of amusement. Could there really be such ferocious characters? Later I read several travel books by Westerners, some of them nothing but praise, others nothing but blame, which thoroughly confused me. Finally, though, I decided: This revolution must have been good for the poor and therefore bad for the rich. Of course, travellers who sympathize with the poor praise Russia, while those on the side of the rich see nothing but bad there.

Later, however, I saw another cartoon by an Englishman showing roads flanked by factories, schools and crèches made of cardboard, with visitors driving through them seated in cars. This was a thrust at those travellers who praised the Soviet Union, implying that they were deceived on conducted tours. I know nothing of politics or economics, but the Soviet Union's export of petroleum and wheat last year, which so horrified the

---

*Lin Keduo was a Chinese metal-worker in Paris, who became unemployed during the economic crisis of 1929 and in 1930 went to the Soviet Union.

people of civilized capitalist countries, settled the doubts
I had harboured for so long. I thought: A window-
dressing state and a nation of killers could never have
this great productive capacity. Those cartoons were
obviously faked.

But the fact is we in China have one foible — we dislike hearing anything good about other countries. After
the purge this applied particularly to any mention of the
achievements of the Soviet Union. If you so much as
breathed a word of these, you were accused of making
propaganda or of taking Russian roubles. And the word
"propaganda" is in bad odour in China, because people
are so used to the way in which dispatches from the rich,
powerful statements made in conferences, or the speeches
of famous personages vanish without a trace as soon as
uttered. They come to believe that all accounts of distant lands or future good are lies, and that "propaganda"
is a polite name for large-scale deceit from selfish motives.

Naturally in China today there are many examples of
this, and those with official sanction can circulate freely;
but not many people read them, because propaganda has
to be confirmed by facts either now or later. What
passes as propaganda in China today is not only bound
to be exposed in future, but also has the bad effect of
making people mistrust all reportage, until finally they
stop reading it altogether. I know this from my own
experience. If the papers carry an article on the sights
of the three capitals* or the new spirit in Beijing and
Nanjing, the headlines alone are enough to put one off.
So I do not even care to read about travel abroad.

This year, though, I came across two books which I
actually finished without having to feel on my guard.
One was Hu Yuzhi's *Impressions of Moscow*, the other

---

* Nanjing, Luoyang and Xi'an. Nanjing was then the Kuomintang capital. During the Japanese invasion of Shanghai, Luoyang
and Xi'an were also designated as temporary capitals.

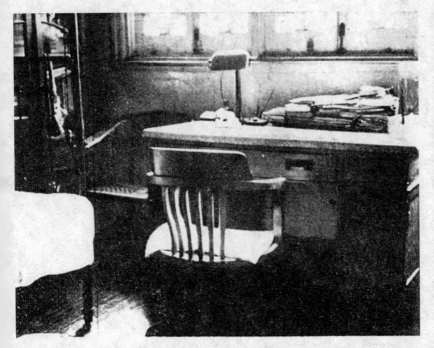

Lu Xun's study in Shanghai

was this *Eye-Witness Account of the Soviet Union*.
Owing to my lack of skill in deciphering handwriting, it
required an effort, but read it I did, because I wanted to
share the experience of this working-class writer who
says, "I had to work to keep myself alive." Though
some parts read like explanations of statistics, and I
could not help finding these dry, they were fortunately
not too many, so I persevered. The reason was that the
author seems to be chatting to his friends. Without any
beautiful phrases or special art, he gives a straightforward, matter-of-fact account. He is an ordinary
fellow, his language is ordinary language, and all he saw
or heard in the Soviet Union shows what an ordinary
country that is too. The people are ordinary, their plans
are all quite rational, and they are simply living like
human beings — there is nothing strange or peculiar
about them. If you are looking for something bizarre or
exotic, you are bound to be disappointed. But this is an
excellent book if you want an unvarnished picture of
the truth.

And this sheds light on the question why the civilized
capitalist countries are so bent on attacking the Soviet
Union. For workers and peasants to live like human
beings is very much against the interests of capitalists
and landlords; hence their greatest wish is to wipe out
the country which serves as a model for toilers everywhere. The more normal the Soviet Union, the more
they tremble. Five or six years ago Beijing was filled
with rumours of nudist parades in Guangzhou, while later
on Nanjing and Shanghai were filled with rumours of
nudist parades in Hankou — proofs of the wish to smear
one's opponent as abnormal. Judging by the descriptions in this book, they would find the Soviet Union most
disappointing. For far from indulging in "abnormal
practices" like sharing wives, patricide, and nudist
parades, the Russians have done many most normal
things, sweeping aside like so much filth "such sacred

inviolable things as religion, the family, property, the motherland and convention"; and a brand-new, truly unprecedented social system has emerged from hell — hundreds of millions of common folk have taken their destiny into their own hands. Only "bandits"* would do such very normal things. Accursed bandits!

But as the author went to the Soviet Union ten years after the October Revolution, he simply describes their "endurance and capacity to work, their courage and self-sacrifice," telling us very little of the bitter struggle they waged to win their present position. Of course this is the task of other writers, and we cannot expect one man to cover everything. But readers should on no account overlook this, otherwise they will be like the man in the Indian parable who wanted to build a high tower but refused to base the pillars on the ground — because he wanted a tower high in the air!

For the reasons already given, I read this book through without feeling on my guard. And another reason why I believe in the good features of the Soviet Union which it describes is that the so-called civilized countries, who a dozen years ago stressed the incompetence and hope-lessness of Russia, trembled last year before its petroleum and wheat. I have also seen certain incontrovertible facts: The civilized countries are sucking China's blood, seizing China's territory, and killing Chinese people. If such great cheats defame the Soviet Union and want to attack it, that is to the credit of the Soviet Union. And this book, to come back to it, confirms me in this view.

Shanghai
April 20, 1932

---

* The name the reactionaries called the revolutionaries.

PREFACE TO *THREE LEISURES*

It is four years, come to think of it, since the publication of *And That's That,* my fourth collection of miscellanea. And last spring some friends urged me to collect what I had subsequently written into one volume. In the publishing world these last few years no one can complain of any dearth of original writing, translations or long treatises on important topics; but there have been very few short reviews or outspoken comments of the sort known as "miscellanea." For the moment I cannot explain why this should be so.

My guess is, though, that the expression "miscellanea" offends high-minded writers who shun it like the plague. This can be seen from the disparaging way in which certain people always refer to me as a "miscellanist," to display their scorn as high-class men of letters. And it seems that while well-known authors may write miscellanea too under pseudonyms, because they are out to settle private scores and afraid to spoil their reputations, or because they have some other ulterior motive the disclosure of which would tie their hands, they let such writing be lost.

Some people certainly think miscellanea my "fatal disease," and I have indeed suffered no little on this score; but I intend to go on collecting and printing these things. It was only the trouble involved in going through magazines, cutting out articles and assembling them that delayed me from starting work for more than half a year. The fighting which broke out in Shanghai on the night of

January 28* grew fiercer and fiercer till I had to evacuate,
leaving my books and papers under fire; for if they were
burned this "baptism by fire" would wash away those
opprobrious epithets "malcontent" and "miscellanist."**
Little did I guess that on my return at the end of March
I should find all my papers intact. Thereupon I started
rummaging through them and making a selection, like
a man just recovered from a dangerous illness who is
curious to peer at his wasted features in the mirror and
finger his wrinkled skin.

First I sorted out what I had written in '28 and '29.
This came to very little; but apart from five or six talks
given in Beijing and Shanghai, for which I had no notes,
nothing else seems to have been lost. I remember now
that these were the two years in which I did the least
writing and could find no publisher. I left Guangdong
in 1927, aghast at the bloodshed there,*** and my stam-
mered comments — I dared not speak outright — appeared in *And That's That*. But once in Shanghai I was
attacked from all sides by the pens of literary pundits.
The Creation Society, the Sun Society and the "respectable gentlemen" of the Crescent Moon Society all con-
demned me. Even those who belonged to no literary
clique, most of whom have now risen to be authors or
professors, kept penning a few quiet gibes at me to demonstrate their superiority. To begin with I was simply
"leisured and moneyed," the "spawn of feudalism" or
"degenerate"; but later I was labelled a "fascist" thirsting
for the blood of the young. At this time I had staying in
my home a Mr. Liao† who said he had been forced to fly
from Guangdong; but finally he told me indignantly, "All

---

* Referring to the attack on Shanghai by the Japanese in 1932,
when Lu Xun's house came under bombardment.
** Terms used by Liang Shiqiu in an attack on Lu Xun.
*** Referring to the White Terror in Guangzhou after Chiang
Kai-shek's coup d'etat on April 12, 1927.
† Lu Xun's student in the Sun Yat-sen University in 1927.

my friends look down on me and are cutting me for living with someone like you."

"Someone like you" — this shows how low I had sunk. Although editing the *Tatler* I had no actual authority; I was not just afraid to write (for details see "My Connection with the *Tatler*"). As for any other writing, it always had to be "milked" out of me. And just then, because of the "encirclement campaign,"* I saw no point in plunging into the fray. That is why I wrote so little.

Now I have collected in this volume all I wrote at that time: what was mistaken as well as what may still be worth reading. As for the writing of my opponents, some of it can be found in *On Lu Xun* and *China's Battle on Literature*, but these are the more dignified and decorous writings which can stand the light of day — they do not represent the whole. I am thinking of collecting some other articles in the nature of "miscellanea" to make up a volume called *The Encirclement Campaign*. A comparison between that and this collection should heighten the readers' interest and help them to understand the other side, all the shifts and subterfuges of shadow-boxing. Such dodges are not likely to die out immediately. Last year's charge "All Left-wing writers are in the pay of Moscow" is just one of many old tricks. Of course, there is no need for young people who are interested in literature and art to learn these, but there is no harm either in knowing about them.

As a matter of fact, I have made a search and can find no sign in my stories or reviews that I ever thirsted for the blood of the young. Nor did I ever dream of such a thing. I believed in evolution, was sure that the future would be better than the past and the young better than the old. Indeed, such respect did I have for the young that if they stabbed me ten times with their daggers I

---

* Referring to the Kuomintang's suppression of revolutionary literature.

only shot back one arrow. Later, however, I realized my mistake. It was not the materialist interpretation of history or some revolutionary writing which befuddled me; but in Guangdong I saw young people divided into two great camps — some of them acting as informers or helping the authorities to make arrests. This exploded my old way of thinking, and I started looking sceptically at the young instead of admiring them unconditionally. I still uttered a few cries of encouragement, though, for young people fresh to the fray — not that it did much good.

I believe this collection comprises everything I wrote during those two years, except that I have selected only those forewords to books which seem to have some relevance today. While looking through old papers, I came across a few articles written in 1927 which were not included in *And That's That*. I fancy that I omitted "Night Jottings" because I meant to put it in another volume; and I left out some talks and letters as being too slight or irrelevant.

However, I am now putting these at the beginning of this volume as a supplement to *And That's That*. To my mind, you need only look at the writings quoted in these speeches and letters to understand what Hongkong was like at that time. I went there twice to speak. My first subject was "The Old Tune Has Been Played Out," the notes of which I have lost. The second was "Silent China" which, sketchy and superficial as it is, I was surprised to find labelled "vicious" and banned by the press. That is what Hongkong was like. But now practically the whole of China is becoming like Hongkong.

One acknowledgement I must make to the Creation Society: They "forced" me to read some scientific literary criticism, which cleared up many questions which had remained unsolved in spite of all written by earlier literary critics. Thanks to this, too, I translated Plekhanov's *The Theory of Art*, to correct the one-sided belief in evolution which I, and others because of me, had held. But I decided to print the materials collected for *A Brief History of Chinese Fiction* as *Anecdotes of Chinese Fiction*, to save students time and trouble; and Cheng Fangwu, in the name of the proletariat, used this as evidence that I had too much "leisure" — "leisure, leisure, and yet more leisure."* Even now this accusation rankles. I do not believe the working class would resort to such a method of condemnation, for workers are not "pettifoggers." So having compiled this volume I am calling it *Three Leisures*, and this is aimed at Cheng Fangwu.

Written after compiling this volume
on the night of April 24, 1932

PREFACE TO *TWO HEARTS*

This is a collection of the miscellanea I wrote in 1930 and 1931.

By 1930 periodicals were growing rare and some could not come out on time, largely because of the daily increasing repression. The *Tatler* and *Torrent* were confiscated so often by the post office and banned by so many local authorities that they simply could not carry on. The only magazine left which would publish my contributions was *Sprouts*, but after five numbers that was also banned, and so we brought out *New Territory*. Hence this volume contains less than ten short articles written that year.

I also gave a few talks in different schools, but nobody took notes and today I myself have forgotten on what subjects I spoke. All I remember is that in one university I talked on "Ivory Towers and Snail Shells." I argued that there could be no ivory-tower art in China because we lacked a suitable environment, lacked even the site for an ivory tower; all we could expect in the near future was probably a few "snail shells." By snail shells I meant the sort of thatched hut to which Jiao Xian, the "recluse" of the Three Kingdoms Period, retired. It must have been rather like the hovels put up by poor folk north of the Changjiang, only smaller; and he spent all his time crouching there, seldom emerging or stirring, going without food, clothes and conversation. For in such a time of murder and looting, of internecine strife between warlords, that was the only way for a dissident to survive. But as a world of snail shells had no art, if we went on like this we could be certain that China would have no art. This speech of mine already smacked strongly of snail shells. Still, before long I was surprised to find myself criticized in the government-sponsored *Republic Daily* in Shanghai by a courageous young man who declared that he despised me utterly because I dared not talk like a Communist. For those living in our Kuomintang Party state after the "purge of the party,"* to talk about communism is a great crime, and a net has been cast all over China for the capture and execution of those who do so; yet unless I do so I am despised by courageous young men loyal to our party state. All I can do is change into a real snail. This is my only chance to escape denunciation.

By this time, however, a hullabaloo was being raised by the big dailies as well as by evening papers accusing Left-wing writers of taking Russian roubles; and the critics of the Crescent Moon Society helped with might and main from the side. Some dailies even picked up the contributions sent by members of the Creation Society to the evening papers, and sneered at me for "surrendering." One newspaper started a column called "Lives of Turncoat Leaders in Literature" and began the series with me — after which, however, they seem to have discontinued it.

I am used by now to that rumour about roubles. Six or seven years ago when The *Tatler* in Beijing passed a few remarks about Professor Chen Yuan and other "respectable gentlemen," the *Jing Bao* in Shanghai printed a letter from Mr. Tang Youren, the "protagonist of Modern Critic," in which he declared that all we wrote and did was dictated by Moscow. These are traditional tactics. At the end of the Song Dynasty men were accused of being "in league with the Tartars," in the

---

* After Chiang Kai-shek betrayed the revolution in 1927, Communists and many Left-wing members of the Kuomintang were massacred in what the reactionaries called a "purge of the party."

early Qing Dynasty of being "in league with foreigners
across the seas." Many have been murdered, invariably
on some such pretext. Indeed, spitting poison has become second nature among Chinese gentlemen and
scholars, but it does not simply show their acumen: it
demonstrates that money is the driving force in this
world. As for my being a "turncoat," there is something
in this accusation. For if I do some soul-searching, I
find that although I did not write about all current
events, I sometimes could not avoid harbouring dissident
ideas. "I deserve death for my crimes, but the emperor
is sagacious."* A loyal subject must never harbour dissident ideas. Incidentally, since it was those men of
letters in government pay who pinned this label on me,
they must have an emperor in their world of letters.

Last year I happened to read some treatises by Franz
Mehring to the effect that, in a decadent society, a dissident who fails in the least to conform is in for big
trouble. And the men who fall on him most savagely
will be members of his own class. They regard him as
a detestable renegade, more detestable than a revolting
slave, for a slave belongs to another class, and therefore
they are determined to liquidate him. This was an eye-
opener to me. So evidently this has been the way in
China and foreign countries, in time past and present —
how true it is that study makes for serenity! This stopped
me from being such a "malcontent" and so, in a different
sense following the example of Three Leisures, I am
making Two Hearts the title of this volume. This does
not prove, however, that I am a proletarian. Members
of one class often end by quarrelling among themselves,
as witnesses the Book of Songs: "Brothers fight at home."
But it does not necessarily follow that they unite to
"resist an attack from without." For instance, the
warlords fight among themselves the whole year round,

---

* A quotation from Han Yu, the great Tang Dynasty prose
writer.

but that does not make one side proletarian. And my incessant harping on myself, of the way I keep "knocking my head against a wall" and of my snail-like conduct, as if all the miseries of the world were embodied in me, a scapegoat for mankind, is a bad failing of middle-class intellectuals. It is true, though, that while I started by simply hating my own class which I knew so well, and felt no regret over its destruction, later on the facts taught me that the future belongs solely to the rising proletariat.

After February 1931, I wrote more than during the preceding year. But as I was writing for magazines of a different type, I had to meet their requirements and wrote very few short pieces like those in *Hot Air*. Moreover, the criticism of my work taught me a lesson. If my comments are too brief, they are easily misunderstood or deliberately distorted. Again, as I do not intend to compile any more collections of long essays like *The Grave* or collections of translations like *Translations Under the Wall*, I have included some rather long articles in this volume and appended my translation of "The Modern Film and the Bourgeoisie." For though films have been popular in China for some time we have seldom seen such cogent articles as this, and all interested in world events really ought to read it. And then regarding the correspondence, if I print my replies only, readers may find them hard to follow; I have therefore included a few of the more important letters I received.

Written after compiling this volume
on the night of April 30, 1932

WE CAN NO LONGER BE DUPED

The imperialists are bent on attacking the Soviet Union. The better the Soviet Union does, the more impatient they are to attack it, for the sooner they will face destruction.

We have been duped too long by the imperialists and their lackeys. Ever since the October Revolution they have been telling us how poor the Soviet Union is growing, what savages and vandals they are. Yet what are the facts? The world has been made to sit up by their export of petroleum and wheat. The leaders of the Industrial Party* — their immediate enemies — have been sentenced to merely ten years' imprisonment. No libraries or museums have been blown up in Leningrad or Moscow. The works of such writers as Serafimovich, Fadeyev, Gladkov, Seifulina and Sholokhov are admired from Western Europe to Eastern Asia. And though I know very little about their art, according to K. Umansky's *Neue Kunst in Russland*, there were twenty exhibitions in Moscow in 1919, and two in Leningrad. From this we can judge the healthy situation today.

But the rumour-mongers are both brazen and crafty. When events refute their lies they bob down, only to come up at once with a fresh crop.

I have just been reading a pamphlet on the likelihood of U.S. economic recovery, the preface to which says that as the Russians have to stand in a long queue

---

*A counter-revolutionary clique unmasked in 1930. Most of its members were engineers or technicians who carried on sabotage under the direction of foreign imperialists.

to buy anything today the situation there must be unchanged. The author sounds quite indignant, as if he
sympathized with those in the queues.

In this case I believe him. Because the Soviet Union
is in the throes of construction work and threatened by
the imperialists, of course many commodities are in short
supply. But we have heard how the unemployed in
other countries queue up in long hunger marches. And
the Chinese people, caught in the meshes of civil war,
foreign aggression, flood, famine and exploitation, are
queuing up in a long death march.

Still the imperialists and their slaves come to tell us
how bad the Soviet Union is, as if they longed to see it
transformed into a paradise where everyone would be
happy. They are disappointed and grieved by the way
things are going. What crocodile tears!

When they open their eyes, you can see them for the
devils they are — they want to take disciplinary action.

While taking disciplinary action, they start spreading
lies again. Terms like "right," "humanity" and "justice"
are bandied about once more. But we can remember
how these terms were bandied about during the Great
War in Europe, to trick us into sending coolies to die for
them at the front. Yet after that in the Central Park
in Beijing they erected that shameless, incredibly stupid
archway with the inscription "Justitia vincit." (It was
later taken down.) But where is justice now? As that
happened a mere sixteen years ago, we have not forgotten it.

The imperialists' interests and ours — I am not speaking of their flunkeys — are diametrically opposed. Since
our sores are their treasures, their enemies must naturally be our friends. They are tottering to ruin, unable
to prop themselves up, but hoping to stave off their final
fate by hating the Soviet Union for its advance. When
slander, curses and hatred prove ineffective, as a last
resort they must prepare to fight — they cannot sleep

till the enemy is destroyed. But what of us? Are we going to be duped again?

"The dictatorship of the proletariat in the Soviet Union means that the intellectuals will starve to death," a well-known journalist warned me.

Yes, that prospect ought to prevent me from sleeping too. But the dictatorship of the proletariat, as I see it, is aimed at bringing about a classless society. The less you sabotage it, the sooner it will succeed and the sooner classes will be done away with, so that nobody need "starve to death." Queues, of course, are a necessary evil for the time, but they will not last very long.

The imperialists' flunkeys want to fight. Let them go with their bosses and fight — our interests are diametrically opposed. We oppose any attack on the Soviet Union. In fact we want to fight the devils who attack it, no matter what honeyed words they use, nor how just they pose as being.

This is our road to life too!

May 6, 1932

FOREWORD TO *THE HARP*

Russian literature after the time of Nicholas II was always written "for life's sake." Whether it was exploring the depths or setting out to solve problems, whether it slipped into mysticism or descended to decadence, its main trend was still "art for life's sake."

This outlook evidently appealed to some of those who introduced foreign literature to China about twenty years ago, for the names of Dostoyevsky, Turgeniev, Chekhov and Tolstoy began to appear in the Chinese press, and some of their works were translated. The Literary Research Society in Shanghai at that time, which was bent on introducing "the literature of oppressed peoples," also regarded them as authors who cried out on behalf of the oppressed.

As all this was a far cry from proletarian literature, naturally the vast majority of the authors introduced simply wept, groaned and complained of poverty and misery, or at the most struggled a little.

Still this was enough to cause a great deal of displeasure in certain other quarters, with the result that two forces turned up to encircle and destroy them. The Creation Society raised the lofty banner of "art for art's sake" and took "Self-expression!" as its slogan, hoping to demolish such "vulgarity" with Omar Khayam's wine cup and the canes of the cultured élite of the *Yellow Book*.* There were also those who had returned baptized

* The magazine brought out in the nineties by Aubrey Beardsley and others.

in the "literary theory" advocated by admirers of English novels for ladies and gentlemen, or of American books written to keep readers happy. The cries and groans of the lower orders made them frown and raise their white-gloved hands to cry deprecatingly, "This scum must clear out of the palace of arts at once!"

And actually China has long had another old-style force of its own stationed up and down the country — those who consider fiction as "light entertainment." As these people look on novels as a means to while away leisure hours after tea or wine, they expect such works to be refined and elegant: on no account must they upset readers or interfere with their fastidious enjoyment. Since this old-fashioned view coincides with the current view of novels in England and America, these three great armies — new and old — joined forces spontaneously to exterminate the literature "for life's sake" — Russian literature.

But as this still had quite a few sympathizers, it continued to grow by devious means in China.

On its native soil, however, it suddenly withered. Many writers had been longing for a change, yet the advent of the October Revolution was a shattering blow they had not bargained for. So D. S. Merezhkovsky and his wife, A. I. Kuprin, I. A. Bunin, L. N. Andreyev and others fled; M. P. Artzybashev, Fyodor Sologub and their like fell silent; the only established authors to go on writing were Valeri Bryusov, V. Veresayev, Marxim Gorky and V. V. Mayakovsky; while later Alexei Tolstoy came back. But no brilliant new literary figures emerged either. During the Civil War and the fierce enemy blockade, the garden of literature was arid and barren.

In 1920 the new economic policy came into force, and the prosperous condition of paper manufacture, printing and publishing helped to revive literature. The hub of activity at this time was the literary group of the Seraphion brothers.

The emergence of this group appears to date from its first meeting on February 1, 1921, in Leningrad, in the "palace of culture." Most of its adherents were young writers whose stand was to oppose every stand. Thus Soshenko said:

From a party member's point of view, I am a man with no guiding principles. But isn't that all to the good? I may describe myself as neither Communist, Social Revolutionary, nor monarchist. I am simply a Russian, and support no particular political party. I probably have the greatest affinity to the Bolsheviks. and I am content to be Bolshevized with them. . . . But I love our peasants' Russia.

This statement gives a clear picture of their stand.

Though the appearance of such a literary coterie was something of a surprise at the time, before long it had won over writers throughout the country. It seems most peculiar to find this un-Soviet literature flourishing in the Soviet Union, but the reason is quite simple. For one thing, the revolutionaries were busy and these young writers were the only ones producing anything worthwhile at the time. Moreover, though not revolutionaries themselves, they had lived through the revolution, and readers could easily respond to the terrors and tension they described, and the exhilaration and gratitude they expressed. Then again, Voronsky who was then in charge of literary activities supported them fully and called them "fellow-travellers." Fellow-travellers are those who accept revolution and advance with it because they are carried away by the heroism of it, but they will not fight to the last or gladly lay down their lives for it. They simply travel together. This name is still used today.

However, there gradually ceased to be any *raison d'être* for the existence of this Seraphion brothers' group, who simply claimed to "love literature" but had no clearly defined ideology, and they started to drift apart and disappear, till finally — like all other fellow-travellers — each was judged according to his merits as a writer.

Four or five years ago, when there was quite a movement in China to introduce Soviet literature, most of the authors chosen were fellow-travellers. There was nothing strange about this. In the first place, this kind of writing was some of the earliest and, being much admired and cried up in Western Europe and Japan, it was readily available for translation into Chinese. In the second place, its nihilistic stand must have appealed to those who introduced these works, though they considered themselves "revolutionary writers."

I have always wanted to introduce the writers of Eastern Europe to China, and have translated works by fellow-travellers too. Now a selection has been made of stories by ten authors, three of them translated by others in whose work I have every confidence. Unfortunately lack of space has made it impossible to include all the best writers and thus make this volume relatively complete; but I believe this defect will be remedied by Cao Jinghua's *Tobacco Pouch* and *Forty-one*.

A brief biography of each author and mention of the text from which the translation was made can be found in the Appendix by those who are interested.

Shanghai
September 9, 1932

ON THE "THIRD CATEGORY"

The last three years have seen very few polemics on art and literature. Apart from those "theorists"* protected by the commander's sword who call themselves "Left-wingers" and find arguments for the freedom of art in Marxism and for exterminating "Communist bandits" in Leninism, practically no one else can open his mouth. The "art-for-art's-sake" writers are still "free" of course, because no one suspects them of accepting roubles. But members of the "third category," that is, those who "cling for dear life to literature,"** cannot escape the bitter premonition that Left-wingers will call them "flunkeys of the bourgeoisie."

In Numbers 3 and 6 of the magazine *Modern Age*, Mr. Su Wen takes up the cudgels on behalf of this "third category." (I should point out here that I say "on behalf of this third category" for convenience's sake, though I know that just as Mr. Su Wen's "group of writers" may well disapprove of such indefinite terms as "perhaps," "more or less" or "influenced," they do not approve of definite terms either, because once you have a definite label you stop being free.) He believes that Left-wing critics call authors "flunkeys of the bourgeoisie" on the

---

* Hu Qiuyuan and some Trotskyites. Hu posed as a Marxist and advocated freedom in art and literature, but he worked hand-in-glove with the Trotskyites and slandered the Chinese Workers' and Peasants' Red Army as "bandits."

** Su Wen opposed the work of popularization, such as the production of serial-picture stories, carried out by Left-wing writers for the workers and peasants. He said, "This will doubtless be opposed by all those who cling for dear life to literature."

least provocation, that they even consider neutrals as partisans, that once a man stops being neutral he risks being dubbed a "flunkey of the bourgeoisie," and that whereas so-called "Left-wing writers" may be "Left" but abstain from writing, the "third category" want to write but dare not. And so the world of letters is a blank. Still, a part at least of literature is said to transcend the class struggle, and this is the literature of the future, the true, immortal literature to which the "third category" cling. Unfortunately, though, the Left-wing theorists have scared everyone off writing such literature, because the authors have a premonition of being branded before they start. People may well have such a premonition, especially those who call themselves the "third category." There may also well be writers, as Mr. Su Wen says, who understand a good deal of theory but find it hard to change emotionally. But when the feelings are unchanged, the degree of theoretical understanding is bound to differ somewhat from cases in which the feelings have changed or changed a little, and this leads to a divergence in views. And from my point of view Mr. Su Wen's view is wrong.

Of course, since Left-wing literature came into being, the theorists have made mistakes and not only do some Left-wing writers simply pose as "Left" but abstain from writing, as Mr. Su Wen claims; others veer from Left to Right and even join the ranks of "nationalist literature" or become owners of bookshops or spies for the enemy party. Still, the Left-wing literature handed down by those writers who have tired of it remains. Not only so, the movement goes on developing and overcoming its failings as it advances upon the hallowed ground of literature.

Mr. Su Wen asks: Why haven't they succeeded in overcoming their failings after three years?

The answer is: True, we must go on overcoming them, perhaps for another thirty years. But while overcoming failings we can forge ahead. We shall not be such fools as to wait till all our failings are overcome before going forward. Mr. Su Wen says as a "joke" that Left-wing writers are accepting payment from capitalist publishers. Now I would like to say in all seriousness that Left-wing writers are still being oppressed, imprisoned and slaughtered by the laws of this feudal-capitalist society. That is why all Left-wing periodicals have been persecuted and only very few are left, while even those which appear occasionally contain very few critical reviews, and those there are do not dub writers "flunkeys of the bourgeoisie" on the least provocation or reject "fellow-travellers." Left-wing writers are not angels sent down from heaven, nor foreign foes who have fought their way in from abroad. They welcome not only those "fellow-travellers" who have gone a little way with them, but even call on all the bystanders at the roadside to advance with them.

Let us ask another question, though. At present the Left-wingers are too crushed to publish many critical articles, but if a day should come when they are in a position to do so, will they dub the "third category" "flunkeys of the bourgeoisie" on the least provocation? I think so long as Left-wing writers have not given their word not to do this and take a gloomy view of things, it is possible — in fact worse is possible. But I believe such predictions are as unnecessary as committing suicide on the off-chance that the earth may crack up some day.

But it is said that Mr. Su Wen's "third category" have "laid down their pens" for such fear of the future. But would they do such a thing because of some imagined evil which they have not yet experienced? Is the grasp of these writers who "cling for dear life to literature" so weak? Would two lovers be afraid to embrace for fear of social censure in the future?

The truth is that the "third category" have not "laid down their pens" because Left-wing criticism is too harsh. The real reason is that no "third category" can exist, and if no such men exist they cannot have "third category" pens, let alone lay them down.

To live in a class society yet to be a writer who transcends classes, to live in a time of wars yet to leave the battlefield and stand alone, to live in the present yet to write for the future — this is sheer fantasy. There are no such men in real life. To try to be such a man is like trying to raise yourself from the ground by tugging at your own hair — it can't be done. You may fume, but it is not because others shake their heads that you stop tugging.

So even this "third category" cannot overstep class. If Mr. Su Wen himself anticipates class criticism, how can any writing get away from class interests? It cannot get away from the fighting either. So, taking a step ahead, Mr. Su Wen protests in the name of the "third category," though he does not want to be accused of "protesting." Meantime, as it is impossible to overstep the present, before he writes a work for posterity transcending class he starts worrying about Left-wing criticism.

This is certainly an awkward predicament. And it arises because fantasy cannot come true. Even if there were no Left-wing literature to complicate matters there could be no "third category," let alone works written by them. But Mr. Su Wen has dreamed up this spectre of a despotic Left-wing literature and lays at its door the crime of preventing the emergence of his illusory "third category" as well as the birth of the literature of the future.

Admittedly there is nothing wonderful about Left-wing writers, who produce serial-picture books and scripts for operas. But they are not as worthless as Mr. Su Wen thinks. They want Tolstoy and Flaubert too. However, they do not want Tolstoys and Flauberts who "strive to write for the future" (because there is no need for them *today*). Tolstoy and Flaubert wrote for their contemporaries. The future is determined by the present, and only something which has meaning today can have meaning for the future. Tolstoy in particular, who wrote tales for peasants, never styled himself one of the "third category" and no amount of attacks from the bourgeoisie could make him lay down his pen. Although as Mr. Su Wen says, Left-wingers are not so stupid as not to know that "serial-picture books cannot give birth to a Tolstoy or Flaubert," they do think these may give birth to artists as great as Michelangelo or Leonardo da Vinci. And I believe that opera scripts and popular tales may produce a Tolstoy or a Flaubert. No one has a word against Michelangelo's paintings today, but were they not actually religious propaganda and serial pictures of the Old Testament? They were done, too, for the "present" of the artist's time.

In brief, Mr. Su Wen is not wrong when he says that rather than deceive others or sail under false colours, the "third category" should do their best to write.

And with even more truth he asserts, "A man must have faith in himself before he has the courage to work."

Yet Mr. Su Wen alleges that the premonition that Left-wing theorists will criticize them has made many lesser and greater members of the "third category" lay down their pens!

"What is to be done?"

October 10, 1932

A DEFENCE OF "SERIAL-PICTURE BOOKS"

I once had a curious experience. At a banquet one day, when I remarked casually that students would undoubtedly learn better from films than from lectures, and that teaching would probably take this form in future, my last words were drowned in shouts of laughter.

Many questions are involved here, of course, the chief being the type of film used — it naturally would not do to show American-style films about money-making and marriage. But I have attended lectures on bacteriology in which films were used, and I have seen books on botany consisting solely of photographs and short explanatory notes. I believe the same thing could be done not only for biology but for history and geography too.

But the shouts of derisive laughter are like a chalk to whiten an enemy's nose,* so that he seems to be clowning.

Not long ago in *Modern Age* I read an essay by Mr. Su Wen in which he condemns "serial-picture books" out of hand from his standpoint as a neutral art critic. True, this comment was made in passing, and the article as a whole was not on painting; but as this question may be exercising the minds of art students, I would like to say a few words on it.

In the histories of art to which we are accustomed we find no reproductions from "serial-picture books," while

---

* The clowns in Chinese opera generally have their noses painted white.

exhibitions of the work of known artists show either "Rome in the Twilight" or "The West Lake at Dusk." Evidently serial-picture books are considered too low to enter polite company. But if you visit the Vatican — not having had the pleasure of travelling in Italy, I have merely seen pictures of the Vatican — you will find that virtually all those splendid frescoes are serial pictures of the *Old Testament, New Testament* and *Acts of the Apostles*. When art historians reproduce one section in a book on art with the title "The Creation of Adam" or "The Last Supper," readers do not think it low-class or propaganda. Yet the originals were obviously propagandist serial-picture books.

The same is true of the East. Once the murals of the Ajanta Caves in India were reproduced by the British, they shone in the history of art. And *The Life of Confucius* in China has long been valued by collectors provided it is a Ming edition. In one case the life of Buddha, in the other the anecdotes of Confucius — these are clearly serial-picture books and propaganda.

Illustrations are intended to beautify books and add to the readers' interest; but since they can do something language cannot do, they are also a form of propaganda. When there are many of these pictures in a series, one can dispense with the text yet still grasp the story; and separated from the text they become independent serial-picture books. The most striking example of this is the work of that famous illustrator Gustave Doré, best known for his illustrations for the *Divina Commedia, Paradise Lost, Don Quixote,* and *History of the Crusades,* all of which have been separately published in Germany. (The first two have also been reprinted in Japan.) With very brief captions he is able to convey the general gist of a book. But does anyone deny that Doré is an artist?

We can still find copies and rubbings of the Song works *Tang Customs* and *Ploughing and Spinning,* while reproductions of Chou Ying's *Private Life of Lady Zhao* and

The Romance of the Western Chamber are still sold in Wenming Bookshop. These are all works of art, both for their age and today.

Since the second half of the nineteenth century the woodcut art has revived, and many artists like to make a series of pictures (Blattfolge), not necessarily all dealing with one subject. For the convenience of art students I will give the names here of some contemporary woodcut artists who have made a name in the history of this art and their works:

First of all, mention must be made of the German artist Käthe Kollwitz. In addition to the six woodcuts she made for Hauptmann's *Die Weber* (The Weavers), she has three works with titles but without commentaries:

1) *Bauernkrieg* (The Peasant War), 7 etchings;
2) *Der Krieg* (War), 7 woodcuts;
3) *Proletäriät* (The Working Class), 3 woodcuts.

Carl Meffert, known in China for his illustrations to *Cement*, is a promising young artist who has made five woodcuts for the German translation of Figner's *Die Jagd nach Zaren* (Hunting the Tsar). He has also the following two folders:

1) *Deine Schwester* (Your Sisters), 7 woodcuts, one inscribed with a poem;
2) *The Apprentices* (I forget the original title), 13 woodcuts.

Then there is the Belgian artist Frans Masereel who, like Romain Rolland, left his country during the Great War because he was against fighting. He is a most prolific artist whose collected works have been published in several volumes, but the individual woodcuts have no titles. Now a popular edition printed in Germany (Bei Kurt Wolff, München) at three marks a volume, is easily procurable. I have seen the following:

1) *Die Idee* (The Idea), 83 woodcuts;

2) *Mein Stundenbuch* (My Book of Hours), 165 wood-cuts;

3) *Geschichte ohne Worte* (A Story Without Words), 60 woodcuts;

4) *Die Sonne* (The Sun), 63 woodcuts;

5) *Das Werk* (Work), woodcuts, the number of which I forget;

6) *Die Passion eines Menschen* (The Sufferings of a Man), 25 woodcuts.

Of American woodcuts, I have seen William Siegel's *The Paris Commune, a Story in Pictures,* published by the John Reed Club in New York. Also the volume of lithographs by W. Gropper entitled *Alay-Oop* (Life and Love Among the Acrobats).

I know very little about English work, because their books are so expensive. But there was a slender volume of fifteen woodcuts with less than two hundred words of commentary by the celebrated Robert Gibbings. It was a limited edition of five hundred, and the English gentlemen absolutely refused to have it reprinted. I am afraid it is now out of print, and each volume may cost nearly a hundred dollars. It is called *The Seventh Man.*

My purpose in listing these works is to prove that not only may picture books be a form of art — they are seated already in the "palace of art." Of course it goes without saying that, as in the case of other kinds of art, the content and technique must reach a high standard.

I do not advise art students to scorn large oil paintings or water colours, but I hope they will pay equal attention to picture books as well as to illustrations for magazines and books, and work equally hard on these. Of course they should study the works of the European masters, but it is even more important to study the pictures in old Chinese books, old Chinese albums of paintings, and the new single-sheet popular paintings. Naturally these studies and the works resulting from

them will not win the same admiration as certain people
bestow on "the masters," but I know the masses will
welcome this work and will appreciate it.

October 25, 1932

ABUSE AND THREATS ARE
NOT FIGHTING

A letter to the editor of *Literature Monthly*

December 10, 1932

Dear Qiying,

The day before yesterday I received and read the fourth number of *Literature Monthly*. Its weakness, I think, is not its lack of variety compared with other periodicals, but the fact that its contents are not as solid as before. Your introduction of new writers this time was an excellent thing, and I am not concerned here with whether they write well or badly; for during the last few years it has been almost impossible for writers whose names have never appeared in print to get anything accepted by magazines; and if this goes on, new writers will have no way of publishing their work. Now that this taboo has been broken, even if only by one number of one monthly, that dispels some of the prevailing dullness, and therefore I approve of it. But I was most disappointed by Mr. Yun Sheng's poem.

One can see at a glance that this poem was inspired by Bednei's satirical poem* in the previous number. But if we compare the two, although Bednei called his poem "vicious," it goes no further than ridicule. This poem, however, contains abuse, threats and attacks made to no purpose — all quite uncalled for.

It starts, for instance, by making fun of the name.

---

* A long poem satirizing Trotsky, translated by Qu Qiubai.

197

Of course if a writer chooses a pseudonym, that throws light on the sort of man he is, and if for instance he calls himself "Blood-and-Iron" or "Nightingale," to poke fun is permissible. But his real surname and place of origin are no indication of his virtues and vices, because these are inherited things in which he has no say. I pointed this out four years ago when someone labelled me "spawn of feudalism," for the fact is it is thoroughly "feudal" to seize hold of such material and then preen yourself on your cunning. Still this practice has grown rather rare in the last few years. I never expected it to crop up again now, and we must admit this is a backsliding.

The abuse at the end of the poem is even worse. Some writers nowadays interlard their dialogue quite unnecessarily with swear-words, as if this makes it proletarian — the more swear-words, the more proletarian. As a matter of fact, very few decent workers and peasants swear each time they open their mouths, and writers should not saddle them with the ways of Shanghai hooligans. If there are foul-mouthed workers, they have a bad habit which writers should correct but on no account spread — otherwise in the future classless society we shall go on abusing each other's ancestors. Besides, even a battle of books is like troop warfare or a bout of fisticuffs: it is best to wait for the right moment to deal your enemy a fatal blow. To keep up a perpetual hubbub is the tactics used in the *Romance of the Three Kingdoms*, while to abuse your enemy's father and mother and then swagger off thinking yourself victorious is pure Ah Q-ism.

Such threats as "you will be carved up like a melon" are quite impermissible too. As I see it, the proletariat make a revolution to free themselves and do away with classes, not to kill their enemies. If a public enemy does not die on the battlefield, the populace can condemn him, but no poet can take up his pen to write a death sentence. Despite all the talk today about "fire and the sword," this is a false charge. No truth can be found in Chinese newspapers, but this is clear from examples from other lands. The proletarian revolution in Germany, though it failed, did not involve massacres; and in Russia they did not even burn the tsar's palace. Yet our writers paint our revolutionary workers and peasants as ogres — this seems to me thoroughly vulgar.

Of course, China's past literature abounds with slander, rumour, threats and abuse, as you can see by reading almost any Chinese history. Today we are still using these things, to an even greater degree. But to my mind this part of our heritage should be made over to the lap-dog writers, for unless our authors strive might and main to do away with it they may become birds of a feather.

I am not suggesting that we smile and bow to our enemies, though. All I am saying is that militant writers should give their minds to "reasoning," and naturally it is legitimate for poets carried away by their emotions to denounce or ridicule others. But they must stop at ridicule or at heated denunciation, and must translate their passions into literature in order to wound or kill the enemy without degrading themselves or disgusting their readers — this is the art of polemics.

I am sending you these ideas just as they occurred to me, for the consideration of your editors. In a word, I sincerely hope to see no more work of this kind in *Literature Monthly* in future.

With best regards,

Yours faithfully,

Lu Xun

PREFACE TO MY SELECTED WORKS

I started writing short stories in 1918, when *New Youth* was calling for a "literary revolution." This movement has now passed into literary history, of course, but there is no doubt that at the time it was a revolutionary movement.

Since what I wrote for *New Youth* was more or less in line with all the other contributions, I think it can actually be considered as "revolutionary literature" of that time.

As a matter of fact, I had no great enthusiasm in those days for a "literary revolution." I had seen the 1911 Revolution, the second revolution,* Yuan Shikai's assumption of the imperial title, and Zhang Xun's restoration of the monarchy, and all this had made me rather cynical. I gave up hope, and lost heart completely. One of the nationalist writers described me this year in their gutter press as "hyper-suspicious." Quite true. At this very moment I suspect their gang of not being genuine nationalist writers, and of being capable of changing sides indefinitely. I suspect my own hopelessness too, though, because I have seen so little of men and affairs. Indeed it was this which emboldened me to write.

"Despair, like hope, is but vanity."**

* This refers to the punitive war against the warlord Yuan Shikai. It was waged in July 1913 by the Kuomintang army under the leadership of Sun Yat-sen.
** A line from Petöfi's *Song of Hope* quoted in "Hope" (Lu Xun, *Wild Grass*).

But why write if I had no enthusiasm for the "literary revolution"? In retrospect, I see it was probably because of my fellow-feeling for the enthusiasts. These fighters, I thought, though alone, had the right ideas. Hence I joined in the shouting to add to their strength. That was the primary reason. Of course, when shouting I could not help slipping in certain exposures of the root of all evil in the old society, mixed up with warnings and the hope that some cure might be found. But to realize this hope I had to take the same line as those pioneers. That is why I cut out some of the gloom and assumed a faint look of gladness, so that my stories might hold out some rays of hope. I refer here to the fourteen stories published later as *Call to Arms*.

This book might also be described as "written to order." But the orders I carried out were those issued by the revolutionary vanguard of that time, which I was glad to obey, not orders sent down by an emperor, or dictated by gold dollars or at the point of the sword.

Later the *New Youth* group broke up. Some of its members rose to high positions, some went into retirement, some moved forward. And I, after seeing this transformation of my comrades of the united front, was left with the label "author" and went on pacing up and down in the desert. But it was too late to get out of writing what I called table-talk for various magazines. When struck by any idea, I wrote a short piece — prose poems to give them a high-sounding title — and these were later printed as *Wild Grass*. If I had more systematic material I went on writing short stories. But as I was now a free lance, unable to form a camp of my own, though technically I had improved a little and my ideas were perhaps less limited, my fighting spirit had diminished considerably. Where were my new comrades-in-arms? I seemed to be in a very bad position.

So I called the eleven stories of this period *Wandering*, hoping that the future would be different.

> *The way stretches endless ahead,*
> *I shall search through heaven and earth.**

But this boast came to nothing. I fled from Beijing and took refuge in Xiamen. In the tower there I simply wrote those few *Old Tales Retold* and the ten essays in *Dawn Blossoms Plucked at Dusk*. The first are stories based on myths and history, the latter simply reminiscences.

After that I wrote no more — I was written out.

So far these are the only five of my books which may by any stretch of the imagination be called literature. It takes very little time to read them all, but the publishers want me to make my own selection. I suppose they think this is a way to save the readers money, and imagine the author is able to make a more intelligent selection than anyone else. I have no objection to the first argument, but think the second highly debatable. As I have neither worked specially hard nor loafed particularly over any of my writings, there are none that I consider exceptionally good or worthy of promotion. So all I could do was make up a volume of twenty-two pieces written in rather different styles and on different subjects, hoping this would satisfy readers. I made a special effort to weed out those which are "most oppressive." For "I did not want to infect with the loneliness which I had found so bitter those young people who were still dreaming pleasant dreams, just as I had done when young."**

But here is no deliberate concealment, as there was

---

* Two lines from Qu Yuan's *Lament* quoted on the frontispiece of *Wandering*.

** A quotation from the preface to *Call to Arms*.

at the time I wrote my *Call to Arms*, for I believe the views of the young people of today and tomorrow have changed.

Shanghai
December 14, 1932

PREFACE TO *IN TWO PLACES*

Here is how this volume came to be compiled —

On August 5, 1932, I received a letter signed by Li Jiye, Tai Jingnong and Wei Congwu, telling me that Wei Su-yuan had passed away in Tong Ren Hospital in Beijing at half past five on the morning of August the first, and they wanted to publish a memorial volume of his work. They asked if I had kept any of his letters. I felt a sudden constriction of the heart. In the first place, I had hoped for his complete recovery, though knowing quite well there was little hope. In the second, though knowing quite well there was little hope, I had sometimes forgotten this, and I might have burned all his letters — letters painfully written as he lay propped on his pillow.

My habit with ordinary letters is to destroy them after answering them, unless they contain controversial ideas or stories, in which case I generally keep them. During the last three years I have had two large-scale incinerations.

Five years ago in Guangzhou, during the Kuomintang purge, I kept hearing of cases in which because A was arrested and letters from B found on him, B would be arrested too. And when letters from C were discovered in B's house, C would also be arrested — and nothing was ever heard of them again. I knew of the "melon-vine case"* some centuries back, when so many people

---

* Jing Qing, a minister during the Ming Dynasty, tried to assassinate one of the royal house. Not only was he executed and his clan wiped out, but several thousand men in his district were killed. The expression "melon-vine case" was first used of this mass execution.

were involved, but I had thought that was a thing of the
past until reality opened my eyes for me and I realized
that it is just as hard to live in the modern world as in
the ancient. Still I did not take this to heart, but remained quite careless. In 1930, when I joined the China
Freedom League and the provincial Kuomintang authorities in Zhejiang asked the Central Government to issue
a warrant for the arrest of "the decadent writer Lu Xun,"
before leaving home I was suddenly inspired to burn all
letters from my friends. This was not to destroy all
traces of "high treason," but because it seemed pointless
to involve others whose only crime was writing to me —
we all know how frightful the least contact with a Chinese yamen can be. After this escape I moved house,
letters started piling up again, and I grew careless again.
I was taken by surprise when I heard in January of 1931
that they were looking for me because they had found
something signed with my name in Rou Shi's pocket
when he was arrested. Naturally I had to leave home
again. But this time, as the impression made on me was
even stronger, of course I burned all letters first.

Because of these two incidents, I started worrying
when I received that letter from Beijing for fear I had
nothing left. And sure enough, even though I ransacked
my trunks and cases, there was nothing there. But
though I could not find a single letter from our friend,
there were quite a few my wife and I had written to each
other. This is not because I set special store by these,
but because I had been in too much of a hurry on those
previous occasions to burn our own correspondence,
which could only involve ourselves. And then these
letters lay for twenty to thirty days in the line of fire,
coming through completely unscathed. Some are missing, it is true, but I probably lost them through my own
carelessness, not through the fault of any official or
soldier.

A man who has not suffered from a sudden catastrophe will not be regarded as anything out of the way; but if he has been in jail or fought at the front, however ultra-normal he may be he will still be considered somewhat special. And that was how we looked on these letters. At first we had let them be crushed at the bottom of a trunk, but the thought of their narrow escape from getting into the courts and from gunfire convinced us that there was something special, something lovable, about them. There are too many mosquitoes on summer nights to allow you to write in peace, so we sorted these letters out in roughly chronological order, and divided them into three lots, calling the whole collection *In Two Places*.

In other words, this collection is of temporary interest to us, though hardly to other people. In it there is no passionate emotion, no beautiful phrases about flowers and moonlight; and as for the language, neither of us had studied *The Epistolary Art* or *The Letter-Writer's manual*. We wrote at random, flouting all literary canons, not caring if we figured in the Language Hospital.* We merely wrote about the student movement, our own affairs, food and the weather. Worst of all, living as we were in a time of total gloom when it was hard to distinguish darkness from light, though there was no difficulty in discussing our own business, when it came to speculating about affairs of state we were often very foolish. Indeed most of our optimistic prophecies, looking back on them now, were empty dreams. If I must praise what is distinctive about this collection, then I think it is its normality. I doubt if anyone else possesses such normal letters. At any rate, they will hardly have preserved them. But we did, and I cannot but consider this a distinction.

---

* A column in a magazine for secondary school students, devoted to examples of ungrammatical or illogical writing.

The odd thing, however, is that there is a publisher willing to print them. If he wants to, let him go ahead. I don't mind. But as this will bring me in contact with readers again, there are two points I must explain to avoid a misunderstanding. First, I am now a member of the League of Left-Wing Writers, and I see from recent book advertisements that as soon as a writer turns Left all his past works are immediately ennobled too, so that even his childhood sobs join the ranks of revolutionary literature. But this is not the case with our book. It has no revolutionary atmosphere at all. Secondly, I have often heard it said that letters are the least artificial form of writing, and the most revealing of a man's true character. But not in my case. No matter to whom I am writing, I always start off with a few hypocritical conventional phrases. Even in the letters here, at the most critical junctures, I nearly always wrote in a somewhat cryptic manner, because we were living under a social system in which "the local authorities," the post office, the college principal . . . could all inspect our letters whenever they pleased. But of course there were quite a few clear statements too.

And then I have changed some of the names in the letters — for different reasons, some good, some bad. Sometimes because it might be inconvenient for a friend if others saw his name in our correspondence, and sometimes just for my own sake, to avoid troubles of the "awaiting trial" variety.

In retrospect, it seems we had our share of trouble during the last six or seven years. As we struggled on some helped us, while others threw stones or jeered and slandered us. But we gritted our teeth, and have managed to survive. During these years the mud-slingers have gradually sunk into deeper darkness, and two of our good friends are no longer with us, namely Suyuan and Rou Shi. We are printing this collection as a me-

mento for ourselves, to express our gratitude to our good friends, and to leave our children a true picture of our times. This is pretty well all there is to it.

December 16, 1932

THE TIES BETWEEN CHINESE AND
RUSSIAN LITERATURES

The literature of Russia, fifteen years ago considered as a semi-barbarous land by the so-called civilized peoples of Western Europe, has triumphed among readers throughout the world. The literature of the Soviet Union, for the last fifteen years regarded as a demon by the imperialists, has triumphed among readers throughout the world. By "triumphing" we mean that its outstanding contents and technique have won readers everywhere, and benefited those readers in many ways.

China has proved no exception.

In *Modern Affairs*, edited by Liang Qichao, we read mysteries like the adventures of Sherlock Holmes, and in *New Fiction* we read scientific fiction like *Twenty Thousand Leagues Under the Sea* by Jules Verne. Then Lin Qinnan translated many of the novels of Rider Haggard, from which we learned of the romances of young ladies in London and the strange habits of savages in Africa. Of Russian literature we knew nothing — unless there were a few "prescient" gentlemen in the know who did not tell us. In another field, however, Russian influence was felt. All the relatively revolutionary young folk of the time knew that young Russians were good revolutionaries and assassins. Sophia* made an indelible impression on them, largely because she was

---

* An anarchist who tried to assassinate Alexander II, but was arrested and executed. Her biography and photograph appeared in the Chinese anarchist magazine *The New Age* in 1907.

beautiful. In much of our native writing today you will find names like Sophia, and this is their origin.

The Russian literature of those days — the late nineteenth century — especially the work of Dostoyevsky and Tolstoy, had a great influence on German literature; but this had no effect on China as very few Chinese at the time studied German. The greatest influence came from the English and American imperialists who translated the selected works of Dostoyevsky, Turgeniev, Tolstoy and Chekhov; at the same time they used Indian primers in the English language to teach our boys and girls the dialogue of Rama and Krishna; but they also gave us the opportunity to read the selected works as well. Stories of detectives, adventurers, English ladies and African savages can only titillate the surfeited senses of those who have eaten and drunk their fill. But some of our young people were already conscious of being oppressed and in pain. They wanted to struggle, not to be scratched on the back, and were seeking for genuine guidance.

That was when they discovered Russian literature.

That was when they learned that Russian literature was our guide and friend. For from it we can see the kindly soul of the oppressed, their sufferings and struggles. Hope blazed up in our hearts when we read the works of the forties, and sorrow flooded our souls when we read those of the sixties. Of course we knew that tsarist Russia was invading China, but that literature taught us the important lesson that there are two sorts of men in the world: the oppressors and the oppressed!

From the vantage point of today, this is common knowledge, not worth remarking on. But in those days it was a great discovery, no whit less so than the ancients' discovery that fire could lighten the darkness and serve for cooking.

By degrees more Russian works were introduced to China and, arousing a response from certain readers, soon spread more widely. I will not speak of individual translations. There were huge tomes like *Russian Drama*, a selection of ten plays, *Studies of Russian Literature*, the bulky supplement of *Short Story Monthly*, as well as two numbers of *Writing of Oppressed Peoples*, inspired by Russian literature, but with the field enlarged to include all small, weak peoples, and with the significant use of the epithet "oppressed."

All this came under attack from the literati, some of whom advocated "nobility" in literature and said it was vulgar to write of low-class people. Yet others compared creative writing to a virgin and contended that translation was simply a go-between, while translating from a translation was even more disgusting. In fact, with the exception of *Russian Drama*, practically all the Russian works at that time were translations of translations.

But Russian literature continued to be introduced and to spread.

When we knew a few more authors, though in L. Andreyev's work we found terror and in M. Artzybashev's work despair and decadence, we learned magnanimity from V. Korolenko and resistance from Maxim Gorky. The enthusiastic response of most readers could no longer be concealed by the selfish distortions of a few critics, and this great pressure finally made the gentleman who had worshipped Katherine Mansfield* make a translation of a translation of Turgeniev's *Fathers and Sons*, while the author who had lashed out at "go-betweens"** translated a translation of Tolstoy's *War and Peace*.

Meanwhile, of course, there was another attack by the allied army of the literati, hoodlums and police dogs. Some said that the translators worked for roubles, others that they had gone over to the enemy. Some laughed

---

* Professor Chen Yuan. See Volume II, p. 168.
** Guo Moruo. In 1920 he complained that readers were more interested in translations than original writing, but translators were only go-betweens — the original work was the bride.

at them for turning "proletarian," others pointed them
out as Communists.   And it is impossible to say how
many books were banned or confiscated, because such
things were usually done in secret.

But Russian literature continued to be introduced and
to spread.

Translations were made of *The Life of Mussolini* and
Hitler's *Mein Kampf,* but no one could introduce a single
great book from fascist Italy and Germany.   *After the
War** does not belong under Hitler's swastika, and *The
triumph of Death*** can pride itself only on "death."
But of Soviet literature we already have Libedinsky's
A Week, Gladkov's *Cement,* Fadeyev's *The Nineteen,*
and Serafimovich's *Iron Stream,* in addition to a great
many short novels and stories.   All these, while exposed
to the open and covert attacks of the literati, took rapid
possession of Chinese readers' hearts, teaching one after
another the bitterness and success of reforms, struggle
and construction.

A month ago, however, there was a lightning change
in "public opinion" about the Soviet Union.***   Last
night's demon has become a good friend this morning.
Most newspapers have a kind word to say about the
merits of the Soviet Union, and naturally sometimes they
touch on literature.   This was because diplomatic relations were resumed.   But our cause for celebration is not
here.   When a selfish man is drowning and about to go
under for the last time, he will clutch at anything within
his reach, whether it is proletarian or totalitarian, not
showing himself a "purist" in the slightest.   But whether
he dies or contrives to crawl ashore, he remains a selfish
man.   Let us take one example.   The *Shen Bao,* generally

---

* By Ludwig Renn.

** By Gabriele D'Annunzio.

*** On December 14, 1927, the Kuomintang severed diplomatic
relations with the Soviet Union.   On December 12, 1932, under
popular pressure, it once more recognized the Soviet Union.

considered one of the "big dailies" in Shanghai, proposes in honeyed terms "the organization of an inspection group to tour the Soviet Union" (Editorial, December 18, 1932) at the same time as it calls Lin Keduo's *Eye-witness Account of the Soviet Union* a "reactionary book" (news of the 27th).

What is worth celebrating is the fact that although the contact between Chinese and Russian literatures started later than that between Chinese and English or Chinese and French, during the last ten years or so our reading public has not cared whether there were diplomatic relations between the two countries or not. Whether translations were allowed or banned did not affect the number of our readers, which did not merely remain constant but increased. It did not merely remain constant throughout the period of severed relations and suppression, but increased despite these things. This shows that the mass of our readers do not look at Russian literature with selfish, "snobbish eyes." Vaguely they know what will grow from this great, fertile "black earth." Indeed, things have grown from it already, as we have seen for ourselves: endurance, groans, struggles, revolt, fighting, changes, fighting, construction, fighting, success.

Today Bernard Shaw in England and Romain Rolland in France have become friends of the Soviet Union too. This is the beginning of a true interchange of culture between us and the rest of the world, growing out of the unceasing cultural exchange between China and the Soviet Union.

That is what we should celebrate.

December 30, 1932

1933

LISTENING TO DREAMS

We are free to dream, but not to tell our dreams. It is true that we dream, but we may be lying if we tell our dreams.

On New Year's Day I received the special New Year number of *Eastern Magazine,* with "New Year Dreams" towards its end. Over a hundred and forty answers have been written on "Your dream of China's future and your own." I appreciated the editor's difficulty. In the absence of freedom of speech it is better to describe dreams. Better discuss the truth in dreams rather than what is false in so-called true statements. But eagerly skimming through this section, I found the editor had failed utterly.

Before receiving this special issue I had met one of the contributors who had seen the galley proofs, and who told me his reply had been chopped and changed by the boss. His dream had been quite different. Evidently capitalists cannot prohibit dreaming, but once the dreams are described, if it is within their power they will interfere and take away your freedom. This was the editor's great defeat.

But instead of troubling with these changes, let us look at the dreams described. As the editor points out, nearly all the contributors are intellectuals. First they all express a sense of insecurity, and then many of them dream of a better society in future — "from each according to his ability," and "universal equality" — which smacks strongly of something "illegal." (This is my interpretation, not the editor's.)

But then he starts being rather "silly," seizing on a

theory from Heaven knows where to divide these
hundred-odd dreams into two main categories. He calls
all those dreams of a better world "propagandistic"
dreams or "heresies." Orthodox dreams ought to "express an individual's thought," and he insists on making
"thought" an empty abstract thing. But Confucius said,
"Each of you should say what he thinks," and finally ap-
proved Zeng Dian's wish, because what he wanted was
in line with Confucius' Way.

Actually there are very few dreams here of the kind
the editor calls "propagandistic." As articles are written during waking hours and the question is like an "intelligence test," each contributor had to provide a dream
appropriate to his present occupation, status and profession. (This does not apply of course to those which have
been chopped or changed.) So no matter how "propagandistic" they seem, there is actually no "propaganda"
for the good society of the future here. Although some
dream of "food for all," others of "a classless society" or
"universal equality," very few indeed dream of what is
needed before building such a society: the class struggle,
the White Terror, air-raids, men tortured to death, boiled
capsicum poured down the nostrils, electric shocks. . . .
Unless men dream of these things, that better world will
never materialize, no matter how brilliantly they write.
It will remain a dream, an empty dream. And describing it will simply teach others to dream this empty dream.

None the less there are men who intend to make this
dream come true, who use deeds instead of words. They
dream of the future and struggle to realize it now. Because of this, many intellectuals are compelled to make
their dreams sound "propagandistic," though in fact they
are just the opposite: they have just been "propagandized."

They let themselves be propagandized for the sake of
bread and butter, now and in time to come.

We are still so fettered by old ways of thinking that

the mere mention of food sounds rather vulgar. Not that I intend the least disrespect to the worthy contributors to *Eastern Magazine*. The editor in his comments quotes Freud's view that "orthodox" dreams "express the secrets of men's hearts and have no social significance." Now Freud considered repression the root of dreams — but why are men repressed? This is bound up with social systems, customs and all the rest of it. Just having a dream is all right, but once you tell it, and are questioned and analysed, it becomes most improper. The editor did not think of this, which is why he ran headlong into the capitalist's red pencil. But to explain dreams in terms of "repression" can hardly be offensive to most people nowadays.

As I imagine, Freud probably had a little money and could eat as much as he liked, so bread and butter were no problem to him: hence his emphasis on sex. And many people with the same background applauded loudly. It is true he also told us that daughters generally love their fathers best, and sons their mothers, because they belong to the opposite sex. But not long after an infant is born, be it boy or girl, it starts pursing its lips and turning its head from side to side. Is it looking for one of the opposite sex to kiss? No, as everyone knows, it wants food.

The truth is that the appetite for food goes much deeper than the sexual appetite. Today when men see nothing mawkish in this endless talk of love and love letters, there is no reason at all why we should taboo talk about food. As these are waking dreams we can hardly avoid a little falsity, especially as the subject is "a dream" and, as the editor has said, "our material needs far exceed our spiritual yearnings." So taking the opportunity when the vigilance of the "censors" (using Freud's expression here) seemed to have relaxed, he published some of them. Actually this is also a case of "pasting up posters and shouting slogans in a dream." It is not positive propaganda though. In fact some slogans may be the reverse of what they seem.

The times are changing so fast and bread and butter are so hard to find and keep that many men, when they think of the present and future, can only describe dreams like this. As we are all petty-bourgeois (I have been called "spawn of feudalism" and "literary bourgeois" but I consider myself a petty-bourgeois), we should understand each other well, and there is no need to try to keep any secrets.

As for those other celebrities who dream of being hermits, fishermen or woodcutters, or taking up some profession quite different from their present one, they simply show a keener presentiment of the fragility of their rice bowl and are trying to enlarge its scope. To fly from the government to the greenwood, from foreign concessions to mountains and marshes — these are much more far-reaching desires than those expressed earlier. But I will not dwell on them here.

January 1, 1933

ON WATCHING FIGHTS

We Chinese are always claiming that we love peace, when actually it is fighting that we love. We like watching other creatures fight, and like watching ourselves fight.

Most common are cock-fighting and cricket-fighting. In the south they make thrushes and other birds fight, and in the north they make quails fight while people with nothing to do gather round to bet on the outcome. In ancient times there were fish-fights, and now conjurors can make fleas fight. I see from this year's *Eastern Magazine* that there are bull-fights too in Jinhua, only they are not like those in Spain; for in Spain a man fights a bull, but with us it is bull against bull.

Let them fight. We will not join in — we simply watch.

The warlords do nothing but fight, and the people will not join in — they simply watch.

But the warlords do not fight themselves either: they make their soldiers fight. So in spite of all these fierce battles year in and year out, the chiefs are quite all right. Their misunderstandings are suddenly cleared up, and they drink happily together, uniting to resist the foe and swearing to serve the country till suddenly. . . . It goes without saying — suddenly of course they start fighting each other again.

But the people let them play their tricks — they simply watch.

Our fighters behave differently, though, towards a foreign enemy. When he is close at hand, they use "non-resistance." When far away, they "advance, shouldering cross-bows."*

The term "non-resistance" is clear enough. As for advancing, "shouldering cross-bows," we have long since forgotten how to make these weapons, and must wait till the archaeologists have found out before we can manufacture them, shoulder them, and advance.

It would be better to use our own soldiers and the weapons already imported to fight ourselves. China has a huge population, so for the time being at least there will always be some left to watch. But of course if we want to do that, we must show ourselves "peace-loving" where foreign foes are concerned.

January 24, 1933

---

* A classical allusion quoted by the warlord Tian Songyao in Hankou.

AN APOLOGY FOR FLIGHT

In ancient times it was most unlucky to be a woman: whatever you did was wrong and the whole world abused you. Now this bad luck has descended on the students: whatever they do they are sharply criticized.

We can remember the fuss the students started making the winter before last. Some wanted to come south, some to go north; but there was no train for them either way. When they reached the capital and respectfully presented their petitions, they were "utilized by the reactionaries," and many happened to knock their heads on bayonets and rifle stocks, while some even got drowned by "falling into the water themselves."

After the post-mortem it was announced that "they were black and blue." I could not understand that.

But who asked any questions or protested? Some people even jeered at them.

There were expulsions too, warning letters to parents, and advice to do research work. For the last year all has been well: there is peace at last. But Shanhaiguan has been lost, and though Shanghai is still a long way off, it is no good in Beijing, for even the research institutes there are in danger. I expect those who live in Shanghai remember what happened last February in Jinan University, the Labour University and Tongji University. . . . How could students stay there to carry on research?

The undergraduates in Beijing are aware of this, for they have memories too. This time they will not knock their heads against bayonets and rifle stocks, or fall into the water themselves so that they turn black and blue. They have invented a new way: that is, to scatter to their homes.

This shows the effectiveness of the education during the last few years.

But people are abusing them again. Boy scouts have actually written on the funeral scrolls of the martyrs: "May they stink for ten thousand years!"

But let us stop to reflect. Even those fossilized curios in the Institute of Language and History are moving away. How can students have an aeroplane each for themselves? If they were knocked silly by Chinese bayonets and rifle stocks and had to hide themselves in research institutes, how can they avoid letting foreign guns and planes drive them out of their research institutes?

Amida Buddha!

January 24, 1933

ON "GOING INTO BATTLE" AND "RUNNING AWAY"

A letter to the editor of *Breakers*

January 28, 1933, in the evening

Dear Sir,

I often read *Breakers* and often exclaim "Bravo!" But Mr. Zhou Muzhai's article "Reproaching Others and Self-reproach" sticks in my gullet. For he says if the undergraduates of Beiping "cannot go into battle, at least they should refrain from running away," and regrets that the enthusiasm of the May 4th period has disappeared completely. As my view is the reverse of Mr. Zhou's, I feel impelled to make a few observations. I belong to the "Running Away Party" and hold, indeed, that if you cannot go into battle, it is your duty to run!

At the end of his article Mr. Zhou says, "I suspect this is one of the consequences of changing Beijing into Beiping."* I believe he has something there. When Beijing still masqueraded as a sort of republic, students could shout without getting into trouble. The ruler in those days was Mr. Duan Qirui, for whom eighteen Shanghai institutions yesterday held that "huge welcome rally on behalf of all Shanghai." Although a military man, Mr. Duan has not yet read *The Life of Mussolini*. And yet, just look what happened. Rifles spat bullets

---

* "Beijing" means northern capital. When Chiang Kai-shek made Nanjing his capital, Beijing was renamed Beiping, which means Northern Peace.

at students who were trying to deliver a petition. That soldiers prefer to shoot at girls is quite understandable from a psycho-analyst's point of view, and quite understandable too from a moral reformer's point of view, particularly if the girls have bobbed their hair. At all events, many students died. But still it was permitted to hold a meeting to commemorate them, and to march past Government House shouting "Down with Duan Qirui!" It was permitted because in those days Beijing still masqueraded as a republic. But then look what happened. Commemorating the dead students in *Modern Critic,* Mr. Chen Yuan, now a prominent Kuomintang professor, observed that it was a pity they had thrown away their lives for a few roubles. When the *Tatler* countered briefly, Mr. Tang Youren, now an important Kuomintang personage, wrote to *Crystal News* claiming that our words and actions were dictated by Moscow. That already smacked of Beiping.

After that the Northern Expedition triumphed, and Beijing came under the Kuomintang's party state. The time had come for all students to start on research, and henceforward the May 4th style of behaviour was reprehensible. It was reprehensible because it could so easily be utilized by the "reactionaries." Great pains were taken by our government, military, scholars, writers, police and detectives to correct this evil tendency. They used orders, weapons, the press, circumstantial evidence, arrests and torture, till last year the students killed while petitioning were said to have "fallen into the water themselves," and no services were held to commemorate them. Only then did we see the fruit of the new educational policy.

I take it that unless the Japanese attack Shanhaiguan again, the world will remain at peace, and "we must settle troubles at home before driving out the invaders." The tiresome thing is that these foreign aggressors are too quick and too many for us, because the Japanese will *not* show enough consideration for Chinese gentle-men. And this is what drives Mr. Zhou to make such a criticism.

Judging by Mr. Zhou's proposal, the best thing is to "go into battle." But this is hard. Had our students been organized and trained, if the second-in-command called for more recruits after the troops at the front had fought and been decimated, it would of course be all right to go. But, alas! Judging by the events of last year they cannot even take a train without paying for it, to say nothing of the fact that most of our undergraduates have been studying the credit system, the history of Turkish literature, the least common denominator and so forth. They could never beat the Japanese. When these under-graduates had a clash with the Chinese police they "fell into the water themselves." How then can they put up any resistance when China's armed forces and police are not yet doing so? We have seen many heroic, full-blooded poems, it is true, on stopping the mouths of enemy guns with corpses or bogging down the Japanese bayonets with hot blood. But these are "poems," sir! The facts are otherwise. We may die like ants without stopping their guns or bogging down their bayonets. Confucius said, "To lead into battle a people that has not first been instructed is to betray them."* Though not an out-and-out devotee of the sage, I think he was right here, for I am one of those against undergraduates "going into battle."

Then what about "not running away"? I am dead against that too. Of course, so far "the enemy has not come." But suppose he does, is it better for unarmed students to curse the invaders and die, or to hide indoors and try to escape with their lives? I think the first is

---

* A quotation from *The Analects of Confucius,* translated by Arthur Waley.

the more dignified way. In future you will be written up as a martyr, but that will not save the country, no matter whether you are one or one hundred thousand. At most another report will be sent to the League of Nations. Everyone is in such raptures over how certain heroes of the 19th Route Army killed some of the enemy last year that they forget the important fact that the whole front fell back a hundred li. In fact, China still lost. And undergraduates have not even weapons. To-day the Chinese press is full of the tyranny of "Man-chukuo" in not allowing private individuals to own weapons, but just see what happens if you keep something for self-defence in the Great Republic of China — that will be the end of you too. This can "easily be utilized by the reactionaries," sir.

If you teach lion-and-tiger tactics, your students will be able to use their claws and teeth. If you teach sheep-and-oxen tactics, in a crisis they may use their pitiful horns. But what tactics are we teaching? We are forbidden even the smallest horns, and when peril approaches we can only run like rabbits. Naturally even running away may not be safe. Indeed no one can say what is safe, for hounds swarm everywhere. We read in the *Book of Songs*:

> *Frisking hares and rabbits*
> *Are caught by hounds.*

But be this as it may, of thirty-six strategies the best is still to "fly."

In brief, my opinion is this: We must not overestimate our undergraduates, or reproach them too severely, for China does not rely entirely upon them. And under-graduates, having run away, should think how best to avoid simply running away in future, how to leave the realm of poetry and tread on solid ground.

I do not know what you think of this, sir. I hope you will publish this letter in *Breakers* for further discussion. I send it for your consideration.

Yours faithfully,

Luo Wu

Postscript on the 29th

I hear that about a fortnight ago over fifty students in Beiping were arrested for holding a meeting. Evidently there are still some who have not run away, but they are accused of "plotting revolt on the pretext of resisting Japan." Clearly, although "the enemy has not come," it is still better to "run away."

THE FACT OF THE MATTER

The facts are often not so pretty as they sound.

For instance this *Free Talk** is not actually free, but we call it *Free Talk*, meaning we can talk here with this sort of freedom.

Or take the current removal of art treasures from Beijing and the refusal to evacuate students. There is reason for these orders, and reason for the criticism of them too. But these are simply words, not the essence of the matter.

You may say that these historical relics are so ancient and unique that they should be removed at once as treasures. And certainly that makes sense. But Beijing is unique too, and after all it is more ancient than all existing relics. We need not speak of Yu,** who was a worm, but at least this place existed in the Shang and Zhou dynasties. Why should we give it up then, and just remove the relics? The fact of the matter is that the art treasures are prized not because they are "ancient," but because after Beijing is lost we can still carry them with us, and realize money for them any time.

Though university students are the "backbone" of the country, they have no market value. If they could fetch five hundred dollars apiece in the European or American market, they would be crated too and moved out of Beijing with the curios by special trains, to be stow-

---

* A supplement of the *Shen Bao*.
** A pseudo-scientific historian had reached the conclusion that Great Yu, the mythological tamer of the flood, was a worm.

ed away in the safes of foreign banks in the foreign concessions.

But university students are too many and too new, more's the pity!

Enough of this idle talk. Let me mourn their fate in the style of Cui Hao's* poem, *Yellow Stork Tower:*

> *The rich and great have flown off with our culture,*
> *Leaving the empty city of culture behind;*
> *Once culture goes it will never return again:*
> *The ancient city will remain bleak and bare.*
> *Now special trains queue up at Qian Men Station,*
> *Bad luck bears down on university students;*
> *The sun shines at the Pass — but who resists?*
> *There is no panic in the red light district.*

January 31, 1933

---

* A Tang Dynasty poet.

STRATEGIC CONSIDERATIONS

The *National Salvation Daily* in the capital contains this notable statement:

> If for strategic considerations we have to give up Beijing for the time being, in order to make the enemy penetrate deeper . . . we should give Zhang Xueliang* stern warning to suppress all resistance by force and not be deterred by bloodshed. (Reprinted in the *Shanghai Daily* of February 9.)

So we shall not be deterred by bloodshed! Oh, excellent strategists!

Indeed, not a little blood has been shed, more is being shed at this moment, and no one knows how much more will be shed in future. All this is the blood of those in the resistance. Why was it shed? For strategic considerations.

Last year when there was fighting in Shanghai,** the strategists said, "For strategic considerations we must retreat to hold the second line of defence." So our troops withdrew. Two days later they said, for strategic considerations, "If the Japanese army does not attack us, our men must not open fire. All soldiers must obey this order." So there was a cease-fire. Then the "second line of defence" disappeared, peace talks started in Shanghai — negotiations, signatures, and all was over.

---

* Then Director of the Kuomintang Generalissimo's Headquarters in Beijing.

** Referring to the fighting on January 28, 1932, when Japanese troops invaded Shanghai.

At that time blood was shed too — no doubt also for strategic considerations; but that is a top military secret, not something the common people can be told. Although those who shed their blood knew the reason, they are silent now. Then why did we fail to entice the enemy to "penetrate deeper"?

Now we know. The enemy failed to be drawn not because our strategists were incompetent, nor entirely because not enough blood was shed by the people in the resistance movement, but for another reason. It seems that the British intervened, and came to a secret understanding with Japan. "See here, Japan," they said, "if you withdraw your forces for the time being from Shanghai, we will help you by making the League of Nations recognize Manchukuo." Then followed all those draft resolutions in the League of Nations, and the attitudes of certain members. What this actually meant was: "Don't come any further in this direction. The loot is for all to share. You can penetrate the north first." Of course there will be further penetration, but for the time being the direction has changed.

So this strategy to "draw the enemy on to Beijing" is unavoidable for the moment. Of course more blood will have to be shed.

Actually, the necessary preparations have now been made: we have all sorts of temporary and war-time capitals, while the cultural relics and university students have been evacuated too. Whatever the enemy — whether yellow-skinned or white-skinned, from a new continent or an old — they can penetrate wherever they please. As for the fear that there may be resistance, we have our strategists who "will not be deterred by bloodshed!" You need not worry.

February 9, 1933

WRITTEN FOR THE SAKE OF
FORGETTING

I

I have long been meaning to write a few words in memory of some young writers. My sole reason is the hope that in this way I may shake off the grief and rage which have assailed my heart now for two years, so that I can relax. To put it bluntly, I want, in fact, to forget them.

Two years ago, in February 1931, during the night of the seventh or the morning of the eighth, our five young writers were murdered.* No Shanghai papers dared report this at the time: they may not have wanted to or may not have thought it newsworthy. *Literary News* alone carried a few articles containing veiled allusions to the matter. In Number 11 (dated May 25), Mr. Lin Mang wrote in his "Impressions of Bai Mang":**

> He wrote a good many poems and translated some by the Hungarian poet Petöfi. When Lu Xun, then editor of *Torrent*, received his manuscript, he wrote to say that he would like to meet him. But as Bai Mang did not care to meet celebrities, finally Lu Xun looked him up himself and encouraged him as best he could

---

* On February 7, 1931, the five young writers Yin Fu, Rou Shi, Li Weisen, Hu Yepin and Feng Keng were secretly murdered by the Kuomintang reactionaries.
** Bai Mang was another name for Yin Fu.

to write. But the young man could not shut himself up in a tiny room to write. He went his own way again and before long he was once more arrested. . . .

This account is actually incorrect. Bai Mang was not so arrogant. It was he who called on me, though not because I had expressed a wish to see him. I was not so arrogant either as to write casually to a contributor I did not know, telling him to call on me. The reason for our meeting was perfectly natural. He had sent in a translation from the German of a life of Petöfi, and I wrote to ask him for the original, which was printed as the preface to the collected poems. He found it more convenient to deliver the book in person than to post it. He was a young man in his twenties with regular features and a dark complexion. I forget what we talked about on that occasion except that he told me that his surname was Xu and he came from Xiangshan; and when I asked why the woman who collected his mail had such a peculiar name (just what was peculiar about it I forget), he said she had peculiar tastes because she was a romantic, but he didn't see eye to eye with her on everything. This is all I remember.

That night I checked his translation roughly with the original and found that, apart from one or two slips, he had deliberately mistranslated the meaning of one phrase. Apparently he did not like the expression "national poet," for in each case he had changed this to "poet of the people." The next day I received a letter from him saying he regretted our meeting: he had talked too much while I had talked too little and seemed so cold that he had felt a certain constraint. I wrote back explaining that it was human nature to speak little at a first meeting, and told him he should not alter the original to suit his own taste. As he had left his book with me I sent him two volumes of Petöfi from my own collection, suggesting that he translate a few more poems for our readers.

He did so, and brought the translations over himself, and this time we talked more. These poems and the life were later published in Volume II, Number 5 of *Torrent*, the last number to appear.

The third time we met was on a hot day, I remember, when someone knocked at the gate and I opened it to find Bai Mang. He was wearing a thick padded gown and dripping with sweat, which made both of us burst out laughing. Only then did he tell me that he was a revolutionary, had just been released from jail, and had had all his clothes and books confiscated, including the two volumes I had given him. He had borrowed this gown from a friend who had nothing thinner, for he had to wear a long gown; so he couldn't help sweating like that. I dare say this is the occasion Mr. Lin Mang was referring to when he said, "He was once more arrested."

Delighted by his release, I immediately paid him for his translations so that he could buy a thinner gown. Still, I was very upset to think of my books falling into the hands of the police — pearls cast before swine. There was nothing special about the books themselves, one being a volume of prose, another of verse compiled by the German translator, who claimed that these were more comprehensive collections than any to be found in Hungary itself. They were printed by Reclam's Universal-Bibliothek and could therefore be bought anywhere in Germany for less than a dollar. But to me they were treasures, for I had ordered them from Germany through the Marusen Bookshop* thirty years before, when I was a passionate admirer of Petöfi. I was afraid, the books being so cheap, that the shop would be unwilling to order them; thus I made my request with considerable trepidation. For a while I carried both volumes about with me; but as times alter men's affections change, and I gave up the idea of translating Petöfi.

---

* A bookshop in Tokyo selling Western books.

I decided it would be a happy fate for these books to be given to this lad who was as devoted to Petöfi as I had formerly been. That is why I took this presentation so seriously that I got Rou Shi to deliver the two volumes for me. It was too bad that they had fallen into the hands of "Three-stripers"* and their like!

II

It was not modesty alone that stopped me from trying to meet contributors. The desire to save trouble was an important factor. I knew from long experience that nine out of ten young people, especially young writers, were hypersensitive and took themselves tremendously seriously. If you were not very careful, misunderstandings tended to arise. So in general I avoided them. Even if we met I was naturally too nervous to dream of asking any favours. The only young writer in Shanghai in those days with whom I dared laugh and chat freely, whom I even asked to do odd jobs for me, was Rou Shi who had taken the books to Bai Mang.

I forget when and where I first met Rou Shi. I believe he once said he had attended my lectures in Beijing, so it must have been eight or nine years earlier. I forget, too, how we became on close terms in Shanghai. However, he was then living in Jingyunli, only four or five doors from my house, and somehow or other we struck up a friendship. The first time he called I fancy he told me his name was Zhao Pingfu (Peaceful Return). But once, when talking about the colossal effrontery of the gentry in his parts, he said a certain local worthy had taken a fancy to his name and told him to stop using it because he wanted it for his son. This makes me suspect that the *fu* in his original name was the one meaning

---

* Members of the police force in the International Settlement of Shanghai at that time, who wore three stripes on their armlets.

"happiness," for that would appeal more to a country gentleman than the *fu* meaning "return." He came from Ninghai, Taizhou, as you could tell at a glance from his brusque Taizhou manner. He was rather stand-offish too, sometimes reminding me of Fang Xiaoru* who I imagine must have been very like him.

He shut himself up at home writing or translating; but after we had met a number of times and found a good deal in common he got hold of a few more young people who shared our views, and we set up the Dawn Blossoms Press. Its aim was to introduce the literature of East and North Europe and to bring in foreign woodcuts, for we felt we should give what support we could to this vigorous, simple art. Then, in line with this aim, we put out *Dawn Blossoms, Modern Short Stories of All Countries* and *The Garden of Art.* We also published the paintings of Koji Kukiwa** to harass the pseudo-artists of the Shanghai Bund, that is, to show Ye Lingfeng up as an impostor.

Rou Shi had no money, though. He borrowed over two hundred dollars to start printing. In addition to buying the paper, he did most of the editing and most of the odd jobs — running to the printers, making prints or proofreading. He was often disappointed, however, and would frown as he related what had happened. All his early works breathe gloom, but actually this was not his character: he believed that men were good. When I described cases of deceit, extortion or friends betrayed, the sweat would stand out on his forehead and his shortsighted eyes would stare in shocked surprise.

"Are such things possible?" he would protest. "Surely not. . . ."

---

*Fang Xiaoru (1357-1402), a Ming Dynasty writer from the same district of Rou Shi. Loyal to Emperor Hui Di, he refused to work for Prince Yan who usurped the throne, and therefore he was killed.

** A contemporary Japanese artist whose work Ye Lingfeng plagiarized.

But before long Dawn Blossoms Press had to close down — I will not go into the reasons here — and for the first time Rou Shi knocked his idealistic head against a brick wall. All his hard work was wasted, and on top of that he had to borrow a hundred dollars to pay for the paper. After that he was less sceptical of my contention that "human hearts are evil," though sometimes he would still sigh, "Are such things really possible?" None the less he went on believing that men were good.

He now sent the stock still left to Dawn Blossoms Press, which was his by rights, to Tomorrow Bookstore and Guanghua Bookshop, hoping to raise a little money on it. At the same time he went on translating for all he was worth in order to pay off his debt. He sold the Commercial Press his translations of *Danish Short Stories* and Gorky's novel *The Artamanovs' Business.* I fear, though, these manuscripts may have been lost in last year's fighting and fire.*

By degrees he became less stand-offish, until finally he dared walk out with girls — friends or girls from his home town — but he always kept three or four feet away from them. This was a very bad habit, for when I met him in the street with an attractive young woman three or four feet away I could never be sure if she was his friend or not. Yet when he walked with me he kept close to my side, supporting me, in fact, for fear I might be knocked down by a car or a tram. This solicitude combined with short-sightedness made me for my part so uneasy that the whole walk was an ordeal for us both. That is why I never went out with him if I could help it. The sight of the strain on him made me feel under a strain too.

Whether motivated by the old morality or the new, if he could help others at his own expense he chose to do so and would take up a new burden.

---

* Referring to the fighting on January 28, 1932, when Japanese troops invaded Shanghai,

Then came a time when he made a decisive change. One day he told me explicitly that he felt obliged in future to write works with a different content and form. I said: That sounds difficult, like switching to a stick when you're used to a knife — how can you manage it? He answered simply: One can learn!

This was no empty boast. He did start learning from scratch. At about that time he brought a friend to see me, a Miss Feng Keng. Some conversation with her made me conscious of a great barrier between us, and I suspected that she was a romantic, eager for quick results. I also suspected that she was responsible for Rou Shi's recent decision to write a long novel. At the same time I suspected myself as well: because Rou Shi's uncompromising answer had shown up the weakness of my argument which meant, actually, taking the line of least resistance, I was perhaps unconsciously transferring my resentment to her. I was, in fact, no better than the hypersensitive young writers whom I dreaded meeting because they took themselves so seriously.

She was a delicate girl, not pretty either.

III

Not till after the League of Left-Wing Writers was founded did I discover that the Bai Mang I knew was the Yin Fu whose poems appeared in *The Pioneer*. I took a German translation of an American journalist's account of his travels in China to one meeting to give him, thinking this might help him to improve his German. But he did not turn up. I had to enlist Rou Shi's help again.

Not long after this they were both arrested, however, and that book of mine was also confiscated, falling into the hands of "Three-stripers" and the like.

IV

When Tomorrow Bookstore asked Rou Shi to edit a periodical, he consented. This publisher also wanted to print my translations, and asked him to find out what arrangements to make about royalties. I copied out my contract with the Beixin Publishing Company and gave this to him. Having stuffed it into his pocket he hurried off. That was late in the evening of January 16, 1931, and little did I know that this was to be our last meeting and our final parting.

The next day he was arrested at a meeting, and I heard that I was wanted by the authorities because he had that copy of my contract in his pocket. The contract itself was plain and to the point, but I had no wish to go to any pointless places to explain it. I remembered a venerable monk described in *The Life of Yue Fei** who "sat cross-legged and departed this world" as soon as the bailiff pursuing him reached the gate of the monastery. He left behind this couplet:

> *As from the east the law arrives*
> *I seek the Western Paradise.*

That was the best way conceivable to slaves of leaving this sea of bitterness. When no "champion of justice" was in sight, this was the ideal way out. Not being a venerable monk, I could not seek nirvana at will. Besides, I hankered after life. So I ran away.

That night I burned old letters from friends and, carrying my small son, went with my wife to a hotel. Within a few days all sorts of rumours had spread to the effect that I had been arrested or killed, but of Rou Shi there was very little news. Some said the police had taken him to Tomorrow Bookstore to find out whether he was an editor there or not; others said he had been taken

---

* A popular novel describing the famous Song Dynasty general Yue Fei (1103-1142) who resisted the northern Tartars.

to Beixin Publishing Company to find out whether he was Rou Shi or not, and he had been handcuffed, sure sign that his case was grave. But no one knew the nature of the charge.

During his imprisonment, I saw two letters he wrote to fellow provincials. The first was as follows:

January 24

I came to Longhua yesterday with thirty-five other prisoners (including seven women). Last night we were put in chains, creating a precedent for political prisoners. This case involves so many people that I don't expect to be out very soon, so I'd appreciate it if you'd take over my work in the bookshop. Everything's all right and I'm studying German with Yin Fu. Please tell Mr. Zhou* not to worry; we haven't been tortured. The police and the security officers have asked me several times for his address, but of course I don't know it. Don't worry.

All the best!

Zhao Shaoxiong

That was on the front of the page.
On the back was written:

I want two or three tin rice bowls. If they won't let you see me, just leave the things for Zhao Shaoxiong.

He had not changed. He was eager to study German and work harder than ever; and he still showed the same concern for me as when we were walking together. Some of his statements were wrong, though. They were not the first political prisoners to be put in chains; but he had always thought too highly of officialdom, imagining it to be enlightened until its cruel treatment of him and his friends. In fact that was not the case. Sure enough, his second letter was very different. He wrote most

---
* Lu Xun's real name was Zhou Shuren.

bitterly and said that Miss Feng's face had swollen. Unfortunately I made no copy of this letter. By that time even more rumours were rife. Some said he could come out on bail, others that he had already been sent to Nanjing. Nothing was certain. And more telegrams and letters were arriving to ask for news of me. Even my mother in Beijing fell ill of anxiety, and I had to write letter after letter to put things right. This went on for about three weeks.

The weather turned colder, and I wondered if they had quilts where Rou Shi was. We had. Had he received the tin bowls? . . . But then we received reliable news that on the night of February the seventh or the morning of the eighth Rou Shi and twenty-three others had been shot at the Longhua Garrison Headquarters. There were ten bullets in his body.

So! . . .

Late at night I stood in the hotel courtyard, surrounded by junk. Everyone was asleep, including my wife and son. I was profoundly conscious that I had lost a fine friend, China a fine young man. I calmed down a little after my first distress, but force of habit asserted itself in the calm and made me string together these few lines:

> Used to the long nights of spring time,
> My hair grows white as I hide with my wife and son;
> Dreams show my dear mother in tears,
> And the chieftain's flag over the city are always
>   changing.*
> Cruel to see my friends become fresh ghosts!
> Raging I turn on the bayonets and write these lines.
> Will they ever see print? I frown
> While moonlight glimmers like liquid on my dark
>   gown.

---

* Referring to the continuous wars among warlords at that time.

The last two lines were not true though, for in the end
I copied the verse out and sent it to a Japanese singer.

But in China at that time we could not publish this
poem. We were sealed in more tightly than in a tin. I
remember Rou Shi had gone home just before New Year
and stayed so long that some of his friends reproached
him on his return. He told me in great distress that his
mother had lost the sight of both eyes, and he could not
bear to leave when she asked him to stay a little longer.
I know the heart of that blind mother and Rou Shi's
devotion. When *The Dipper* was first published, I wanted
to write something about Rou Shi, but could not. All I
could do was to select Käthe Kollwitz's* woodcut *The
Sacrifice*, which shows a mother giving up her son in
agony of spirit. And I alone knew that this was to commemorate Rou Shi.

Of the four other young writers killed at the same time,
I had never met Li Weisen and had only seen Hu Yepin
once in Shanghai and exchanged a few words with him.
The one I knew relatively well was Bai Mang or Yin Fu,
for we had corresponded and he had written for my
magazine. But I can find nothing of his today. I must
have burned all his contributions on the evening of the
seventeenth, before I knew he was among those arrested.
I still have his *Poems of Petöfi*, and looking through this
I found just four lines of his translation penned beside
one of the "Wahlspruch" (maxims):

> *Life is a treasure,*
> *Love even dearer;*
> *But to win freedom*

---

* Käthe Kollwitz (1867-1945), a progressive German woodcut
artist. Her works expose the evils of capitalism and express the
people's feeling of revolt. After these young writers were murdered, she and other progressive writers and artists abroad protested to the Kuomintang reactionaries.

I would throw both away!

On the second page is written Xu Peigen, which I suspect was his real name.*

V

Two years ago today, I was lying low in a hotel while they went to the execution grounds. A year ago today, I was escaping through gunfire to the International Settlement while they lay buried none knows where. Only this year on this day am I sitting at home again while everyone is asleep, including my wife and son. Once again I am profoundly conscious that I have lost fine friends and China fine young men. I grow calmer after my distress, but force of habit asserts itself in my calm and has made me write.

If I go on, I shall still be unable to publish what I write in China today. When a lad, I read Xiang Ziqi's *Reminiscences* and blamed him for writing a few lines only, then finishing when he had barely begun.** But now I understand.

It is not the young who are writing obituaries for the old, but during the last thirty years with my own eyes I have seen the blood shed by so many young people steadily mounting up until now I am submerged and cannot breathe. All I can do is take up my pen and write a few articles, as if to make a small hole in the mud through which I can draw a few more wretched breaths. What sort of world is this? The night is so long, the way so long, perhaps I had better forget and remain

---

* Xu Peigen was in fact Bai Mang's brother, head of the Kuomintang Bureau of Aviation.

** Xiang Ziqi, a third century writer who, after his best friend was killed, wrote *Reminiscences* to express his grief. This is a short poem consisting of little more than 150 words.

silent. But I know, if I do not do so, a time will come
when others will remember them and speak of them. . . .

February 7-8, 1933

WHO IS THE PARADOX?

George Bernard Shaw is not making a world cruise.* He is travelling to see reporters' faces all over the world, and to be quizzed by reporters all over the world — but he has not passed his test.

He dislikes being welcomed and interviewed by reporters, yet they insist on welcomes and interviews, and after the interviews they poke fun at him.

He tries to keep out of sight, yet they insist on seeking him out, and when they have found him they write at great length about him. Yet they insist that he courts publicity.

He does not want to talk, yet they insist on his talking, and when he says a little they force him to say more. When he has said more, the papers dare not print his remarks in full and blame him for saying too much.

He tells the truth, yet they say he is joking, laugh loudly at him and blame him for not laughing himself.

He speaks frankly, yet they say he is satiric, laugh loudly at him and blame him for thinking himself intelligent.

He is not a satirist, yet they insist on calling him one, though they despise satirists and use futile satires to satirize him.

He is not an encyclopaedia, yet they insist on treating him as one, questioning him about everything under the sun. And when he has answered they grumble, as if they knew more themselves.

---

* On February 17, 1933, while on a world cruise Shaw stopped at Shanghai.

He is on holiday, yet they force him to expound general principles. And when he has said a little they are annoyed, and complain that he has come to "spread communism."

Some despise him for not being a Marxist writer. But if he were one, those who despise him would not look at him.

Some despise him for not being a worker. But if he were one, he would not have come to Shanghai and those who despise him would not be able to see him.

Some despise him for not being an active revolutionary. But if he were one, he would be imprisoned with Noulens* and those who despise him would not mention him.

He has money, yet insists on talking about socialism. Refusing to work, he insists on making pleasure cruises. He insists on coming to Shanghai, insists on preaching revolution, insists on talking about the Soviet Union. He insists on making people uncomfortable. . . .

So he is contemptible.

His height, his age, his white hair are contemptible. His dislike of welcomes and avoidance of interviews are contemptible. Even his affection for his wife is contemptible.

But now he has gone, this Shaw whom all describe as a "paradox."

But I think we should wait a little. We had better recognize him as one of the great writers of the world. Gossip and monkey business will not enable us to crush a great writer. Besides, it is better to have Shaw, so that we have more to talk about.

For the end of the paradoxical Shaw, or the solution of Shaw's contradictions, will come only when the con-

---

* A progressive foreigner residing in Shanghai. On June 17, 1931, the Kuomintang government arrested him and his wife, and imprisoned them in Nanjing. Soong Ching Ling and others formed a committee for their defence.

Lu Xun, Bernard Shaw and Cai Yuanpei

Mr. and Mrs. Bernard Shaw and Col. Vrionis

tradictions of society are solved, and that is no joking matter.

The night of February 19, 1933

ON SEEING SHAW AND THOSE
WHO SAW SHAW

I like Shaw. I admired and began to like him not through his works or life, but simply because of a few epigrams I read and because I was told he was always tearing the masks from gentlemen's faces — I liked him for that. Another reason is that China keeps producing men who ape Western gentlemen, and most of them dislike Shaw. I tend to believe that a man disliked by the men I dislike must be a good sort.

But on the eve of Shaw's visit to China, I had no intention of seeking him out.

During the afternoon of the sixteenth, Mr. Kanzo Uchiyama* showed me a telegram from the Kaizo-sha Press, and asked me if I would call on Shaw. I decided that if they wished me to I would.

On the morning of the seventeenth, Shaw had disembarked at Shanghai but hidden himself no one knew where. After several hours had passed it looked as if we should not see him. But just after noon I received a note from Mr. Cai Yuanpei saying Shaw was having lunch with Madame Sun,** and I should go there at once.

So I hurried to Madame Sun's house. The moment I entered the small room next to the sitting-room I saw Shaw in the seat of honour at a round table having lunch with five others. As I had seen his photograph and heard that this was a man with a world reputation, I realized

---

* The manager of a Japanese bookshop in Shanghai.
** Soong Ching Ling.

in a flash that here was a great writer, though in fact there was no evidence of this. It did strike me, though, that with his snow-white hair, healthy colour and genial expression, he would make a first-rate model for a painter.

They were halfway through lunch. It was a simple vegetarian meal. A White Russian paper had predicted that there would be innumerable attendants, but there was only one cook.

Shaw did not eat much, unless of course he had eaten a great deal at the beginning of the meal. In the middle he started using chopsticks, but very awkwardly — he could not pick anything up. The admirable thing was that by degrees he became more skilful, till finally he got hold of something quite firmly. Then he looked round to see if the others had noticed his success, but no one had.

Shaw at table did not strike me in the least as a satirist. And he said nothing unusual. For instance, among other things he remarked that friends are best because you can always keep in touch with them, whereas a man does not choose his parents or brothers and is therefore forced to leave them.

As soon as lunch was over, three photographs were taken. As we stood side by side, I was conscious of my shortness. And I thought, "Thirty years ago I should have done exercises to increase my height. . . ."

At two there was a reception at the Pen Club, and I went with them by car to the large Western-style building called the World College. Upstairs we found about fifty persons assembled: the writers of literature for literature's sake, the writers of national literature, social stars, the magnates of the theatre and so forth. They gathered round and bombarded him with questions, as if he were the *Encyclopaedia Britannica*.

Shaw also made a short speech. As these gentlemen were all men of letters, he said, they knew all about per-

formances like this. The actors, who were in the profession themselves, must understand these things better
than a mere writer like himself. That was really all
there was to it. In short, today's meeting was like a
visit to the zoo. Now the animal had been seen, that
should be enough. . . .

Everyone roared with laughter, no doubt taking this,
too, for satire.

Dr. Mei Lanfang and some other celebrities also asked
questions, which were answered, but we can pass over
that.

Then came the ceremony of presenting gifts to Shaw.
These were brought forward by Mr. Shao Xunmei,
renowned for his manly beauty. There was a box of
small clay masks like those of the classical theatre, and
another gift which I heard was a stage costume, but
which I could not see as it was wrapped up in paper.
Shaw accepted these with pleasure. According to an
article published later by Mr. Zhang Ruogu, Shaw asked
a couple of questions, and Mr. Zhang made a satirical
answer. But unfortunately Shaw "did not hear it";
actually I did not either.

By the time someone asked why he was a vegetarian
there were quite a few photographers about, and thinking
my cigarette was out of place I went into another room.

At three we went back to Madame Sun's house for an
interview with some newspapermen. There were forty
to fifty people waiting there, only about half of whom
were admitted. First came Mr. Tsuyoshi Kimura, four
or five men of letters, half a dozen Chinese reporters,
an English one and a White Russian one, and three or
four photographers.

On the back lawn the newspapermen arranged themselves in a semi-circle round Shaw and, as a substitute
for the world cruise, offered an exhibition of reporters'
faces. Again Shaw was bombarded with questions, as if
he were the *Encyclopaedia Britannica*.

Shaw seemed in no mood for talking. But the newspapermen would not let him off, so he talked. As soon
as he said much, the reporters stopped taking such co-
pious notes.

I thought, "Shaw cannot really be a satirist if he talks
so much."

This quiz ended at about half past four, and as Shaw
seemed very tired by then I went back with Mr. Kimura
to Uchiyama Bookstore.

The next day's papers were infinitely more striking
than Shaw's actual conversation. Quite different accounts
were given of the same thing said at the same time and
in the same place. Apparently the interpretation of the
English varied according to each listener. For instance,
on the question of China's government, the Shaw of the
English press said the Chinese should choose for themselves rulers they admired. The Shaw of the Japanese
press said there were several Chinese governmnts. The
Shaw of the Chinese press said no good government could
win the people's hearts.

Judging by this, Shaw is not a satirist but a mirror.

But most of the comments on Shaw in the press were
unfavourable. Everyone had gone to hear satire which
would amuse and suit him; instead of which he had heard
satire which annoyed and injured him. So they all used
satire to strike back at Shaw, declaring he was nothing
but a satirist.

In this contest between satirists, I think Shaw is still
the greatest.

I asked Shaw no questions and he asked me none. I
did not realize that Mr. Kimura would want me to write
my impressions. I often read other people's impressions,
which are written as though the subject's heart was
laid bare to them the moment they set eyes on him, and
I do admire such perspicacity. In my own case, though,
I have not so much as consulted a manual of physiogno-
my. So even though I meet a famous man, if you want

me to pour out a flood of my impressions, I very soon dry up.

However, as the request came all the way from Tokyo to Shanghai the least I can do is send these few notes by way of response.

The night of February 23, 1933

PREFACE TO *BERNARD SHAW*
*IN SHANGHAI**

What we call "men" today always wrap themselves in something: brocade, cloth, gauze — any of these will do. Even those reduced to begging at least own a pair of ragged trousers. Even so-called savages wear a little skirt of grass or leaves. If they take these off in public, or have them torn off by others, we say they are indecent.

But in spite of this, people still want to look at them. Some stand still to watch, some trail after them. All gentlemen and young ladies hide their eyes, but some of them peep out from between their fingers. All like to see other people naked, but watch out for their own neat clothes.

Most of men's talk is also wrapped up in anything from brocade to leaves. If this is torn away, others like to listen yet are afraid to listen. Wanting to hear, they crowd round. But fearing to hear, they give such talk a special name to lessen its effect on them, and call those who talk this way "satirists."

I believe this is the reason why Bernard Shaw's visit to Shanghai caused even more of a sensation than that of Tagore, let alone Boris Pilniak or Paul Morand.

Another reason is that "tyranny makes men sneer." But that was said of England, and may not apply to a people who from time immemorial have only been able to

---

* A collection, compiled by Qu Qiubai, of articles on Shaw from the Shanghai press. Its purpose was to "show the real Shaw and the true character of many other people."

"signify their anger by looks on the road."* Of course, times have changed after all, and the "humour" of a foreign satirist is needed to make everyone roar with laughter.

Another reason I will not mention here.

But the main thing is to watch out for our own clothes. So everybody hopes for different things. The lame hope he will advocate using crutches, those with scabies hope he will praise hat-wearing, those who use rouge hope he will taunt sallow-faced matrons, and the writers of nationalist literature are counting on him to crush the Japanese troops. But what is the result? You can tell the result is not too satisfactory by the great number of people who are complaining.

Herein, too, lies Shaw's greatness. From the fact that the English, Japanese and White Russian papers, apart from spreading certain rumours, have unanimously attacked him we can see that he is certainly not being used by imperialism. As for certain Chinese papers, we need not speak of them, for they are followers of the foreigners. They have followed behind like this for a long time. It is only on "non-resistance" or "strategic considerations" that they march in the van.

Though Shaw was in Shanghai for less than twenty-four hours, he gave rise to many stories. This could hardly have happened with any other writer. And as this was no trifling event, this book is undoubtedly an important record. In the first three sections the faces of men of letters, politicians, warlords, hooligans and pugdogs are reflected in a flat mirror. I do not agree that Shaw is a distorting mirror.

The backwash of this, reaching Beijing, made a British reporter draw the conclusion: Shaw does not like being welcomed by the Chinese. A Reuter's telegram of the

---

*A quotation from *Guo Yu* (Records of the States). It describes the subjects of a Zhou Dynasty tyrant, who were too afraid to speak out.

twentieth said that the amount written about Shaw in the Beijing press "showed the traditional callousness of the Chinese."* And Dr. Hu Shi, even more transcendent, asserted that the noblest welcome was not to entertain him at all.

"A beating is no beating, and no beating is a beating!"**

This really is a great mirror. It really is a great mirror which makes men conscious that here is a great mirror. And from the antics of those who want to look in it or do not want to look in it, men's hidden selves are revealed. Some of those in Shanghai, though they neither write nor speak as brilliantly as the foreign journalists and Chinese scholars in Beijing, are none the less quite clever. The number of traditional masks is limited. Though some articles have not been included and others may be published later, the main features are probably all here.

Written by lamplight, February 28, 1933

---

* On February 20, Shaw reached Beijing. A Reuter report said, "The government papers this morning published news of the spread of large-scale fighting, yet still devoted a great deal of space to Bernard Shaw's arrival in Beijing. This shows the traditional callousness of the Chinese."

** According to a Song Dynasty anecdote, a small official named Qiu Jun called on a monk who treated him very rudely. But when a general's son arrived, the monk treated him very well. Qiu Jun demanded the reason. "A welcome is no welcome," lied the monk, "and no welcome is a welcome." Qiu slapped his face and said, "In that case, a beating is no beating, and no beating is a beating!"

FROM SATIRE TO HUMOUR

To be a satirist is dangerous.

If he satirizes the illiterate, those who are killed and imprisoned, or the oppressed, well and good: he can make the "educated intellectuals" who read his essays laugh, and heighten their consciousness of their own courage and superiority. But the satirists today are satirists precisely because they satirize this society of "educated intellectuals."

Because the object of satire is this society, each individual in it feels stung. Then one by one they come out secretly to kill the satirist with their satire.

First they accuse him of cynicism. Then by degrees they all give tongue together, calling him a slanderer, a mischief-maker, vicious, vile, an academic bandit, a Shaoxing pettifogger, and so on and so forth. But satire aimed at a society often "persists a fearfully long time." Even if you get a foreigner who has been a monk or some special evening paper to attack it, it is no use. This is enough to make a man choke with rage!

The crucial thing is this: the object of his satire is society, and so long as society does not change, his satire will remain. But you are attacking him as an individual, and so long as his satire remains, your attacks will be useless.

So to beat such a vile satirist, you will have to change society.

Still those who satirize society are in danger, especially during an age when some "men of letters" have openly or secretly turned into "the teeth and talons of the ruler."

Nobody wants to be the chief target in a persecution of writers; but so long as a man is alive and has some breath left, he will want to work off his feelings under the pretext of laughter. Laughter should not offend anyone, and there is still no law that citizens must pull long faces. We can take it, then, that laughter is not illegal.

I suppose this accounts for the "humorous" trend in literature since last year. Of course in many cases it is simply laughter for laughter's sake.

But I am afraid this cannot go on for long. "Humour" is not one of our native products, the Chinese are not a "humorous" people, and this is not an age in which it is easy to have a sense of humour. So even humour is bound to change. It will either become satire directed against society, or degenerate into our traditional "joking" or "hanky-panky."

March 2, 1933

FROM HUMOUR TO GRAVITY

Once "humour" inclines towards satire, in addition to losing its own character it begins to be satirized and persecuted. If it degenerates into "joking," it has a longer life and a smoother time; but it becomes more and more like a native product, and ends up as a sort of Westernized Xu Wenchang.* A proof of this can be seen from the fact that amid all this talk of "Buy Chinese!" we find advertisements for "home-made imports."

Besides I am really afraid there will soon be a law ordering all citizens to pull long faces. Laughing was not illegal to begin with. But then unhappily the north-eastern provinces were lost, the whole nation was aghast, and when patriots sought the cause for our loss of territory they discovered that one reason was the young people's love of pleasure and addiction to ballroom dancing. When laughing boys and girls were skating merrily in Beihai Park, a large bomb was dropped; and though no one was hurt a big hole was made in the ice, which prevented further skating.

Then unfortunately Shanhaiguan was lost, and Jehol became hard-pressed. This made famous scholars and writers feel more "hard-pressed" too. Some write dirges, others battle songs, yet others speak of the right attitude to writing. Abuse is disgusting, poking fun is not civilized either; but we are asked to write seriously and to look serious as well, to supplement "non-resistance."

But men cannot remain so placid. When the enemy

---

* (1521-1593), a writer and painter at the end of the Ming Dynasty about whom many funny stories were told.

is at the gate and they have no arms to resist him, they will at least rage inwardly. Thus they have to find some substitute for the enemy. Thereupon those who laugh are in trouble, for they are called "utterly heartless." So those who are cunning pull long faces like everyone else, in order to avoid trouble. "A wise man keeps out of trouble," as our ancient sages taught. Then "humour" goes up to heaven, and "gravity" reigns supreme over all that is left of China.

Once we understand this, we know why in the old days all women, whether chaste or lewd, could not laugh or speak in public; and why all women mourners today, whether sad or not, must wail aloud by the roadside.

This is "gravity." But to tell the truth is "vicious."

March 2, 1933

HOW I CAME TO WRITE STORIES

How did I come to write stories? I sketched the reasons in my preface to *Call to Arms*. I should add here that times have changed since I first took an interest in literature: in China then fiction was not considered as literature, and its writers could not rank as men of letters. Thus nobody thought of making a name in this way. I had no thought, either, of elevating short stories to the level of literature. I simply wanted to use them to reform society.

I did not set out to write, being more interested in introducing and translating — short stories in particular, especially those by the writers of oppressed peoples. For in those days there was a great deal of talk about driving out the Manchus, and some young people found moral support in these monitory, insurgent writers. So though I never read a single book on the art of writing fiction, I read not a few stories, some for my own enjoyment, most because I was looking for material to introduce. I also read histories of literature and literary criticism, to find out different writers' characters and ideas in order to decide whether they were suitable to introduce to China or not. There was nothing at all scholarly about this.

As I was looking for monitory, insurgent works, I inevitably turned towards Eastern Europe and read many books by writers from Russia, Poland and the Balkan states. At one point I was searching eagerly for stories from India and Egypt, but to no purpose. I recollect that my favourite authors at that time were the Russian,

Gogol and the Pole, Sienkiewicz. Also two Japanese — Soseki Natsume and Ogai Mori.

After coming back to China I taught in school, and for five or six years had no time to read stories. I need not go into my reasons for starting again, having already done so in the preface to *Call to Arms*. I started writing short stories not because I thought I had any particular talent, but because I was staying in a hostel in Beijing and had no reference books for research work and no originals for translation. I had to write something resembling a story to comply with a request, and that was "A Madman's Diary." I must have relied entirely on the hundred or more foreign stories I had read and a smattering of medical knowledge. I had no other preparation.

But the editors of *New Youth* came to press me again and again till I wrote something. And here I must remember Mr. Chen Duxiu, who was the one who urged me the most strongly to write.

Of course, a man who writes stories cannot help having his own views. For instance, as to why I wrote, I still felt, as I had a dozen years earlier, that I should write in the hope of enlightening my people, for humanity, and of the need to better it. I detested the old habit of describing fiction as "entertainment," and regarded "art for art's sake" as simply another name for passing the time. So my themes were usually the unfortunates in this abnormal society. My aim was to expose the disease and draw attention to it so that it might be cured. I did my best to avoid all wordiness. If I felt I had made my meaning sufficiently clear, I was glad to dispense with frills. The old Chinese theatre has no scenery, and the New Year pictures sold to children show a few main figures only (though nowadays most of them have a background too). Convinced that such methods suited my purpose, I did not indulge in irrelevant details and kept the dialogue down to a minimum.

After finishing something I always read it through twice, and where a passage grated on my ears I would add or cut a few words to make it read smoothly. When I could not find suitable vernacular expressions I used classical ones, hoping some readers would understand. And I seldom used phrases out of my own head which I alone — or not even I — could comprehend. Only one of my critics spotted this, but he dubbed me a "stylist."

The happenings I described generally arose from something I had seen or heard, but I never relied entirely on facts. I just took one occurrence and modified or expanded it till it expressed what I had in mind. The same was true of the models for characters — I did not pick on specific individuals. My characters were often a mixture of a mouth from Zhejiang, a face from Beijing and clothes from Shanxi. Those people who said such-and-such a story was aimed at so-and-so were talking nonsense.

One difficulty, however, of writing this way is that it is hard to put down your pen. If you finish a story at one sitting, by degrees the characters come alive and play their parts. But if something happens to distract you, and you do not go back to the story for a long time, the characters may have changed and the story may turn out quite differently from what you intended. When I started "Buzhou Mountain," for instance, I wanted to describe the awakening of sexual desire, its creation and decline. But in the middle I read an article by a moralist attacking love poems, to which I took great exception. So in my story a little creature ran up between Nü Wa's legs. This was not only unnecessary but destroyed the scope of my plot. Still, probably no one else can recognize such places. In fact, our eminent critic Mr. Cheng Fangwu says that was my best story.

If you base a character on one particular individual, I imagine you can avoid this trouble, but I have never tried it.

I forget who it was that said that the best way to convey a man's character with a minimum of strokes is to draw his eyes. This is absolutely correct. If you draw all the hairs of his head, no matter how accurately, it will not be very much use. I keep trying to learn this method, but unfortunately have not mastered it.

I never used any superfluous padding, or forced myself to write when I felt I could not; but that was because I had another source of income at the time and did not live by my pen. That can hardly be considered a general rule.

Again, while writing I paid no attention to any criticisms whatsoever. Because if Chinese writers were childish in those days, Chinese critics were even more so. If they did not laud you to the skies, they damned you utterly; and had you taken them seriously you would either have thought yourself a prodigy or committed suicide to expiate your crimes. Criticism can only be of use to writers if it condemns what is bad and praises what is good.

I often read foreign critical essays, however, because those critics were not prejudiced for or against me, and although they wrote of other authors, there were many judgements which I could apply to myself. But of course I made a point of finding out their political affiliations too.

All this was ten years ago, since when I have neither written nor advanced. When the editor asked for an article on this subject, what could I write? This hodgepodge is all I can offer.

The night of March 5, 1933

"WHEN THE LIGHT COMES...."

The third degree in Chinese prisons is an open secret. Last month the League for Civil Rights brought up this problem.

But *The North-China Daily News* run by foreigners published a "Dispatch from Beijing" written on February 15, which reported that Dr. Hu Shi had visited several prisons in person and told this reporter "in a most friendly manner" that, "according to the careful investigation he made, there is not the least evidence of such a thing. . . . They found it quite easy to talk with the prisoners, and once Dr. Hu Shi even talked with them in English. Regarding the prisons themselves, he (Dr. Hu Shi) declared they were not satisfactory; but although the prisoners talked freely (sic) about their bad treatment, there was not the slightest hint of third degree."*

Although I was not privileged to take part in this "careful investigation," ten years ago I visited the Model Prison in Beijing. Though it was called the Model Prison, talking with the prisoners was not "free" at all. You were separated by a window, three feet apart, with a jailer at your side; your time was limited and no secret signs were allowed, let alone the use of a foreign language.

But this time Dr. Hu Shi "talked with them in English" — *most* extraordinary! Either Chinese prisons have improved out of recognition to become so "free," or the jailer was frightened by the "English" and took Dr.

---

* Translated from the Chinese.

Hu Shi for a compatriot of Sir Lytton, and a person of consequence.

Fortunately I recently saw Dr. Hu Shi's comment on the Three Chief Cases of the China Merchants Steam Navigation Company: "Open indictment is the only weapon against corrupt politics. When the light comes, the darkness will disappear."

Then everything was clear to me. In prison, talking with prisoners in a foreign tongue is forbidden; but an exception was made at once for Dr. Hu Shi, for he can make "open indictments," he can talk with foreigners in "a most friendly manner," and he is the "light." When the light comes, the darkness will disappear. So he preferred an open indictment to the foreigners against the League for Civil Rights, for that is where the darkness lies.

But I do not know whether the prison authorities will allow anybody else to talk to the prisoners in English, now that this "light" has gone home.

If not, that means that once the light disappears, the darkness comes back again.

But this "light" is too busy with university affairs and the Indemnity Fund Committee to pay many visits to the "darkness." So I fear before his next careful investigation of the prisons, the prisoners may not have the good fortune to speak English freely. Alas, light goes only with the "light," and the light in prisons is really too evanescent.

But they cannot blame anyone else for this, for the prisoners should never, never have broken the law. Gentlemen never break the law. If you doubt my word, look at this "light"!

March 15, 1933

MODERN HISTORY

For as long as I can remember, the open spaces in all the towns I have visited have been used by "showmen" or "circus men."

In general there are only two kinds of shows.

In one type a monkey is made to wear a mask and clothes, flourish a sword or a spear, and ride round in a few circles on a goat. Or else a bear, fed on slops till it is nothing but skin and bones, performs a few tricks. In the end a collection is taken.

In the other type a stone is put in an empty box, which is wrapped round and round in a large handkerchief, and a white pigeon is produced. Or a showman stuffs his mouth with paper, lights it and breathes out flames from his mouth and nose. After which a collection is taken. Upon receiving the money, one fellow complains that it is too little and refuses to go on, while another reasons with him and asks the audience for five more coins. Then sure enough someone gives one, and he asks for another four, another three. . . .

When they have enough, another trick starts. This time they put a child into a vat with such a small mouth that only the small tuft of hair on his head can be seen. To get him out, you have to pay. When enough has been collected, a man kills the boy by some means with a sharp knife, covers him with a sheet, and leaves him lying stiff and stark. To bring him to life again, you have to pay.

"At home we look to our parents. Outside we look to our friends. . . . Hurrah! Hurrah! shouts the showman gravely and sadly, making a pretence of dropping coins.

He swears at other children if they go closer to have a good look. If they pay no attention, he hits them.

Sure enough there are plenty of people who give coins. When the number is more or less what was expected, the showmen pick up the coins and collect their things. The dead boy scrambles to his feet, and goes off with them.

The spectators scatter too, looking very foolish.

The open space is quiet again for a while, but presently the whole thing starts again. According to the proverb: Everyone can do tricks, but not all tricks are the same. Yet in fact for many, many years they have been the same; and yet there are always people to watch and give money. In between, though, there must be a few days of quiet.

This is all I have to say, and it signifies very little, just that after everyone has given money, there will be a few days' quiet before the same thing starts all over again.

I see now that I have chosen the wrong title. This is really neither fish nor fowl.

April 1, 1933

THE CHINESE PEOPLE'S "LIFEBELT"

"Even ants love their lives." Since the common folk of China have always described themselves as the "ant-people," if to preserve my life I keep looking for a relatively safe place to which to move for a while, I doubt if any but heroes will laugh at me.

But I seldom take news at its face value, and often hold a different view. For example, when the papers said that air-raid precautions were being taken in Beijing, I was sceptical; but the moment I saw that cultural relics were being moved south I realized the old city's danger. And judging by the curios' destination, I can guess where happiness is located in China.

Now, one batch after another, the curios have concentrated in Shanghai. This shows that after all the foreign concessions there are safer than anywhere else.

But this means rents are bound to go up.

This is another big blow for the "ant-people." So we must think of other places.

After much reflection, I have thought of a "lifebelt." This is neither the interior nor the frontier, but a sort of circle between the two, in which a man may manage "to prolong his days in this — world."

At the frontier,* planes are dropping bombs. According to Japanese papers, they are wiping out "bandits." According to Chinese reports, they are massacring the people and reducing villages and towns to rubble. In the

---

* The region of Jehol.

interior,* planes are dropping bombs too. According to Shanghai papers, they are wiping out "Communist bandits" and have inflicted heavy damage on them. We do not know what the Communist papers say. Anyway, at the frontier there is endless bombing, and in the interior there is endless bombing. Though over there the bombing is done by outsiders and over here we are doing it ourselves, while the bombers are different the people bombed are the same. Their only hope not to be "blasted to smithereens" is to stay between these two places — provided no bombs fall there by accident. So I call this the Chinese people's "lifebelt."

When the bombing from outside comes further in, the "lifebelt" will shrink into a "lifeline." When it goes further, people will escape to the already bombed interior, and the "lifebelt" will become a "zero."

As a matter of fact, everyone shares this premonition. One proof of this last year was the virtual disappearance of such talk as "Our China has a vast territory, rich resources and a great population." One gentleman making a speech went so far as to describe the Chinese as a "weak, small people."

Of course, the rich and mighty will think this nonsense, for they have planes and "foreign homelands" too.

April 10, 1933

---

* Referring to the Red Army bases in Jiangxi and elsewhere. At this time Chiang Kai-shek had thrown 90 divisions into his fourth all-out offensive against the Red Army.

ON WRITING AND THE CHOICE
OF A SUBJECT

If you keep on writing on one subject, you come to
the end of it. If you still insist on fresh angles, others
may feel you are making a fool of yourself. But if you
go steadily ahead and get friends to lend a helping hand
every day, people will grow used to it. Then not only
can you do it — you can put it across as well.

For instance, the most important subject today is
"Pacify internal foes and resist external ones."* A great
deal has been written on this subject. Some say that to
pacify the interior we must first resist outside foes. Some
say the two things should be done together. Some say
that unless we resist external foes we cannot pacify internal ones. Some say that by resisting attacks from
outside we will pacify the interior. Some say that pacifying the interior will enable us to resist attacks from
outside. Some say that to pacify the interior is more
urgent than to resist external foes.

So now the subject seems quite exhausted. It looks as
if the limit has been reached.

Therefore if we want to introduce a new angle, we
shall look like utter fools, or — to use the most current
term of abuse today — like "traitors." This is because
only three possible angles are left: "Pacify the interior
and stop resisting foreign aggression," "Invite the foreign foe to pacify the interior," and "Outside and inside

---

* The Kuomintang slogan for suppressing the Communists and
resisting the Japanese.

are the same, so no resistance is needed."

Although these seem queer ideas to write about, such things have happened. And we need not go back to the Northern and Southern Dynasties either, but have only to look at Ming Dynasty history. While the Manchus were waiting ready to pounce, inside China they treated human life as grass and slaughtered good citizens — this is the first type. When Li Zicheng* entered Beijing, because the rich and mighty could not bear to let their slave become emperor, they asked the "great Manchu army" to defeat him — this is the second type. As for the third type, not having read the *Qing Dynasty History*, I cannot speak with any certainty. But judging by old precedents, we should say that the Manchu imperial house was actually descended from a son of the Yellow Emperor who had gone north; and because of their great nobility and virtue they gained the empire. In short, we are all one big family.

Later historians would naturally try to refute this, and famous moderns are against the bandits too. But this is something that only happens later or in modern times; it was not the case in those days when vultures and dogs were in power. Wasn't the eunuch Wei Zhongxian** worshipped in the Confucian Temple during his lifetime? In those days all their doings were shown in the best light possible.

At the end of the Qing Dynasty the Manchus did their best to suppress revolution, and their slogan was: "Give the country to a friendly power rather than to our own slaves." When the Hans heard this they were furious. But actually they had done the same thing themselves. We can see from the way Wu Sangui*** asked the

---

* Leader of the great peasant revolt at the end of the Ming Dynasty.

** A notorious powerful eunuch of late Ming Dynasty.

*** A Ming Dynasty general who invited the Manchu troops to occupy Beijing.

Manchus to invade China, that "all men are the same at heart" when their own interests are threatened. . . .

April 29, 1933

Note: My original title was "Pacify Internal Foes and Resist External Ones."

May 5, 1933

A NEW DRUG

When his name crops up we remember him; but it is true that since the September 18th Incident we have heard no more of Mr. Wu Zhihui's remarkable talk, and he was said to be ill. Now a little voice has emanated from Nanchang; but it has been ridiculed even by those "nationalist" writers who have assumed new colours and who have also made no sound since the September 18th Incident.

Why is that? Precisely because of this Incident.

If we think back we can remember the great role played by Mr. Wu's pen and lips all through the end of the Qing Dynasty, the May 4th Movement, the Northern Expedition, the Kuomintang Purge, and the period of confusion which followed. But now the moment he opens his mouth even those shady characters start to jeer. Since the September 18th Incident the planes really seem to have shaken Mr. Wu, senior statesman of Kuomintang China — or else to have emboldened the shady characters.

So after the September 18th Incident the situation has changed.

A fable in an old book* tells how during the reign of a certain emperor, most of the imperial concubines were ill, and no cure for them could be found. Finally a famous physician turned up and made out a miraculous prescription: so many lusty young men. The emperor was forced to agree to this. When he went after several days to investigate, he found all his concubines in excel-

---

* A collection of anecdotes by Chu Renhuo of the Qing Dynasty.

lent spirits, while some haggard, cadaverous men pros-
trated themselves before him. The emperor was shocked
and asked, "What are these?" The ladies answered
rather sheepishly, "These are the dregs of the medicine."

Judging by the last few days' papers, Mr. Wu is rather
like the dregs of medicine — perhaps even the dogs will
trample on him. He is a wise, most balanced individual,
however, who will certainly not go all out and let others
suck him dry. But as the situation has changed since
the September 18th Incident, it is true that a new drug
should be sold, and the jeering at him actually shows
the nature of the new drug.

This new drug needs to be both potent and mild. If
we compare it to writing, it must first describe heroes
dying for their motherland, and then beauties dying for
love. On the one hand it should praise Hitler's government, and on the other the Soviet Union's achievements.
A love song must follow a battle song; after a discussion
of brothels should come a discussion of morality. On
the Day of National Shame it should write of weeping
willows, and on May Day reminiscences about roses. It
must attack its master's enemy while expressing apparent
dissatisfaction with its master. . . . In a word, whereas
a simple prescription was used before, from now on a
more composite drug will be sold.

Though the composite drug may seem a cure for all
ailments, quite possibly it will prove useless too. It
may neither cure nor kill. But because patients taking
this medicine stop looking for a better cure, their illness
may grow worse till it ends in uncalled-for death.

April 29, 1933

A KINGLY CULTURE

The kingly culture of China is indeed "shedding lustre on all quarters of the globe."[*]

When Pu Yi's[**] sister-in-law ran away with a cook, taking over thirty thousand dollars with her, she was arrested and tried by a Chinese court, which decreed that she should be returned to "her husband's custody." Though Manchukuo is a sham, there is nothing sham about a husband's authority.

When the Moslims in Xinjiang made trouble, a Pacification Commissioner was sent to them.[***]

When Mongolian princes became homeless vagrants,[†] a special Relief Committee for Mongolian Princes was organized.

Our consideration for Tibet was shown when the Panchen Lama was asked to read sutras and incantations.[††]

---

[*] A quotation from the *Book of History*.

[**] The puppet ruler of Manchukuo.

[***] A reference to the Turfan Revolt of January 1933. Two Kuomintang generals in Xinjiang were at loggerheads. In May 1933, the Nanjing government sent a Pacification Commissioner to settle their dispute.

[†] After the Mongolian People's Government was set up in 1921, some reactionary princes fled to Inner Mongolia. In 1932 a few of them went to the Xinjiang-Gansu border and started robbing merchants and travellers there. In February 1933, the Kuomintang formed a committee to look after these brigands.

[††] In April 1933, abetted by the British imperialists, the rulers of Tibet plotted to set up an independent Tibet and Xikang. To win over the Panchen Lama in Nanjing, the Kuomintang invited him to perform services.

But the most compassionate policy of our kingly culture can be seen from our treatment of the Yao minority in Guangxi.*   According to the *Evening News,* to
carry out this "compassionate policy" we killed three
thousand out of thirty thousand Yao, and sent three
planes to their district to "lay eggs," so that "amazed by
this godlike might they surrendered."   Then Yao representatives were chosen to visit our coastal cities and see
the civilization of their sovereign state, such as the might
of the red-turbaned Sikh police.**

And the red-turbaned Sikhs told them, "Don't make
such a noise."

These "barbarians" so long under our rule have been
making a great deal of noise lately, the reason being
that all of them are indignant.   Once a kingly culture
is in its heyday, "When the conqueror goes east, the western barbarians murmur. When he goes south, the northern barbarians complain." Of course, this is only natural.

But we still rush east and west, and fight north and
south, never slacking off for a moment.   It may be a
hard life, but the "moral victory" is ours.

After the husband's authority in puppet Manchukuo
has been protected, after the Mongolian princes have
been relieved, after the lama has read his incantations,
after the Moslims are truly pacified, after the Yao have
surrendered — what will be left to do? Naturally we can
only cultivate our virtue in order to subjugate "distant"
Japan. By then our Sikh-police type of duty will have
been done.

Ah, we simple fellows are lucky to live in such a brave
age. All we can do is pay close heed, shout for joy, and

---

* There was a Yao uprising in March 1933.
** The International Settlement in Shanghai, controlled by the
British, was policed by Sikhs.

dance with pleasure.*

May 7, 1933

This article was suppressed by the censor's office. As I am lucky enough not to be a Yao and to live in a foreign concession, no Chinese plane will come to "lay eggs" over me. But as the order "Don't make such a noise!" applies to all, I cannot shout for joy. I shall just have to remain silent, shamming dead to save the state!

The night of May 15, 1933

* A quotation from Sun Yat-sen's "Letter to Li Hongzhang," written in 1894.

ABOVE AND BELOW

There are two kinds of bombing in China: bombing from inside, and bombing from outside.

Here is an example of the first kind:

There has been no fighting recently, but planes have been sent to bomb the bandit area. From morning till evening on the seventh, the third and fourth squadrons flew in formation to the west of Yihuang and the south of Chongren, where they dropped about three hundred bombs weighing a hundred and twenty pounds each. All the places that might be used by the bandits as shelters were demolished, making it impossible for them to recover their strength. . . . (A dispatch from Nanchang, in the *Shen Bao* of May 10.)

Here is an example of the second kind:

This morning at six, enemy planes bombed Jixian, killing more than ten civilians. Miyun was also strafed four times, by two planes each time. More than a hundred bombs were dropped. The damage is now being investigated. . . ." (A Beijing dispatch in the *Evening News* of the same day.)

In this connection, Shanghai school children have started to buy planes, and Beijing school children to dig air-raid shelters.* This brings up two remarkable as-

---

* In March 1933, to raise funds to suppress the Communists, the Kuomintang government made children in Shanghai collect money for planes. In May that year, Beijing school children stopped class every morning to dig shelters.

pects of the theme: "Without pacifying internal foes we cannot resist external ones," and "To pacify the interior is more urgent than to resist outside foes."

Happy are those who live in foreign concessions. But if we close our eyes and take a wider view, we realize that in China there are government troops above, and "Red bandits" and people "influenced by the Reds" below; while outside there is the enemy above, and civilians not "under the influence of bandits" below. "The damage is now being investigated," and in this land of peace pagodas are being built.* When Buddha was born, he pointed with one hand to the sky and with the other to the earth. "Above and below I shall reign supreme," he said. And that's how it is.

But if we close our eyes again and think harder, we are faced by a difficult problem. If bombing the interior from inside is slower than bombing from outside, the two lots of planes will surely meet — and then what shall we do? Should we stop "pacifying the interior" and turn round to make a counter-attack? Or should we go on bombing the interior, letting the bombing from outside come further in to join us in bombing the "bandits" until they are wiped out, when we can "resist" and drive the others away?

This is only a joke. Such a thing could never happen. But even if things came to such a pass, the problem could still be solved. Go abroad for a rest-cure or worship Buddha in the hills — then everything will be all right.

May 16, 1933

I remember that my original manuscript ended: "Go abroad for a rest-cure, have a boil on your back, wor-

---

* In 1933 a memorial pagoda was built for Sun Yat-sen in Nanjing.

ship Buddha in the hills, or suffer from diabetes* — then
everything will be all right."

The night of May 19, 1933

---

* In 1933 Wang Jingwei had a boil on his back, and declared
that he was suffering from diabetes. He made this a pretext to
go abroad. Dai Jitao, then head of the Examination Yuan, set
up a Buddhist shrine in his government office.

A MENTAL RESERVATION

These last few days the newspapers have reported that when Huang Fu, the newly appointed head of the Political Reorganization Committee, arrived by special train in Tianjin, seventeen-year-old Liu Gengsheng threw a bomb at him.* The criminal was immediately arrested and, as witnesses said he had been sent by the Japanese, the next day he was bound and taken outside the new station, where his head was cut off and displayed as a warning to others.

Although twenty-two years have passed since the Qing Dynasty turned into a republic, the sections on nationalism and civic rights in the draft constitution have only just been written and not yet published. Last month when a bandit was executed in public in Hangzhou, thousands are said to have rushed to enjoy the sight. Though this is obviously a little inconsistent with the first clause of the Section on Civic Rights, which says "Raise the status of the nation," it is quite in accord with the second clause of the Section on Nationalism — "Uphold the national spirit." North and south have been unified now for eight years; so if Tianjin also hangs up one small human head to demonstrate the national unity, this is nothing to wonder at.

Moreover, though in China we say that "women and the young are hard to deal with," the moment anything

---

* Liu was a workman who happened to be crossing the railway tracks at the time. He did not throw the bomb. The incident was manufactured by the Kuomintang to hide the fact that Huang was going north to sign a cease-fire agreement with the Japanese.

happens, in addition to the telegrams, declarations and inscriptions drawn up by old men, some of them over ninety, there are also fine stories about child patriots and girls who volunteer for the army, to put men in their prime to shame. Our people always seem "intelligent when children, not so good when grown up," but on reaching old age they are rejuvenated and judging by the obituary notices dead men are even more remarkable. So it is not strange in the least that a lad of seventeen should throw a bomb.

But my reservation is about this claim that he was sent by the Japanese, for that would make him a traitor. For the last twenty years there have been constant crises in China, but all those considered traitors by the general public have been over thirty, though later they have gone perfectly unscathed. As for children and young people, how many times have they taxed their childish powers, physical as well as mental, running about in sandstorms or through the mud with their clay or bamboo collecting-boxes, trying to be of some slight use to China! Although they have no foresight, and the money they collect at the cost of sweat and blood is usually gulped down by tigers and wolves, at least their patriotism is genuine — they have never been traitors.

How odd that this time there should have been an exception. Still, I hope we will reserve judgement over this verdict, and look at the facts again. We need not wait for three years, five years or ten. We shall learn the truth before the head hanging there has decomposed. We shall know who is the traitor after all.*

Let us wash away the filth spattered on our children's and young people's heads!

May 17, 1933

---

* On May 31, a fortnight after Lu Xun wrote this article, Huang signed a cease-fire agreement with the Japanese, by which China gave up her four north-eastern provinces and granted Japanese military forces free access to parts of north China.

This article, as well as the next three, was suppressed by the censor.

July 19, 1933

MORE MENTAL RESERVATIONS

Talking about the charge against Liu Gengsheng made me think how difficult it is to speak or write in China today. To be safe, it is best to say nothing: otherwise, on your own head be it.

Here are a few examples.

Twelve years ago Lu Xun wrote "The True Story of Ah Q," no doubt with the intention of exposing the national failings, though without making it clear whether he included himself in the criticism or not. But this year people have started calling him Ah Q — this is retribution for evil here on earth.

Eight or nine years ago some true men and gentlemen started a paper in which they claimed that their opponents made trouble in different colleges because they had been bribed with Russian roubles. But four or five years later, the true men became professors and the gentlemen department heads, who lived on Russian funds. Indeed they protested loudly when the fund was stopped. Though this was a case of good requited here on earth, it was also on their own heads.

But even if those who use the pen are careful, they cannot help leaving loop-holes. To take a recent example, the press has been filled with words like "enemy," "traitor," "bogus" or "puppet state." You have to write like that to show your patriotism: otherwise readers will complain. Who could have foreseen that the order would be issued: "Resistance to the enemy should be practical, and as words like 'traitor' or 'enemy' are too provocative and pointless, in future they should not be used"? Moreover when Commissioner Huang Fu reached Beijing and expressed his views, he said, "China must take a passive role whether we fight or make peace. It is hard to say what we should do. All kinds of danger threaten our state, and we must make one last supreme effort." (Both quotations are from the Beijing dispatch in the *Evening News* of the eighteenth.)

Luckily, the papers now carry only such headlines as "Japanese Planes Threaten Beijing," without unduly "provocative" expressions, though we still use the term "traitor." Since the Japanese are not our "enemy," how can Chinese be "traitors"? This does seem a big loophole. Fortunately we Chinese are not afraid of "provocative" expressions. Even if heads are cut off and hung up in the streets for the enjoyment of Chinese and foreign ladies and gentlemen, nobody will ever protest.

Such being the case, we know how hard it is to speak.

Since the massacre of scholars in the Qing Dynasty, men of letters have not dared to write historical anecdotes. If anyone now could forget the terror of three centuries ago and cull the choicest items from the press, he could compile an immortal work. Of course, he need not be hypersensitive either, or substitute such terms as "sovereign state" or "divine intelligence."

May 17, 1933

REFUTING TALK OF "IN NAME
BUT NOT IN FACT"

A recent "Eye-witness Account from the Fighting Zone" contains this passage:

This reporter met a company commander recently transferred here from the front, who said that our army had spent three or four hundred thousand dollars, not counting the cost of timber . . . on fortifications in Shimenzhai, Haiyangzhen, Qinhuangdao, Niutouguan and Liujiang. . . . After working hard on this construction, we planned to defend these positions to the last; but as soon as Lengkou fell, we received orders to retreat. Then all these positions, into which so much labour and money had gone, were not used at all but casually abandoned. He felt very bad about it. After the "Non-resistance General" left and the command was changed, the men's morale improved . . . but again they were disappointed. "How unlucky we are to have been born Chinese!" he said. "And more unlucky to be soldiers in name but not in fact!" (A report from a special correspondent in the *Shen Bao* of May 17.)

The naïveté of this officer goes to prove that you cannot discuss politics with fools who have never received "instruction." First, he thought that "non-resistance" would disappear with the "Non-resistance General."* This

---

* Referring to Zhang Xueliang, Commander of the Northeastern Army, who, by order of Chiang Kai-shek, gave up the three northeastern provinces without putting up resistance to the Japanese invaders. In April 1933, Chiang forced him to resign and go abroad, to appease the people's anger.

shows an ignorance of logic: the general is one individual, while non-resistance is an "ism," and the individual may go while the "ism" remains. Secondly, he imagined that after spending three or four hundred thousand dollars on fortifications we must defend them to the last. (At least the fellow did not consider attacking.) This means that he has no sense of strategy: fortifications are built to show the common people, not to defend to the last; for the genuine strategy is to "lure the enemy to penetrate deeper." Thirdly, though ordered to withdraw, he had the presumption to feel bad. He clearly has no grasp of philosophy: his mind needs to be reformed. Fourthly, his "morale improved." This was premature. It shows that he does not understand his fate, for the Chinese are born to suffer. No wonder such a stupid officer exclaimed repeatedly that he was born unlucky, and even felt he was a soldier "in name but not in fact." Actually he has no inkling of who is really something "in name but not in fact."

As for the privates who are lower in rank than this company commander, it goes without saying that all they can do is declare, "Frankly, as things stand now, if we cannot resist the invaders we shall revolt." (From the same report.) This is outrageous talk. The ancients said, "Without a threat from outside, the state will perish." I never really understood this before, for if there was no enemy how could we lose our country? Now this soldier's words have made it clear. The country may be lost to those who "revolt."

To conclude: if we do not want the country to perish, we must find more threats outside, and teach those fools who feel bad a good lesson, to make them the same "in fact as well as in name."

May 18, 1933

ON NOT TRYING TO UNDERSTAND
THOROUGHLY

All statements must have their commentary, especially those made by important world figures. Some writers find it most tiresome if they have to comment on their own writings. But important world figures are different, for they have whole flocks of secretaries, followers or disciples to make their commentaries for them. There is another type of statement, though, on which no comment should be made.

For instance, that Number One world figure, the president of the United States, has issued a "peace" declaration, apparently aimed at stopping different armies from crossing their frontiers. But at once the commentators said:

> As for the stationing of American troops in China, that is permitted by previous agreement, and is not therefore included in the ban proposed by President Roosevelt. (A Reuter's dispatch from Washington on the sixteenth.)

Or let us look at these words of the president:

> All countries of the world should take part in a solemn and binding non-aggression pact, and solemnly reiterate their duty to limit and cut down armaments. Moreover, provided the signatories fulfil their obligations faithfully, they should agree not to send armed forces of any description across the frontier.

If we comment on this seriously, its actual meaning is:

All countries which have no "binding" and "solemn" agreements or do not "agree" can send forces of any description across their frontiers. At least we in China must not rejoice prematurely, for according to this explanation there is good reason for the Japanese army to have crossed its frontiers. Besides, the American troops in China have already been declared an exception. Still, such serious comments are rather disconcerting.

Again there are many different interpretations of the classic clause "We swear never to sign any treaty betraying our country."* One commentator** says, "Now nobody dares to speak of compromise with Japan, or do anything of that sort." The key word here is "dares." However, to dare or not to dare sign a treaty is a problem for those who wield pens — those who wield weapons need not study such difficult questions, and no signing of treaties is needed to shorten the line of defence or lure the enemy deeper into our territory. But even those who wield pens will not confine themselves to signing their names, for that would be too simple. So we have something else known as "carrying on negotiations at the same time." Then another comment is made: "The third party, which advocates non-recognition, has most improperly been negotiating . . . and condemning useless resistance." This report comes from the Japanese News Agency. These comments that let out secrets are very annoying too; so this must undoubtedly be a Japanese "rumour."

In any case, such statements are so nebulous that it is best not to make any comment, especially not the type of comment which disconcerts or annoys people.

In my young days when we read that Tao Yuanming "enjoyed reading but did not try to understand thoroughly," my teacher explained that this meant he did not look up the commentaries but simply read the text. Though

---

* A statement of Chiang Kai-shek.
** Wang Jingwei.

there are commentaries, there are certainly people who
do not like us to read them.

May 18, 1933

PREFACE TO THE WORKS OF
LI DAZHAO

I first met Li Dazhao at a meeting to which I was asked by Chen Duxiu to discuss how to run *New Youth,* when we can be said to have made each other's acquaintance. I do not know whether he was already a Communist or not. At all events, he impressed me most favourably: sincere, modest and rather quiet. Although many of the contributors to *New Youth* wrangled in public and in private to build up their own position, to the very end he never did so.

His appearance is hard to describe. As he had quite a cultured and yet quite a simple and normal air, he looked a cross between a scholar, official and merchant. I have not met merchants of this type in the south, but you find them in Beijing as secondhand booksellers or stationers. On March 18, 1926, he was in the crowd when Duan Qirui's lot fired on the unarmed students who were presenting a petition. One of the soldiers seized him and asked who he was.

"A shopkeeper," he answered.

"What are you doing here then? Clear off!"

The soldier shoved him away, and so he escaped.

Had he said he was a teacher, it might well have cost him his life then.

But the next year he was killed by Zhang Zuolin.*

---

* The Communist leader, Li Dazhao, was murdered in prison in 1927 on the orders of the warlord Zhang Zuolin.

When General Duan massacred forty-two people, including some of my students, I really felt pretty bad. General Zhang seems to have massacred about a dozen — as I have no list I cannot be sure of the number — but the only one I knew was Li Dazhao. After hearing this news in Xiamen I kept seeing his oval face, almond eyes and moustache, blue cotton gown and black jacket, next to a shadowy gallows. I felt rather bad, but much less so than before. This is an old foible of mine: I am never so upset by the death of contemporaries as when young people die.

When I heard recently of the public funeral to be held in Beijing, I calculated that it was seven years since the murder. This was highly fitting. I forget the charge framed for Li Dazhao by the generals — doubtless simply "endangering the Republic." But in these seven short years incontrovertible facts have proved that it was not Li Dazhao who gave away the Republic's four provinces,* but the generals who assassinated him!

In that case, a public funeral should surely be permitted. But I see from the papers that the Beijing authorities have forbidden a sacrifice on the way and arrested some of the mourners. I do not know why, but assume this time it was for "disturbing public order." If that is the case, an incontrovertible rebuttal comes even more swiftly. Look! Is it the people or the Japanese soldiery who have disturbed the peace of Beijing?

But the blood of revolutionary pioneers is no longer a novelty. Take my own case for example. Seven years ago, on account of a few martyrs, I gave vent to a good deal of stirring, empty talk. Since then I have grown accustomed to stories of electric torture, firing squads, decapitation and secret murders. By degrees my sensibility has become so numbed that nothing shocks me any more and I have nothing to say. I fancy the

---

* Referring to the Japanese occupation of the Northeast.

"vast crowds" who, according to the papers, go to see the heads displayed as a public warning, can hardly feel more excited than during a lantern festival. Too much blood has flowed.

But apart from his warm blood, Li Dazhao has left some writings. Unfortunately it is difficult for me to comment on these. As we worked in different fields, though he and I were comrades-in-arms in the time of *New Youth* I paid very little attention to his articles, imagining that a rider need not notice how bridges are built any more than a gunner need study horsemanship. I did not know then what a mistake this was. So all I can say today is that while, of course, his arguments may not be appropriate today, even so they will be immortal, because they are the work of a pioneer, and a landmark in revolutionary history. On the other hand, the piled-up tomes of dead and living swindlers are already beginning to totter, so that even bookshops have to make a sacrifice and sell them at a twenty or thirty per cent reduction.

Judging by incontrovertible facts, both past and present, the case is as clear as daylight!

The night of May 29, 1933

Postscript

Mr. T — asked me to write the foregoing, because Li Dazhao's work was to be published by the G — Press with which he was connected. As he would not take a denial, I wrote this brief preface, and it was printed soon after in *Breakers*. Later, however, I heard that the owner of the copyright had asked the C — Press to publish the writings. They have not yet been printed, and may not appear for some time. Though I regret my bad manners in writing a quite uncalled-for preface, I want

to preserve this with my other work as a reminder of
this case.

The night of December 31, 1933

MORE ON THE "THIRD CATEGORY"

Dai Wangshu* has sent a letter all the way from France describing how André Gide joined the French A.E.A.R. (a revolutionary writers' association), and protested violently against German fascism at a mass meeting on March 21. He has reported Gide's speech, which was published in the June number of *Modern Times*. It is not uncommon for French men of letters to come out on the side of justice. Earlier examples are Zola's indignant partisanship of Dreyfus and Anatole France's oration at Zola's grave. A more recent one is Romain Rolland's denunciation of war. But this case gives me even keener pleasure, as the question is a topical one and I too detest fascism. However, during his report Mr. Dai points out the "stupidity" of China's Left-wing writers as well as their tyranny which resembles that of warlords, and on this I would like to say a few words. I do not want to be misunderstood and taken to be making excuses in the hopes that China will receive aid from the "third category" similar to that offered to the oppressed in Germany — not at all. In point of fact, China's burning of books and papers, closure of bookshops, and imprisonment or murder of writers actually happened long before Germany's White Terror, and protests have been made by revolutionary writers throughout the world. All I want to do here is discuss a few points in his letter which must be raised.

After describing how Gide joined the movement to resist fascism, our correspondent goes on:

* A poet.

In the French world of letters, we can call Gide one of the "third category". . . . From 1891 . . . onwards, he has always remained loyal to his art. But writers loyal to their art are not necessarily "accomplices of the bourgeoisie," and revolutionary authors in France do not have such a stupid view (it might be better to call it clever tactics). That is why Gide spoke amidst enthusiastic acclamations from the public.

In other words, "a writer loyal to his art" is one of the "third category," and China's revolutionary authors are fools enough to describe all such men as "accomplices of the bourgeoisie." But now Gide has proved that this does not necessarily follow.

There are two questions here which should be answered.

In the first place, do China's Left-wing theorists really consider all "writers loyal to their art" as "accomplices of the bourgeoisie"? As far as I know, they do not. No matter how foolish Left-wing theorists are, they cannot fail to understand that "art for art's sake" started as a revolution against certain social conventions. But if we go on using this old slogan to hamper the growth of the new fighting literature by open and secret means, the slogan becomes reactionary, not simply an "accomplice of the bourgeoisie." And not all "writers loyal to their art" can be lumped together. For writers of every class have their "self," which is a part of their class. Those loyal to their art are also loyal to their class, irrespective of whether they belong to the bourgeoisie or the proletariat. This is a clear and obvious fact, which Left-wing theorists can hardly fail to grasp. But when Mr. Dai substitutes "loyal to their art" for "art for art's sake," he is certainly demonstrating the utter "stupidity" of Left-wing theorists.

In the second place, is Gide really one of what is called in China the "third category"? Not having read Gide's books, I am not qualified to comment on his work. But

I believe that although writing and speeches differ in form, the ideas they contain must be the same. Let me quote two sections from his speech as reported by Mr. Dai:

> Someone may say, "It is the same in the Soviet Union." Possibly, but the aim is completely different. Besides, a certain extremism is unavoidable if you want to build up a new society and give freedom of speech to those who have always been oppressed and denied that freedom.
>
> Why is it and how is it that I now support what elsewhere I have opposed? It is because in Germany's terrorism I have seen the most deplorable and detestable past being brought to life again, whereas in the social construction of the Soviet Union I have seen unlimited promise for the future.

This is surely clear enough. The method is the same, but he supports it in one case and opposes it in the other because of differences in aim. After the Soviet Union's October Revolution, the Seraphion brothers and their associates who laid stress on art were also called "fellow-travellers," whereas in fact they were not so positive. This year a special volume has been printed in China of articles about the "third category." Can we, looking through this, find that Gide and the sentiments of our self-styled "third category" have anything in common? If not, then I dare affirm that Gide is not one of the "third category."

But just as I deny that Gide is like China's "third category," Dai Wangshu feels that the difference between Left-wing writers in China and in France is the great difference between intelligence and stupidity. After attending the meeting to express indignant sympathy for Germany's Left-wing artists, he remembered the stupidity and tyranny of China's Left-wing writers. Then he could not control his emotion.

I do not know whether there has been any reaction in China to the terrorism of the German fascists. Like our warlords, our writers and artists delight in civil war. While France's revolutionary writers have joined hands with Gide, our Left-wing writers are doubtless still considering the "third category" as their sole enemy!

There is no need to refute this, because the facts speak for themselves. There was a slight reaction here, but as this is not France it took rather a different form. And for some time now there have been no articles in the magazines "considering the 'third category' as the sole enemy." The civil war is over, and the warlord atmosphere has disappeared. Dai Wangshu has guessed wrong.

But are China's Left-wing writers as intelligent as those of France appear to be to Mr. Dai? To my mind, they are not and should not be. Before all voicing of opinion is silenced, it is very necessary to reopen and extend the discussion on the "third category." Mr. Dai has glimpsed the secret of the French revolutionary writers, and feels that in time of crisis it may be "clever tactics" for them to join hands with the "third category." But as I see it, simple reliance on "tactics" is not enough. For clever action, accurate views are needed. Just by looking at Gide's speeches, we can see that he does not hold aloof from politics, and it is wrong to dub him recklessly one of the "third category." One can welcome his attitude without any secret tactics. But the so-called "third category" in China is rather a complicated case.

The original meaning of "third category" was those who stand outside opposing camps or battles between A and B. But in point of fact, there cannot be any such people. Men are fat or thin, and in theory there ought to be a third category which is neither, but actually there is not. When comparisons are made, men are either rather fat or rather thin. It is the same with the "third category" in the arts. Though artists may look impartial and uncommitted, they always lean slightly to one side or the other. Normally they may hide this, deliberately or otherwise, but in time of crisis they will reveal it clearly. Thus Gide shows his Leftist tendencies, and other men may also expose themselves clearly by a few words. So of this heterogeneous crowd some may advance with the revolution, and cry aloud together. Some may seize the chance to injure, weaken or distort the revolution. It is the task of the Left-wing theorists to analyse them.

If this is equivalent to "civil war" between warlords, then the Left-wing theorists must go ahead with this civil war, to distinguish clearly between the two camps, and pluck out the poisoned arrows shot at them from behind.

June 4, 1933

IN PRAISE OF NIGHT

The lovers of night are not only the lonely and the leisured, or those who cannot fight or fear the light.

Men often talk and act quite differently by day and by night, in sunshine and under lamplight. Night is a mysterious garment which Nature has woven to cover all men so that they may be warm and calm, so that by degrees, without thinking, they may take off their artificial masks and clothes, and wrap themselves stark naked in this boundless mass so like dark cotton.

Although it is night, there are light and shade. There are glimmerings, twilight, and pitch darkness in which you cannot see your hand in front of you. Those who love the night must have ears to hear it and eyes to see it, to see all the darkness while in the darkness themselves. Gentlemen go from the lamplight to dark rooms, where they stretch and yawn. Lovers go from the moonlight into the shade of trees, where in a flash their looks change. The fall of night blots out all the sublime, confused, abrupt and splendid articles written on shining white paper in the daytime by men of letters and scholars, leaving only the night air with its begging, fawning, lying, cheating, boasting and devilry, to form a bright golden aura over their learned heads, like that seen in Buddhist paintings.

So the lovers of night receive the light given by it.

A fashionable young lady in high-heeled shoes taps briskly along under the street lamps; but the shiny tip of her nose shows that she is merely learning to be fashionable, and if she stays long in the bright light she will reap disaster. The obscurity of a whole row of closed shops lends her a helping hand, enabling her to slow down and catch her breath. Only now does she realize how refreshing the cool night breeze is.

So both lovers of night and fashionable young ladies receive the boon given by night.

When the night is over, people get up cautiously again and go out, even husbands and wives looking different from five or six hours ago. Then all is noise and bustle. But behind high walls, in tall buildings, ladies' chambers, dark prisons, sitting-rooms and secret offices, there is still shocking, palpable darkness all around.

The broad daylight and the noisy coming and going are simply a cover for the darkness, the golden lid on a cauldron of human flesh, the cold cream on a devil's face. The night alone is honest. Because I love the night, I am writing this at night in praise of night.

June 8, 1933

PUSHING

Two or three months ago, I believe the papers carried the news that a newspaper boy who stepped on to a tram to sell a paper accidentally trod on the gown of a passenger who was alighting. This man was very angry, and pushed the boy so hard that he fell under the tram, which had just started moving and could not stop. So the boy was killed.

The man who pushed the boy down has disappeared. But judging by the fact that his gown was trodden on, he was wearing a long gown; so even if not a "high-class Chinese," he must at least have belonged to the upper classes.

Walking in the streets of Shanghai, we often come across two types of men who charge straight ahead and never step aside from pedestrians they meet head-on or overtake. One type do not use their hands, but stride forward on long legs as if there were no one there; and unless you step out of the way, they will trample on your stomach or your shoulders. These are the foreign masters. They are all "high-class," with no difference between higher and lower as among the Chinese. The other type have crooked arms and out-turned palms like the pincers of a scorpion. They push their way along, not caring whether the people they push over fall into a pool of mud or fiery pit. These are our compatriots, the "high-class" ones. When they travel by tram, they take the third-class carriages converted from second-class. When they read papers, they read only the gutter press. Their

The five volumes of essays written between 1927 and 1933

The line spectrum of calcium, written between 1874 and 18__

mouths water as they sit there reading; and when they start moving again, they push.

To board a tram, go through a door, buy a ticket or post a letter, such a man pushes. To go out of a door, get down from a tram, escape from trouble or fly for his life, he also pushes. When women and children stagger and fall before him, he walks over them — walks over their corpses if he happens to have killed them. On he goes, licking his thick lips, quite unaffected. During the Dragon Boat Festival someone raised the cry "Fire!" in a theatre, and the pushing started again. A dozen young people who were not strong enough were trampled to death. Their corpses were laid outside on the ground, and a crowd of over ten thousand is said to have gone to see the sight. Oceans of men, and more pushing.

The upshot of pushing is a broad smile and the comment: "What fun!"

Living in Shanghai, you cannot hope to avoid being pushed and trampled, and this pushing and trampling is going to spread even further. They want to push down all the weak low-class Chinese, to trample down all the low-class Chinese. That will leave only high-class Chinese to congratulate each other:

"What fun! To safeguard our culture, we must not grudge any material sacrifice — and what importance had they anyway?"

June 8, 1933

EXPERIENCE

It is a fact that some of the experience handed down to us by the ancients is exceedingly precious, having cost many lives and remained of great value to posterity.

I could not help being struck by this when turning the pages of the *Materia Medica*.* This well-known book is indeed a mine of wisdom. Of course, some of the entries are inevitably fantastic; yet the efficacy of most of these drugs could only be so well known after a long process of trial and error. Most amazing of all are the accounts of poisons. It has always been our way to flatter the old-time sages and to consider that all remedies were discovered by a certain emperor Shen Nong** alone, who tasted seventy-two poisons one day but did not die because he had antidotes for them all. But such legends have lost their hold upon men's hearts. Most of them already know that all things were devised by degrees by men now nameless. This is true of architecture, cooking, fishing, hunting and husbandry; and medicine is no exception. If you think in those terms, this is a very big thing. No doubt when the men of old first fell ill they tried a little of this and a little of that, died if they ate poison, were unaffected if they ate something inappropriate, and recovered when they ate the right thing — after which they knew for what ailments it was a cure. Knowledge acquired in this way was first roughly jotted down, and

---

* A pharmacopoeia in fifty-two volumes by Li Shizhen (1518-1593).
** A legendary emperor to whom many inventions are attributed.

gradually grew into huge tomes like the *Materia Medica*. Indeed, from the fact that the entries in this book belong not to China alone, but include the experience of the Arabs and Indians, we can imagine how many lives were lost when first these drugs were tried.

Sometimes, however, the outcome of many men's experience is unfavourable, as in the case of the proverb: "Sweep the snow from before your door, and never mind the frost on your neighbour's roof." Unless you are very, very careful, when you try to help others it is all too easy to be slandered, and another couplet sums up the result of such unfortunate experience:

> *The yamen gate is opened wide;*
> *If you've right but no money — keep away!*

So if something is not a man's own affair, he keeps well out of harm's way. I imagine in early times they were not so callous; but when beasts gained the upper hand and many lost their lives for meddling, they naturally took this course. That is why in China, especially in the towns, if someone falls down seriously ill in the street or is hurt when a cab overturns, plenty of onlookers crowd round, some of them actually enjoying the sight, but very few stretching out a helping hand. This is one of the disadvantages of unhappy experiences.

In short, experience whether good or bad is always won at a great price. The cost of even the smallest is bound to be staggering. For instance, in recent times some newspaper readers have stopped paying any attention to declarations, telegrams, speeches or comments, no matter how eloquently phrased or grandiloquent. They may even go further and treat such things as jokes. These are not so important as "First language was invented, and then clothes."* But this mite of experience has cost us a great tract of territory and many human lives and

---

* A quotation from *The Thousand-Character Classic*.

property. Not our own lives, of course. If they had been,
we should not have the experience. It is because all experience can only be possessed by the living that I am not
taken in by those who scoff at my fear of death, and will
not commit suicide or risk my neck. That, too, is why I
am writing this. For this also is one tiny fruit of experience.

June 12, 1933

PROVERBS

On a casual view, proverbs may seem to exemplify the thinking of one age or country, but in fact they are merely typical of a part. Take for example the proverb: "Sweep the snow from before your door, and never mind the frost on your neighbour's roof." This is a maxim for the oppressed, bidding them respect their betters, pay their taxes, subscribe to levies, know their place, be neither insolent nor unruly, and — above all — mind their own business. It does not apply to oppressors.

The opposite of a despot is a slave: a tyrant in power is almighty, but once out of power he becomes utterly servile. Sun Hao* was a super-tyrant, but after surrendering to Tsin he became an absolute flunkey. Emperor Hui of Song** was a proud sovereign, but once a prisoner he submitted to every insult. A dictator treats all others as slaves, but when there is a master over him he is bound to call himself the slave: this is a fixed, unchanging principle.

The men who, under oppression, believe the maxim: "Sweep the snow from before your door, and never mind the frost on your neighbour's roof," start behaving in a totally different way the moment they have the power to bully others. Now it is: "Never mind the snow before your door, but sweep the frost from your neighbour's roof."

We have seen many such cases during the last twenty

---

* The last king of Wu in the Three Kingdoms Period.
** The last emperor of the Northern Song Dynasty, who was captured by the Golden Tartars.

years. The job of generals is to train soldiers and fight. Whether their troops are for civil war or to resist invaders, "the snow before their door" is leading an army; yet they will interfere with education and uphold morality. The job of educators is to teach. Whether they are successful or not, "the snow before their door" is education; yet they will make pilgrimages to see Living Buddhas and expound traditional medicine. Humble folk go with the troops as transport workers, and boy scouts collect money from door to door. The bosses do what they feel like at the top, and the little men mill about beneath, till everyone's doorstep is in a shocking state, and everyone's roof is a mess.

When women show their arms or the calves of their legs, this appears to shock the hearts of worthy men. I remember how much disapproving talk there was, the ban that was proposed, and the decrees against such practices later. But this year, to my surprise, they have started saying, "Clothes should barely cover the body, not waste material by trailing down before or behind. . . . In such difficult times as these, the evil consequences of this are easily foreseen." And the magistrate of Yingshan in Sichuan has ordered his police to go out and cut off the skirts of all those in long gowns in the streets. Long gowns are wasteful, true; but to assume that not wearing them or cutting off their skirts will prove a palliative for "difficult times" is strange economics indeed. The *Han History* has an apt phrase for this: "Their words are the law of the state."

The ideas and views of each individual are determined by the class to which he belongs. This may sound as if I am advocating some unmentionable class again, but it is the actual truth. And this is why proverbs do not represent the thinking of a whole people. The old literati, who thought themselves omniscient, boasted to everyone, "A scholar, without leaving home, knows all that goes on in the world." As the common people believed them, this gradually spread as a proverb. But in point of fact, "A scholar, even if he leaves home, does not know what is going on in the world." Since a scholar has merely the mind and eyes of the literati, of course he cannot see clearly or judge correctly all things beneath the sun. At the end of the Qing Dynasty when they wanted a "Reformation," they kept sending "talented men" abroad on tours of inspection. But read their notes today! What struck them most was a waxwork figure in some museum which played chess with a living man. Kang Youwei, that great sage of Nanhai, travelled in eleven countries, but not till he reached the Balkans did he realize the reason for all the "regicide" abroad. Their palace walls were too low, he said.

June 13, 1933

THE ART OF THE NUMBER-TWO CLOWN

Among the different roles in Eastern Zhejiang opera is one known as the "second painted-face," or to use a more dignified term, the "number-two clown." The difference between him and the clown is this: instead of playing a bullying, reckless rake or some official's servant who makes use of his master's power, he takes the part of a young gentlemen's bodyguard or fawning protégé. In short, his social status is higher than the clown's, but his character is baser.

A loyal servant is played by an actor whose face is not painted, who gives good advice and then dies for his master. A bad servant is played by a clown, who does bad things and perishes in the end. A number-two clown is different, however. He looks not unlike a gentleman, knows something of lyre-playing, chess, calligraphy and painting, and can join in drinking games and solve riddles; but he has powerful backing and bullies the common people. When someone is persecuted, he laughs coldly and feels pleased; when someone is slandered, he threatens him and shouts. He is not always consistent, however, for he quite often turns round to point out his young master's faults to the audience, wagging his head and grimacing as he says, "Look, this fellow is going to get into trouble this time!"

This last trick is typical of the number-two clown, for he is neither as stupid as the loyal servant nor as simple as the bad one. He is an intellectual. He knows quite well that his patron is an ice mountain which cannot last very long, and later he will have to serve someone else. Therefore while he is being fed and basking in reflected glory, he has to show that he is not really on his noble master's side.

Of course operas written by number-two clowns do not have this character. Certainly not. Neither do operas written by clowns or rakes, for they see only one side of his character. No, this number-two clown is a creation of the common people, after they have seen through his type and extracted its essence.

So long as there are powerful families, so long will there be despotism, then there will be number-two clowns, and the art of the number-two clown. If we take a paper and read it for a week, we shall find him now complaining about the spring, now extolling the war, now translating some speech by Bernard Shaw, now talking about the marriage problem. But from time to time he must express his indignation and dissatisfaction with the government — that is his last trick.

This last trick is supposed to show that he is not a flunkey. But the common people understand, and have long ago presented this type on the stage.

June 15, 1933

RANDOM THOUGHTS

Those adept at governing a state see methods of govern-ment everywhere. Thus in Sichuan someone felt that long gowns wasted cloth and sent patrols to cut them short. In Shanghai a famous man is about to clean up the tea-houses, and it is said that there will be three major reforms: the first is to pay more attention to public hygiene, the second is to keep fixed hours, and the third is to spread education.

The first reform, of course, is very good. As for the second, although bells ringing at opening and closing time will remind us rather tiresomely of our school days, if we want to drink tea we shall have to put up with it, so that is all right too.

The most difficult is the third. When the "ignorant masses" go to tea-shops, apart from asking for the news and gossiping, they like to listen to stories like those about Lord Bao.* These tales are old, and fact is mixed with fiction. One talks aimlessly and the others listen casual-ly, sitting there to the end. If you tell stories about living men instead, they will probably neither believe them nor want to hear them. If you just tell the secrets and inside story of the enemy, they may not be very in-terested, for your "enemy" may not be theirs. The re-sult will be too bad for the tea-shop owner, for his business will drop off.

At the beginning of the reign of Guang Xu in the Qing

---

* A magistrate of the Northern Song Dynasty, whose wisdom and justice were legendary.

Dynasty, there was an opera company in my home town which called itself the Jade Company but did not live up to this name, for it gave such poor performances that no one wanted to see them. The country folk, who are no whit inferior to great men of letters, made up a song about it.

> Above, the actors staged a play;
> Below, the audience ran away;
> They bolted doors to make them stay,
> But then the people climbed the wall,
> Till not a soul was left at all,
> Just poles the pedlars had let fall.

You cannot force people to accept things. If they do not want to look, it is no use dragging them over. For instance, there are certain magazines with money and powerful backing which you would expect to have a tremendous circulation; yet they have very few subscribers and just a handful of contributors, so that only one number comes out every two months. The satire is already the babble of old men of a past generation, and it looks as if for good non-satirical writing we shall have to wait for the next generation.

June 15, 1933

ON BATS

Men generally dislike creatures that come out at night, probably because they do not sleep as human beings do, and it is to be feared they may observe secrets while men slumber soundly or stir in the darkness.

But though the bat also flies by night, it has a good reputation in China. Not because it preys on mosquitoes and is a friend of man, but more on account of its name which has the same sound as the Chinese word for "good fortune." It is thanks entirely to this that its not too distinguished features appear in paintings. Another reason is that the Chinese have always wanted to fly and imagined other creatures as flying too. Taoist priests want to take wing to heaven, emperors to soar up as immortals, lovers to become birds which flit in pairs, and sufferers to fly from their misery. The thought of "winged tigers" makes men shiver with fear, but when money flies their way they fairly beam. As the flying machines invented by Mo Zi* are lost, we have to raise funds to buy aeroplanes from abroad now. This is not strange in the least for we laid too much stress in the past on spiritual culture — compelled to by circumstances, for the best of reasons. But though we cannot actually fly, we can do so in imagination; so when we see creatures like rats with wings, we are not surprised. And famous writers even use them as themes for poems, and compose

---

* A philosopher of the Spring and Autumn Period. According to the *Han Fei Zi*, he spent three years making a wooden hawk and flew it for a day before it broke.

316

such fine lines as: "At dusk I reach the temple where bats are flying."*

The Westerners are not so high-minded or big-hearted. They do not like bats. If we look for the reason, I think Aesop is probably to blame. In his fables we read that when the birds and beasts held their meetings, the bat went to the beasts and was turned away because he had wings; then he went to the birds and was turned away again, because he had four legs. In fact, because he had no proper stand at all, everyone disliked him as a fence-sitter.

In China recently we have picked up some old foreign allusions too, and sometimes make fun of the bat ourselves. But though such fables are pleasant, coming from Aesop, who lived in a time when zoology was in its infancy, it is different today when even a child in primary school knows quite well what species whales or bats belong to. If a man still takes these old Greek fables seriously, it simply shows that his knowledge is on a par with that of the ladies and gentlemen who took part in those meetings in Aesop's time.

Professor Liang Shiqiu, who thinks goloshes are a cross between straw sandals and leather shoes, has a similar mental level. Had he lived in ancient Greece, he might have been second only to Aesop; but today, unfortunately, he is born too late.

June 16, 1933

---

* From a poem by Han Yu, famous Tang Dynasty prose writer.

TO LIVE BY ONE'S WITS

The Shanghai expression "putter" has to be translated
as "loafing" in standard Chinese. As for "living by one's
wits," it should be easier for outsiders to understand if
translated into the classical expression: "All is grist that
comes to the loafer's mill."

How strange that loafing should be a way of life! Yet
if you ask a man in Shanghai, or question a woman about
her husband's profession, you may receive the frank
reply: "He lives by his wits."

The man who asks the question is not surprised either,
any more than if the answer were "Teaching," or "Working in a factory." If the answer were "He has no job,"
then he would begin to be worried.

To live by your wits in Shanghai is quite respectable.

Nearly all the news we read in the Shanghai papers are
the exploits of these fellows. Without them, the local
news would not be so lively. Still, in spite of the great
scope of their achievements, their methods boil down to
three and seem legion only because they are not all used
at once.

The first method is cheating. Tempt those who are
greedy, pretend to be sorry for those with a grudge, make
a show of generosity to those fallen on hard times, and
tell a bad-luck story to the generous. In this way you
can fleece the other fellow.

The second method is blackmail. If cheating is not
effective or is discovered, look angry and start threatening. Accuse the other of being rude or slandering one
of improper conduct, say he owes you money, or give

no reason at all — this is also counted as "reasoning with him." In this way also you can fleece him.

The third method is running away. When either or both of the above-mentioned methods has proved successful, make off like the wind, leaving no track behind. In case of failure, also make off like the wind, leaving no track behind. If the matter is serious, leave the district and lie low for a time until the trouble has blown over.

Everyone knows that such a profession exists, yet no one is shocked.

When men can live by their wits, those who work will naturally starve. Everyone knows this, yet no one is shocked.

But the fellows who live by their wits have some admirable qualities: they admit quite frankly that they "live by their wits!"

June 26, 1933

THE "TOMINS"

In *Free Talk* on June 29, Mr. Tang Tao spoke of the "Tomins," a degraded caste in eastern Zhejiang. He accepted the view put forward in *Anecdotes About the Tomins* that these people were despised as descendants of the Song Dynasty general Jiao Guangzan, who surrendered to the Golden Tartars. By the time of the first emperor of the Ming Dynasty, the word "Beggars" was inscribed on their gates, since when they have lived in wretched circumstances, despised by all.

Born as I was in Shaoxing, I often came across Tomins in my childhood, and heard from the lips of my elders the same explanations for their degradation. Later I had my doubts. It seemed to me that the first Ming emperor, who showed no disrespect even to the defeated Mongols, would never have troubled about a general who had surrendered to the Tartars in the preceding dynasty. Besides, when we look at the Tomins' professions, there are clear signs that they have been musicians or singsong girls. Their ancestors may therefore have been good and loyal citizens at the beginning of the Ming Dynasty who opposed the first emperor and Emperor Yong Le. Furthermore, the descendants of good men usually suffer hardships, while the descendants of traitors may not be degraded. To take an obvious example, the descendants of General Yue Fei are still grave-keepers in Hangzhou, where they lead a miserable life; but what of the descendants of Qin Hui, Yan Song, etc.?*

---

* Notorious traitors of the Song and Ming dynasties.

I do not mean to settle these old scores here, though. I simply want to point out that the Tomins in Shaoxing are a sort of freed slaves, who were probably freed during the Yong Zheng period. They therefore all have trades, which are naturally low ones. The men collect junk, sell chicken-feathers, catch frogs, or perform in operas, while the women call on their patrons during festivals to offer congratulations, and help in marriages and funerals. Here, then, is a trace of their former servitude. But as they leave as soon as the job is done, and are well tipped for it, they are obviously freed.

All Tomins have definite patrons, and cannot just go to any house. When the mother-in-law dies, the daughter-in-law takes her place, and so the relationship is handed down from generation to generation like a family heirloom. Only when a Tomin family is so poor that they have to sell the right, are they separated from their former masters. If some patron, for no reason, tells a Tomin not to come again, it is a serious insult. I remember after the 1911 Revolution my mother said to a Tomin woman: "In future we shall all be equal, so you needn't come here any more." But the woman was very angry, and answered indignantly, "Whatever are you saying? We shall go on coming here for thousands of years."

So for a few tips they are not only content to be slaves, but want to find more masters and pay to buy the right to servitude. I dare say this is something inconceivable to free men outside the Tomin caste.

July 3, 1933

SAND

Of late our literati have kept lamenting that the Chinese are a dish of loose sand and quite hopeless, shifting the blame for our troubles to the people as a whole. In fact this is unfair to most Chinese. Though the common people do not study and may not have a clear judgement, they are quite capable of banding together over something which they know affects their interests. The old methods were public penances, insurrection and revolt; while today they still use petitions and similar tactics. If they are like sand, it is because their rulers have made them so. In classical parlance, they are "well-governed."

Is there no sand, then, in China? There certainly is. Not the common people but their rulers, great and small.

We often hear the expression "official promotion and a fortune." In fact the two are not synonymous. Men want official promotion in order to make a fortune: the first is the way to the second. So though high officials rely on the central government, they are not loyal to it. Though small officials rely on the local yamen, they do not love or defend it. The superior may issue an order for honest dealing, but the petty bureaucrats will pay no attention, counteracting this command with false reports. They are all self-centred, self-seeking grains of sand, out to better themselves while they can; and each particle is an emperor, who lords it over others whenever he can. "Tsar" has been translated into Chinese as *"shahuang"* or "sand-emperor," and that is the most appropriate title for this lot. Where do their fortunes come from? They squeeze them out of the common people. If the common

people were to band together, their fortunes would be
hard to make; so obviously they must do all they can to
change the country into loose sand. Since the people are
ruled by these sand-emperors, the whole of China is now
"a dish of loose sand."

But beyond the sandy desert are men who band together and walk in as if to "an uninhabited land."

This means a big change for the desert. For such
times, the ancients had two extremely apt comparisons:
the chiefs become apes and cranes, the common people
insects and sand.* The rulers take off into the blue like
white cranes, or climb up trees like monkeys. "When
the tree falls the monkeys scatter." But as there are other
trees, they will not come to grief. The people are left
below as ants and dirt, though, to be trampled underfoot
or killed. If they cannot oppose the sand-emperors, how
can they stand up to the sand-emperors' conqueror?

At such a time, however, there is always someone to
flourish a quill or wag a reproving tongue. Then the
common people are catechized severely:

"What are you going to do now?"

"What are you going to do in future?"

They suddenly remember the people and, keeping
silent on all other matters, demand that the people save
the situation. This is like asking a man bound hand and
foot to catch a robber.

But this is precisely the final act of the sand-emperor's
good government, the last gasp of apes and cranes, the
end of self-adulation and self-betterment, the inevitable
consummation.

July 12, 1933

---

* A quotation from the *Bao Pu Zi:* "During King Mu's southern expedition, the whole army was transformed. The chiefs
became apes and cranes, the common people insects and sand."

SURPLUS KNOWLEDGE

Owing to surplus production in the world, there is an economic crisis. Although more than thirty million workers are starving, the surplus of grain is still an "objective reality," without which the United States would not give us flour on credit and we could not suffer the "calamity of a bumper harvest."

But there can be a surplus of knowledge too, which causes an even more serious crisis. They say that the further education spreads in Chinese villages today, the quicker will be the bankruptcy of the countryside. No doubt this is the calamity of a bumper mental harvest. Because cotton is too cheap, the Americans are doing away with their cotton fields. Similarly China should do away with knowledge. This is an excellent method learned from the West.

The Westerners are very able. Five or six years ago the Germans complained that they had too many college students, and some politicians and educationists raised a hullabaloo to advise young people not to enter university. In Germany today they not only give this advice but are in the process of doing away with knowledge: burning certain books, ordering writers to swallow their own manuscripts, and shutting up groups of university students — this is known as "solving the unemployment problem." Aren't we complaining in China today that too many students are studying literature and law? Not just these subjects either. We even have too many high school students. So a "strict" examination system should be used like an iron broom — sweep, sweep,

324

sweep! — to sweep most young intellectuals over to the "masses."

How can surplus knowledge cause a crisis? Isn't it a fact that about ninety per cent of the Chinese are illiterate? Yes, but surplus knowledge is "objective reality" all the same, and so is the crisis that ensues. When you have too much knowledge, you become either too imaginative or too soft-hearted. If you are too imaginative, you tend to think too much. If you are too soft-hearted, you cannot bear to be ruthless. Either you lose your own equanimity or interfere with that of others, and that is how calamity comes. Therefore knowledge must be done away with.

But just doing away with knowledge is not enough. A suitable practical education is needed. The first requirement is a fatalist philosophy — men should be resigned to fate, and even if their fate is a sad one should rest contented. The second requirement is a sense of expediency. Watch to see how the wind is blowing, and learn something about the power of modern weapons. These two practical courses of study at least should be promoted immediately. The method of promotion is very simple. In ancient times a philosopher who opposed idealism said that if you doubt whether a bowl of flour exists or not, you had better eat it and see whether you feel satisfied. So today if you want men to understand electricity, you can give them an electric shock and see if they suffer or not. If you want to impress them with the effectiveness of aeroplanes or such things, you can fly an aeroplane over their heads and drop bombs, to see if they are killed or not. . . .

With a practical education like this, there will be no surplus of knowledge. Amen!

July 12, 1933

THE CHINESE IMAGINATION

Foreigners who do not know China often say the Chinese are entirely practical. Actually this is not the case. We Chinese are a most imaginative people.

In ancient times just as today, everyone knew that a man with many wives who was too incontinent must pay his debt to nature sooner or later, even if he took aphrodisiacs every day. Yet our ancients cherished the strange fantasy that intercourse with women was one way to become immortal, the example being Peng Zu,* who had many wives and lived for hundreds of years. This method was once as popular as alchemy, and titles of many works on the subject can be found in old catalogues. It cannot have worked very well in practice, however, for today no one seems to believe in it any more, which is most unfortunate for lustful heroes.

Another small fantasy was that a man could blow a white ray from his nostrils which would travel any distance — near or far — to kill his enemy. Then the white ray would return, and the murderer would never be found. In this way you could kill people without any trouble, quite nicely and cosily. As late as the year before last, some men wanted to go up Wudang Mountain** to learn this art; but last year this fantasy was squeezed out by the Big Swords Battalion,*** while today even the battal-

---

* A legendary figure.
** A Taoist centre in Hubei Province.
*** Troops sent to resist the Japanese armed only with big swords.

ion's fame has died. This is most unfortunate, too, for patriotic heroes.

Recently, however, we have got hold of another fantasy, namely that we can save the country and make money at the same time. Though all these lotteries look very much like gambling, and there is only a "chance" of making money, still it is true that we link the two things together. Of course, there is the kingdom of Monaco which supports itself on the proceeds of gambling. But judging by common sense, gambling may ruin your family or the country, while to save the country you have to make a little sacrifice — do something quite different at least from making money. Yet in China today we have found that the two have certain features in common, though we are still in the experimental stage.

Then there is another small fantasy: You do not need a white ray, but by means of a few advertisements, a few anonymous letters or a few articles written under pseudonyms can kill your enemy without staining your foreign suit or house with blood. By doing so, in fact, you win fame and wealth. This is also in the experimental stage, and we cannot say what the result will be, but if we look through the existing histories of literature and art we shall not find a single such case. So probably this will prove a vain effort too.

> Wild gambling saves the state,
> And lust will bring you immortality;
> With folded hands you kill your enemy,
> By spreading rumours you win property.

If anyone wants to compile another book of famous rhymes ancient and modern, he might, I think, include these four lines.

August 4, 1933

KICKING

Two months ago I spoke about "Pushing." This time it is "Kicking."

According to the *Shen Bao* of the ninth of this month, on the evening of the sixth three lacquer-workers, Liu Mingshan, Yang Akun and Gu Hongsheng, were enjoying the breeze on the Butterfield and Swire Wharf in the Bund in the French Concession, when a police patrol drove away some gamblers near them. Liu and Gu were knocked into the water by a Russian policeman, and Liu was drowned. According to the Russian, of course: "He fell in himself." But Gu in his evidence said:

> I went with Liu and Yang to the wharf to get some breeze. Liu was sitting on the ground by an iron bench . . . and I was standing beside him. . . . When the Russian policeman came and kicked him, Liu stood up to get out of the way. Then another kick made him fall into the water. I wanted to pull him out, but it was too late. When I turned to grab that Russian, he shoved me into the water too. But I was saved.

"Why did he kick him?" asked the judge.

"I don't know," said Gu.

To "push," you have to raise your hand. But there is no need to take such trouble for the lower orders, and here "kicking" comes in. In Shanghai there are experts in kicking: the Indian police, the Annamese police, and now the White Russian police, who use the tactics employed in tsarist days against the Jews on us here. After all, we

are people who "swallow insults." So provided we do not
"fall in," we generally pass it off with a laugh, or some
such remark as: "I've eaten a foreign ham!"

After the Miaos were defeated they fled to the mountains, driven there by our Yellow Emperor. When the
Southern Song Dynasty fell, the last survivors fled to
the sea, where it is said they were driven by our emperor
Genghis Khan. And there in the end Lu Xiufu leaped
into the sea with the infant emperor on his back. So we
Chinese have long had this tradition of falling into the
water ourselves.

Some philanthropists say that the only things free to
the poor in this world are water and air. This is not
true, however. For in fact how can the poor have the
same water and air as others? If they are enjoying the
breeze on a wharf, they may be kicked into the water for
no reason and drowned. If they try to help a friend or
catch the criminal, they are pushed in themselves. If
everyone comes to help, they may be suspected of anti-
imperialism; and while of course this is not forbidden
in China, we must be on our guard lest "reactionary elements take this chance to stir up trouble." In each case
the result is a kick or a push, and you end up in the water.

Time marches on, and today there are steamboats and
aeroplanes everywhere. If the last emperor of Song were
alive now, he would certainly not have to jump into the
sea, but could go abroad while the common people fell
into the water in his place.

Yet simple as this is, it is complicated too, which is
why the lacquer-worker Gu answered, "I don't know."

August 10, 1933

"PESSIMISM IN THE CHINESE WORLD OF LETTERS"

Some gentle men of letters are particularly prone to shed tears. They say that writing has been as chaotic of late as the fighting between warlords, and therefore they cannot help lamenting. What upsets them most is slander.

Actually ever since men stopped hiding their works in the mountains for posterity and the "forum" of letters came into existence, it was inevitable that there should be tussles, and even abuse and slander. We can pass over the Ming Dynasty as too remote. In the Qing Dynasty, Zhang Shizhai and Yuan Zicai, Li Chunke and Zhao Huishu* were as inimical as water and fire. Later there was the fight between the *People's News* and the *New People's Gazette*** and that between the *New Youth* group and others, all of them very fierce fights. At the time, too, outsiders shook their heads and sighed. But the issue did not become clear till some time had passed, and by then the blood on the battlefield had been washed away by rain and dew, and those who followed imagined there had been peace in the previous generation's world of letters. The same is true abroad. Nowadays most of us simply know that Hugo and Hauptmann are outstanding writers, unaware that there were arrests and fights in the theatre when their plays were first performed. In fact

---

* A historian, a poet and two calligraphers who were jealous rivals.

** Two late Qing Dynasty papers, one advocating a republic, the other a constitutional monarchy.

some more detailed histories of literature have pictures of these fights.

So whether in China or abroad, in times ancient or modern, there is bound to be some chaos in the world of letters, which makes gentle literati feel "pessimistic." Still, many so-called writers and their works are bound to perish, and only those who deserve to survive will live on, to show that the world of letters is a proper place after all. In fact it is these pessimists who increase the chaos by saying there is reason on both sides, without examining the situation or passing censure, but considering all writers birds of one feather. This is no way to end the chaos. But not everything is like that: there are bound to be some clear distinctions between right and wrong. Remember Lin Qinnan's stories attacking the literary revolution, which were written not so long ago — where are they now?

The recent slander does seem quite a cut above the ordinary, yet actually it is no worse than that of old, as is shown by the tales which have come down about the persecution of writers at the start of the Qing Dynasty. Besides, those who play at this game are not necessarily writers. Nine out of ten of them profess to be authors, but in spite of their trade-signs their lack of genuine goods shows that these are brigands selling dumplings of stolen human flesh. If some of them happen by any chance to have a smattering of learning, they are now revealed in their true colours and expose their own degeneration. This is not what makes for chaos in the world of letters. On the contrary, it makes for increasing clarity and lucidity.

There is no putting back the clock, and no need for pessimism in the world of letters. Pessimism comes when fence-sitters refuse to find out the rights of a case, yet insist on taking an interest in letters, or remain decadent.

August 10, 1933

SHANGHAI GIRLS

If you live in Shanghai, it pays better to be smart than
dowdy. If your clothes are old, bus-conductors may
not stop when you ask them, park attendants may inspect
your tickets with special care, and the gate-keepers of
big houses or hotels may not admit you by the main
door. That is why some men do not mind living in poky
lodgings infested by bedbugs, but insist on pressing their
trousers under the pillow each night so that the creases
are sharp the next day.

But it pays even better to be a well-dressed woman.
That is most evident in the shops, where the assistants
are extremely patient no matter how long the customers
go on picking and choosing, unable to make up their
minds. Of course, if they take too long the penalty is
a little mockery or mild flirtation. If the women will
not have this, they may receive the usual treatment —
contemptuous looks.

Those females accustomed to life in Shanghai soon
become well aware of the glory of all their sex, knowing
at the same time the danger inherent in it. Hence the
manner of fashionable women is both provocative and
wary, seductive and on the defensive. They appear
friendly yet hostile to the opposite sex, pleased and angry
simultaneously. And adolescent girls are also infected
by this manner. We sometimes see them shopping, their
heads on one side, pretending to be angry, as if face to
face with some enemy. Of course the assistants can flirt
with them, too, just as they do with grown women; and

the girls understand the significance of this flirting. In brief, they mature early.

Yet in the daily papers we often see news of the abduction of small girls or rape.

It is not only the demon king in the *Pilgrimage to the West* who insists, when he wants human flesh, on eating boys and girls. In the homes of the rich and great here on earth, they have always taken young girls to wait on them, satisfy their lust, show their superiority, seek immortality and restore their vitality, just as those who are tired of ordinary rich fare like sucking-pigs or tippy tea. Today this is true of shopkeepers and workmen as well; but it is the result of the frustration of their life, and should be compared with the search of starving men for roots and bark. It has nothing in common with the way in which the rich and great satisfy their lust.

But in brief, even young girls in China are in danger.

This danger makes them mature even earlier, so that in spirit they are women, while their bodies are still those of children. The Russian writer Sologub once created a girl of this type, describing her as a child with grown-up eyes. Our Chinese writers, though, use different, approving epithets "chic and petite."

August 12, 1933

SHANGHAI CHILDREN

Last year, because of the fighting, the neighbourhood round North Sichuan Road outside the International Settlement was quiet for many months. This year it is as lively as ever again: the shops have moved back from the French Concession, the cinemas have been open for some time, and in the parks you often see lovers strolling hand in hand, which was not the case last summer.

Walk into any lane in the residential district, and you will see buckets of night-soil, portable kitchens, flies swarming in all directions and children milling around, some engaged in active devilry, others swearing like experts — a microcosm of utter chaos. On the main roads, however, your eyes are caught by the splendid, lively foreign children playing or walking — you see scarcely any Chinese children at all. Not that there are none, but with their tattered clothes and lack-lustre expression they pale into insignificance beside the others.

The main run of Chinese families seem to have two ways only of bringing up children. The first is to let them run wild without any control, allowed to swear or even fight. Standing before or inside their own gates they are petty tyrants, conquerors; but outside they are like spiders without a web — quite incapable of anything. The second is to treat them with invariable harshness, scolding or beating them till they shrink into their shells and become slaves or marionettes, whereupon their parents praise their "obedience," and preen themselves on the success of their training. When these children are let out, they are like small birds freed for a moment from a cage. They can neither fly, sing nor hop.

At last China too has picture books for the young, the chief characters in which are naturally children. But most of the boys and girls in these books look either savage or stupid. If not actual hooligan types or juvenile delinquents, they are "good children" with bent heads, round shoulders, downcast eyes, and completely blank expressions. This is due in part to the artists' limitations, but still these drawings are based on real children and serve as models for them too. If we look at pictures of children of other lands, the English seem well-behaved and quiet, the Germans boisterous and proud, the Russians sturdy and warm-hearted, the French smart, the Japanese intelligent — none of them show any trace of this Chinese listlessness. The spirit of a land can be seen not only from its poetry, but also from its pictures, including those children's pictures which are generally disregarded.

Stupidity and lethargy are enough to make men decadent. The child's environment determines the future man. Our moderns talk of love, of small families, of independence and of pleasure; but very few raise the question of children's education at home or at school, and of social reform. The men of old merely knew how to be "horses and oxen for their sons and grandsons." That was wrong, of course, but we must admit that it is even more wrong to think only of the present and forget the future, "letting our sons and grandsons remain horses and oxen."

August 12, 1933

A STROLL ON AN AUTUMN
EVENING

Though it is autumn by the calendar, the heat is no less intense than in summer. So when electric lights took the place of the sun I was still out for a stroll.

Dangerous? Danger keys men up, and makes them feel their own strength. Strolling through dangers is an excellent thing.

There is still some quiet in the International Settlement, in the residential district. But the tenements where middle-class Chinese live are like a furnace, with their portable kitchens, two-stringed violins, mahjong games, gramophones, buckets of night-soil and half naked bodies. More seemly are the precincts of the houses of upper-class Chinese or classless foreigners, with their wide avenues, verdant trees, pale awnings, cool breeze and moonlight. But dogs bark there too.

Being country born and bred, I like to hear dogs bark. Distant barking late at night is a wonderful sound. As the ancients said, "The dog barks like a panther." If you happen to be skirting a strange village, a huge hound may leap out at you with a sudden bark, and that keys you up as if you were entering battle — most exciting.

Unfortunately here all I could hear was a lap-dog. It slunk furtively after me with shrill barks: Yap, yap! Disgusting sound.

I gave a cold laugh as I strolled on, because I knew how to shut its mouth. All you have to do is go and say a few words to its master's gate-keeper, or throw it a juicy bone. I could have done either, but did not.

It went on yapping.

Disgusting sound.

I gave a wicked smile as I strolled on, for I had a stone in my hand. As my wicked laugh died away I raised my hand, and got it on the muzzle.

With a yelp it disappeared. I strolled on and on, through a rare solitude.

Autumn was here, and I went on strolling. The yelping went on too, but more furtive than ever. The sound had also changed. It was further away, and even the creature's muzzle was out of sight.

I gave no more cold or wicked laughs, but strolled on listening contentedly to that yelping.

August 14, 1933

CLIMBING AND HURTLING

Professor Liang Shiqiu once remarked that the poor always want to climb, to climb up and up till they become rich. Indeed, not only the poor but even slaves are climbers, who consider themselves as immortals when their chance comes. So of course the world is at peace.

Though very few are able to climb to the top, each thinks he will be the one. Then naturally they remain contented with their lot as ploughmen, peasants, dung-collectors or poor teachers. Hard-working and thrifty, saddled with a miserable fate, they battle with nature and climb up, up, up for all they are worth. But there are so many climbers that the one path up is fearfully crowded. The simple souls who climb according to the rules seldom get to the top. The intelligent who have drive push them aside or down, to tread on them and climb up over their shoulders and heads. Most people simply climb, convinced that their enemies are not above but beside them — the men who are climbing with them. Most of them will put up with anything as they struggle up step by step on hands and knees, only to be pushed back again. But they climb on once more, never stopping for a rest.

However, as there are so many climbers and so few get to the top, by degrees good men lose hope. And thus in the end there may be a passive revolt. That is why in addition to climbing, hurtling was invented.

This happens when you know your lot is too hard and want to stand up. Then a shout goes up behind you: Hurtle through! And while your numbed legs are still trembling, someone hurtles past. This is much easier than climbing as there is no need to use your hands or knees: just bend forward and hurtle past. If you hurtle well, you will get half a million dollars, wives, wealth, children and status. If badly, at the worst you will have a fall and land on the ground. But that does not matter, as you were on the ground to begin with, and you can start climbing again. Besides, some people just hurtle for the fun of it, and are not afraid of falling.

Climbing is a time-honoured custom, whether from the position of the humblest scholar to the first in the palace test, or from a pimp to a compradore. But hurtling seems to be a recent invention. If we look into the matter, probably the nearest thing to this in ancient times was when "the young lady threw a silk ball."* When the young lady was about to throw the silk ball, all stout fellows who wanted to marry looked up, gaping, with mouths watering profusely. Unfortunately the ancients were too stupid to insist on seeing the colour of their money, otherwise they could surely have raked in tens of thousands.

The fewer the chances for climbers, the more men try to hurtle. And every day those already at the top provide them with chances to do so, bidding them make a little outlay, and promising them that they will enjoy fame and profit and lead the life of immortals. So though there is even less chance of successful hurtling than of climbing to the top, everybody wants to try his luck. After climbing they hurtle, and if hurtling fails they go back to climbing. . . . And so it goes on till their dying day.

August 16, 1933

---

* According to popular lore, a rich girl threw a silk ball into the street, promising to marry the suitor who caught it.

THE CRISIS OF THE ESSAY

A month or so ago I seem to have read an obituary in some paper, which said that the deceased had been a well-known collector of bric-a-brac, and ended by expressing the fear that with his death all China's collectors of curios had died.

Unfortunately I did not pay much attention at the time, so I have forgotten the name of the paper and the collector.

Most young people today may not know what is meant by "bric-à-brac." But those from old families, who number scholar-dilettantes among their forbears and have not gone down too much in the world or sold the heirlooms they consider useless to the rag-and-bone man, may find among their dust-shrouded junk a tiny mirror on a stand, a curious rock, figures carved in bamboo, animals cut in old jade, or bronze three-legged toads with a green patina. Such things are bric-à-brac. In the days when these objects were set out in the study, each had its own splendid title. The three-legged toad, for instance, might be called "The Toad-in-the-Moon Ink-pot." The last collector would certainly know all these names, but today they have disappeared with the glory of the objects they adorned.

Of course bric-à-brac was not for the poor, but neither was it displayed in the homes of high officials or millionaires, who like miniature gardens of pearls and jade, or polychrome porcelain. Bric-à-brac was simply a "highbrow hobby" of the literati, who owned at least a dozen acres of fertile land outside, and several quiet and tasteful studies at home. Even if a scholar moved to Shanghai, he must live in relative leisure. He would have a hotel room booked indefinitely, with a writing desk and an opium couch, and when he had smoked his fill and felt at peace, he would fondle and enjoy his curios. But today this state of affairs has foundered in the evil tide of world events, like a small boat on an angry sea.

Even in "times of peace and prosperity" though, bric-à-brac never had any real importance. A square inch of ivory engraved with the *Preface to the Orchid Pavilion* is still called a "work of art," but if you hang it on the Great Wall or lay it at the feet of some eighteen-foot Buddha at Yungang, it is too small to see; and even if enthusiasts point it out, it simply looks ridiculous. Besides, now that wind and sand buffet our faces and wolves and tigers swarm, who has time to appreciate the amber pendant on a fan, or a jade ring? To please the eye, men want huge buildings that will tower in the wind and sand: solidity and greatness, not a fine finish. For satisfaction, they want daggers and javelins: sharpness and strength, not elegance.

In art, the demand for bric-à-brac has been shattered like a dream, as the author of that obituary knew for himself. But the demand for essays and short articles — the bric-à-brac of literature — is growing stronger and stronger. Those who make the demand imagine that by means of soft reproaches and gentle groans they can refine rough hearts and make them polished. They want men to lose themselves so completely in the *Selected Essays of the Six Dynasties* that they will forget they are clinging to a tree only the top of which remains above the flood.

But all we need just now is struggle and battle.

And the continued existence of short articles and essays depends solely on struggle and battle. The "idle talk" of the Jin Dynasty died out with that regime. At the

end of the Tang Dynasty poetry degenerated, but short
prose compositions flourished. Still, Luo Yin's *Traduc-
tions* consists almost entirely of indignant tirades. And
while Pi Rixiu and Lu Guimeng considered themselves as hermits and were so called by others, if we
read the essays in their collections, far from having forgotten the world they are the bright spot and spearhead
in a welter of rubbish. Though the essays of the late
Ming Dynasty are rather decadent, they are not entirely
devoted to the wind and the moon, but embody resentment, satire, attacks and destruction. This type of writing touched the Manchu rulers and their ministers on
the raw, and it took the sword-points of many tyrant-
aiding generals and the pen-points of many collabora-
tionist scholars before they finally crushed it in the reign
of Qian Long. What followed was bric-à-brac.

Naturally bric-à-brac could not go too far. But during the May 4th Movement it did develop, when
short prose compositions were almost more successful
than novels, plays or poetry. Certainly these contained
some struggle and battle, but as English essays were
often taken as models, there was also a little humour
and dignity. Sometimes the style was mannered and
well-knit too, to show the old literature that what it had
considered its monopoly could be achieved equally well
in vernacular writing. After that the path forward was
quite obviously sharper struggle and battle, grounded as
it was in the "literary revolution" and the "ideological
revolution." The trend today, however, is to encourage
those features held in common with the old essays —
tolerance, elegance, preciosity — to provide bric-à-brac
for discriminating scholars. It is hoped, moreover, that
if young people learn to enjoy this bric-à-brac, their
roughness will turn into elegance.

But today there are no more big writing desks. And
although opium is now sold openly, opium pipes are
banned, so that smoking is still far from easy. To hope

that the people in fighting zones or famine areas will enjoy literary bric-à-brac is, as everyone knows, an even stranger illusion. Though this type of writing is so fashionable at present in Shanghai, where the gossip of teashops and taverns fills all the small papers, its authors are actually in the same plight as those light women who no longer ply their trade at home but have to put on powder and paint and mince out to the main roads by night.

This is how we have reached a crisis in essay-writing. But I use the word crisis in the medical sense, as the parting of the ways between life and death, which may lead straight to death or to recovery. Works which are opiates will perish along with those who administer or take narcotics. The essays which live on must be daggers and javelins which, with their readers, can hew out a blood-stained path to a new life. Undoubtedly they may also bring pleasure and relaxation, but they are not "bric-à-brac," much less consolations or opiates. The pleasure and relaxation they provide are a form of sustenance, a preparation for labour and for battle.

August 27, 1933

SOME THOUGHTS IN EARLY
AUTUMN

On the smallish patch of ground outside the door two armies of ants are fighting.

The name of Eroshenko, the writer of folk tales, is fading from readers' memories, but I have just remembered a strange fear he had. When in Beijing he once told me quite seriously, "I am afraid that in future they may invent some method by which — in no time at all — men can be turned into fighting machines."

Such a method was actually invented long ago. Only it is rather involved, not something that takes "no time at all." If we look at foreign books and toys for children, the main purpose of which is to teach them how to use weapons, we can see that here is the equipment for making fighting machines, and the process must start with innocent children.

Not only human beings but insects know this. There is a "soldier" ant which does not make nests or look for food, but spends all its life attacking other ants and seizing their young to be its slaves. But the strange thing is that it will not capture grown-up ants, because they are difficult to re-educate. It invariably takes young ants or larvae to grow up in its robber's den with no memory of the past, to be stupid, loyal slaves for ever. For not only will these serve it, but when the soldier goes out on a raid they will follow to help carry the young ants and larvae of their own kind which it attacks.

But you cannot make one simple rule like this for

human beings. That is why men are "the flower of creation."

Yet the manufacturers will not give up. When the children grow up, they not only lose their innocence but become dull and stupid too, as we see so often. The economic depression makes publishers unwilling to publish big volumes on science or literature, but school textbooks and children's books flood the market like the Yellow River breaking through its dam. What are these books about? What will they do to our children? I have seen no comments on these questions from those warlike critics, for it seems few men are interested in the future.

When the papers carry little news about the disarmament conference, it shows that war is popular in China; and the indifference to such news as there is shows that it goes against our inclinations. Of course wars must be fought, and to follow soldier ants to carry the larvae of the defeated is a sort of triumph for slaves. But for men, "the flower of creation," this is surely not enough. We must fight, certainly. We must smash the ant-heaps which manufacture war machines, smash the sugared pills which poison our children's minds, smash the plots to destroy our future. This alone is a worthy task for human fighters.

August 28, 1933

THE SECRET OF BEING A JOKER

Kierkegaard* is a Dane with a gloomy outlook on life, whose works always breathe indignation. But he says some amusing things too, as in the passage below:

A theatre catches fire. The clown steps to the front of the stage to announce the fact to the audience, who think it a joke and applaud. Then the clown announces again that there is a fire, but they roar with laughter and clap more loudly than ever. No doubt the world will end amid the general applause of these laughter-loving people who take everything as a joke.

What amuses me, however, is not this passage alone but the way it reminds me of these jokers' cunning. When there is a job to be done, they help out; when their masters are bent on crime, they become accomplices. But they help in such a way that in case of bloodshed no bloodstain is found on them, nor any reek of blood.

For instance, if something serious has happened and everyone is taking it seriously, the joker starts clowning to make the thing look funny, or exaggerates some irrelevant aspects of it to distract attention. This is known as "playing the fool." If murder has been done, he describes the scene of the crime and the hard work of the detectives. If the one killed is a woman, so much the better: he can refer to her as "the lovely corpse" or introduce her diary. If it is an assassination, he tells the life story of the victim, relates his love affairs and the

---

* Sören Azbye Kierkegaard (1813-1855), Danish philosopher and theologian.

anecdotes about him. . . . Passions are bound to cool down eventually, but cold water — or, to be more refined, green tea — will speed up the cooling-off process. Then this fellow playing the fool becomes a man of letters.

If a serious alarm is raised before men have grown completely apathetic, of course that is bad for the murderer. But then the joker can play the fool again, cracking jokes and making faces on one side, so that the man who has raised the alarm looks like a clown himself to everyone, and his warnings sound laughable. The joker shrinks and shivers to show how rich and mighty the other is. He bows and sighs to show the other's pride. Then the man who raised the alarm is considered a hypocrite. Luckily most of these jokers are men: otherwise they could accuse the one who gives the warning of attempted seduction, making public a great many indecent details, and finally pretend to kill themselves for shame. When there are jokers all around, the most serious talk loses its force and amid the suspicion and laughter an end is made of everything unfavourable to the murderer. This time the joker appears as a moralist.

When there are no incidents of this kind, jokers collect tittle-tattle for the newspaper supplements every week or ten days with which to stuff readers' heads. After reading this for six months or a year, your mind is stocked with stories of how a certain great man plays mahjong or a certain film star sneezes. This is naturally quite amusing. But the world will come to an end amid the laughter of these laughter-loving people.

August 28, 1933

FROM DEAFNESS TO DUMBNESS

The doctors tell us that many of those who are dumb have nothing wrong with their throats and tongues. Having been born deaf, however, and unable to hear grown-ups talk, they had nothing to imitate. And thinking that all other people just opened their mouths to gibber, they did the same. So Brandes, deploring the decline of Danish literature, says that original writing has virtually died out, and no human or social problems can rouse any interest or any discussion except in the papers and magazines. There is no notably original writing. And on top of that, practically no attention is paid to introducing foreign culture. So spiritual deafness leads to dumbness. (See his preface to the first volume of *Mainstreams in the Literature of the Nineteenth Century*.)

This criticism may be applied to literary circles in China, and it is not fair to hold our oppressors entirely responsible: the pioneers of the May 4th Movement and its later opponents should take their share of the blame. The former were so anxious for quick results that they did not translate any worth-while books, while the latter rounded on translators and abused them as matchmakers. Some young people lent a helping hand too, going so far at one time as to accuse translators of "showing off" when they gave the original proper names in footnotes for the convenience of readers.

What is the position today? There are quite a few three-roomed bookshops on Fourth Avenue, but the shelves are filled with booklets, and a fat volume is as hard to find as gold in dust. Of course, not all tall, stout fellows are great men, and a flood of words is not necessarily a classic, especially when it includes "cut-outs" from other works. Still, a small "ABC of something or other" cannot embody all learning and art. Though it is true that a stream is not as clean or limpid as a cup of clear water, if you distil part of the stream you will get many cups of clear water.

As a result of years of playing the market, the world of letters is barren; and though literary forms are now in rather better trim, there has been a decline in fighting spirit. By certain shrewd investments and mutual praise, writers win fame in no time; but their desperate bragging only makes their inflated carcases seem more hollow. And they mistake this emptiness for loneliness, and tell readers about it in all seriousness, even displaying their inner putridity as a secret treasure. Of all writing today, prose is comparatively the most successful; but if we look at this year's anthologies, even the three most famous are not up to much, like "sable eked out with dog fur." Children brought up on husks will never be strong, and future achievements will be yet more insignificant, like "der letzte Mensch"* described by Nietzsche.

But all ways of bringing in spiritual sustenance, such as introducing new trends in foreign thought or translating world classics, have been blocked by those who make men deaf and dumb, so that even the flunkeys of foreigners and the protégés of the rich laugh at us sarcastically. They want to stop young people's ears and turn their deafness into dumbness, so that they wither away and become "der letzte Mensch." And they will not stop until all we can read is the pornography sold by pimps and rich men's sons. It is absolutely imperative for writers and translators who are willing to come down to the earth to fight on, and this means doing all we

---

* The last men.

can to bring in some genuine spiritual sustenance for
our young people, and packing those makers of the deaf
and dumb back inside their dark holes and vermilion
gates.

August 29, 1933

MORE THOUGHTS IN EARLY
AUTUMN

During the night of August 30 sharp reports burst out
all around, and at once I imagined "resistance" had
started again. I soon calmed down, however, when I
realized that these were firecrakers. And I wondered
what festival this could be. . . . The next day I found
out from the paper that there had been an eclipse of the
moon, and those sharp reports had been a display of
might on the part of our Chinese brothers and heterodox
brothers (we call ourselves the descendants of the Yellow
Emperor; but since the descendants of Chi You* can
hardly all have died out, I call them our heterodox
brothers) to save the moon from the jaws of the Heavenly
Hound.

A few days before that there had been another very
lively night. Up and down the streets and lanes were
set tables loaded with cakes and water melons, the melons
swarming with flies, aphides and mosquitoes, while at
separate tables monks chanted incantations: *"An-ya-
hong! Hong!"* They were celebrating mass for the dead
and feeding the hungry ghosts. At the Buddhist Feast
of All Souls,** all ghosts, whether hungry or not, hurry
here from the nether regions to see the sights of Shanghai. Then all devout believers act as hosts, asking monks

---

* A legendary leader who was overcome by the Yellow Emperor.
** The fifteenth of the seventh lunar month.

to chant and scatter grains of white rice, to give the spirits a good square meal for once.

As a layman, I have never paid much attention to heaven or the nether regions, but on these occasions I never fail to be struck by the superb imagination and discrimination of those Chinese and heterodox brothers still in the world of men. To mention nothing else, in less than two years the flags of four great provinces and nine small islands have changed colour, and soon another eight islands will follow suit.* Not only are we powerless to save them, but simply raising the subject may get us into trouble. (This sentence after printing was altered into "impossible under the circumstances.") So the most discriminating act is to save the moon; for no matter how loudly the firecrackers go off, the Heavenly Hound will not bite us, and the elders on the moon (if elders there be) will not come forward to stop us or dub us reactionaries. It is the same with saving human beings. Millions of people suffer from war, drought, flood, plagues of locusts . . . but how can the humble folk lucky enough to have escaped this time come to their rescue? Obviously it is much, much better to rescue spirits, which is easy and redounds to your credit like the good deeds of those great ones who celebrate the feast of All Souls and build pagodas. This is what is meant by the saying: "If men take no thought for the future, trouble will beset them now," or by "The superior man attends to great and distant affairs."

Another wise maxim of the ancient sages is, "Though a cook does not cook well, the priest will not take his place." The common people need not raise an outcry,

---

* The four provinces mentioned here are the Northeast Provinces Liaoning, Jilin, Heilongjiang and Rehe (Jehol), which were occupied by the Japanese in 1931. The nine islands are the Nansha Islands; the eight islands are the Xisha Islands; both are Chinese islands in South China Sea; they were occupied by the French and later by the Japanese, and returned to China after the Second World War.

but can leave affairs of state to the rulers of the state. For all the sage emperors and enlightened kings in history, far from despising the common people, have given them an even nobler freedom and right, entrusting to them the entire responsibility for saving the universe and the spirits. This is the foundation of peace, the time-honoured tradition which can hardly be lightly swept aside. Last year, I remember, just after the fighting stopped in Shanghai, when the Japanese troops were by degrees boarding transports or withdrawing into barracks, one night those sharp reports broke out again. This was still the period of "protracted resistance," and the Japanese, who did not understand the essence of our national character, thought another Chinese army had come to recapture that territory. At once they posted sentries and mobilized soldiers, creating perfect chaos until they found out that we were saving the moon and they were clutching at shadows.

"Oh! Oh! *Naruhodo* (I see)."

Overcome with amazement and respect, they resumed their former peaceful dispositions. This year they did not even post sentries, influenced no doubt by China's spiritual culture.

Are invaders and oppressors today like the tyrants of old, who would not even permit their slaves to have hallucinations or dreams?

August 31, 1933

SOME JOTTINGS

The *Shen Bao* of September 20 carried an item of news from Jiashan, some extracts of which are as follows:

Shen Hesheng and his son Linsheng of Dayao Village in this county were kidnapped by the bandit Shi Tang the Younger, who demanded a thirty-thousand-dollar ransom. As the Shens are only moderately well-to-do, the family delayed in taking action. Then the bandits took Shen and his son, with some other victims kidnapped in Jiangsu, to north of Dingpeng, where they tortured them cruelly. Cloth strips, pasted over their backs, were painted with unboiled varnish. When this had dried a little the cloth was pulled off, bringing the men's skin with it and causing such excruciating pain that they screamed for mercy in a heart-rending manner. The local people who saw this took pity on them, and sent the sad news to the Shen family, warning them that unless they paid up immediately the two men were not likely to return alive. The cruelty of these bandits is appalling!

"Torture" stories appear constantly in papers all over the country, yet we shudder only at the time of reading, and very soon forget — for truly this is too much to remember. But methods of torture are certainly not invented in a day, and must be handed down from earlier generations. This method used by Shi Tang the Younger, for instance, is an old one. The literati may scorn such reading, but most of the lower orders know that episode in the *Story of Yue Fei,* in which Qin

Hui wants Yue Fei to admit that he is a traitor and, to extort a confession, uses strips of hemp and glue. Personally, I doubt this talk of unboiled varnish, because varnish takes such a long time to dry.

The invention and improvement of torture is the work of tyrants and sadistic officials. It is, indeed, all they are good for, and they have the time to go into it thoroughly. This is how they awe the people and get rid of traitors. But, as Lao Zi said so well, "If you measure by pecks and bushels, people will rob you of your measures."* Those eligible for torture will start playing the same game. It surely was appalling when Zhang Xianzhong had a man flayed alive. But he had the precedent of Emperor Yong Le, who flayed that "disloyal minister" Jing Qing.**

Slaves brought up on "torture" themselves think that the right treatment for others.

But masters and slaves differ in their view of the effects of torture. The masters and their flunkeys usually have some education and can foresee the probable pain which the enemy will suffer. They can therefore devise new tortures and introduce improvements. All slaves, on the other hand, are bound to be fools. They cannot "judge others by themselves," much less "share the same emotions." Once they are in power, they may use traditional methods, but they are not so cruel as those educated men who have imagination. Serafimovitch in *Iron Stream* describes how some peasants who killed a nobleman's daughter were surprised when her mother wept bitterly. "Why are you crying?" they asked. "Many of our children have died, but we never shed a tear." They were not cruel. They were surprised

---

* Actually this is a quotation from Zhuang Zi.
** Emperor Yong Le usurped the throne from Emperor Jian Wen. Jing Qing, a minister of Emperor Jian Wen, refused to work with the usurper

simply because they did not know how precious a human life could be.

Slaves used to being treated like pigs and dogs assume that men are no different from pigs and dogs.

No wonder, then, that those happy beings who have slaves or semi-slaves fear nothing but a "slave revolt."

To prevent a "slave revolt" they use more torture, and so torture is becoming less and less effective. A firing squad has long ceased to be a novelty, and the display of a head or a corpse can only amuse the populace for a short time. Still there is no decrease in the number of robbers, kidnappers and criminals, and even kidnappers are beginning to use torture. A cruel education makes men indifferent to cruelty. Thus when first some citizens were killed for no reason, a shout of protest was raised; but today a killing is as common as eating or drinking. The people have been conditioned to have thick skins like those scabby, pachydermatous elephants. But precisely on account of these thick skins, they tramp on impervious to cruelty. The sadistic officials and tyrants did not foresee this, and even had they foreseen it they could have done nothing to prevent it.

September 20, 1933

WRITTEN AT RANDOM

We cannot tell what autumn was like in the earliest geological epochs, but in modern times there is little variation from one year to another. If the autumn before last was a stern one, this is a dismal one, and it looks as if the life of this earth is going to be considerably shorter than the astronomers predicted. Human affairs change most rapidly, however, and poets in particular are struck by the differences between different autumns, conveying them in tragic or pathetic language to ordinary mortals, to enable them to muddle along together. This is also the reason for the spate of new poems.

The autumn before last did seem a tragic one. Townsfolk raised money, boys and girls risked their necks, and battle cries poured from the poets' pens, as if they were determined to "lay down brushes and take up spears." As poets are sensitive souls, who have known from the start that their compatriots are empty-handed and unarmed, all they can do is praise those who die for the country; and that accounts for the emptiness which we sense hidden in their tragic notes. I remember a passage from "Oh, Countrymen, Awake!" a poem by Mr. Shao Guanhua published in the *Republic Daily:*

> *Oh, countrymen, awake!*
> *Kick open all faint hearts*
> *And feeble minds.*
> *See where*
> *Our countrymen's blood spurts out,*
> *Our countrymen's flesh is hacked,*
> *Our countrymen's corpses are hanging!*

357

When drums first roll at the front before an advance, the effect may be "exciting." But when they roll a second time, the effect is less stimulating, and by the third time the soldiers are exhausted. While if drums continue to roll when no preparations are being made for battle, they may have the reverse effect and make men who are tense relax. That is why I compare this to "wailing at a funeral." It makes an excellent send-off for the dead, conclusion for a burial, and means by which the survivors may live on in peace and happiness in new surroundings. Throughout our past literature there have been tragic essays penned to help turn "enemy" into "emperor" and "rebel" into "royal," though naturally not all come from the same hand. In the eyes of poets, however, it appears such talk is nothing but "frenzied barking."

Still, facts are even more ruthless than the critics. In a mere two years, the volunteer troops have become "bandits,"* and some of the "heroes of the resistance" have settled down in Suzhou,** while there is even doubt about the war funds.*** On the anniversary of September 18 in the Chinese Settlement, prison vans followed the armed patrols on their rounds, not in order to arrest enemies or traitors, but as a splendid conveyance thoughtfully provided for any "reactionaries" who "meant to seize the chance to stir up trouble." The weather was wretched too, with high winds and driving rain. The papers said this "cyclone" was heaven and earth weeping over China, but between heaven and earth — in the world of men — the day passed "peacefully."

So this has become a "peaceful" if somewhat dispirited autumn, like the season when a mourner lays aside

---

* The Kuomintang described as "bandits" those guerrillas who continued to resist the Japanese in the Northeast.
** Su Bingwen, who fought in the Northeast.
*** People all over China contributed money for the war, but much of this was embezzled.

mourning. Poets, however, find such times suit them best. I heard low groans and comfortable words in "Autumn Dusk," published in *Current News* on September 25 and by the author of "Oh, Countrymen, Awake!"

> Every autumn my spirits droop, and at dusk in autumn I shed tears. I am well aware that my depression is whipped up by the buffeting autumn wind, and it dawns on me that my surroundings are absolutely appropriate to autumn. Softly I caress the sound waves which autumn sends out to Nature. I know that fate has made me an "autumnal" man. . . .

In China today we often see fashionable young ladies chased by hooligans or young revolutionaries chased by detectives. We seldom see men of letters or writers chased. If we could do a little sleuthing for a few months or years, we should discover how many poets turn somersaults to suit the times.

Of course, a live man wants to go on living. Even slaves, the lowest of the low, struggle to survive. But at least they know they are slaves. They endure hardships, burn with resentment and struggle to free themselves — sometimes they succeed in doing so. Even if defeated for a time and fettered again, they are simply slaves. But utterly damned are those who try to find "beauty" in slavery, praising and caressing it or being intoxicated by it, for they try to reconcile themselves and others to being slaves for ever. This slight difference between slaves gives rise to the difference in society between peace and disturbances, and the striking difference in the world of letters between escapist and fighting literature.

September 27, 1933

TEA DRINKING

When a certain department store had another sale, I went and bought two ounces of good tea at twenty cents an ounce. To start with I brewed a whole pot, and wrapped it in a padded jacket to keep it warm. But when I drank the tea with due respect, it tasted much the same as my ordinary tea. The colour was muddy too.

I realized this was my mistake. Good tea should be drunk from a bowl with a lid. So that was what I did next. And indeed, after I had brewed the tea this way it was clear and sweet, faintly fragrant yet slightly bitter. Yes, this really was good tea. It required tranquillity and leisure though, and as I was in the middle of writing "Living on Religion," when I picked up the bowl to drink the aroma had somehow got lost again and once more it tasted just like ordinary tea.

To have good tea and be able to appreciate it is one of the "refined pleasures." But in order to enjoy this one must have leisure and a trained, connoisseur's palate. Judging from this trifling experience, I imagine that when a man doing heavy manual labour is thirsty, even if you give him the choicest "Dragon-well" tips or "Pearly-orchid,"* he will not find them very different from hot water. The same is true, in fact, of "autumn ennui." Sensitive souls and literary men may feel: "Ah, this autumn ennui!" Wind and rain, clouds and shine cut them to the heart, and this is one of their "refined

_____
* Two of the finest brands of tea.

360

pleasures." But old peasants simply know that this is the season for getting in the rice.

Thus it is sometimes taken for granted that such refined sensitivity is not for men of common clay, but is a hall-mark of the upper-class elite. I fear this means that this hall-mark is pretty well finished. While sensitivity to pain makes us suffer, it also enables us to guard against danger. A man lacking this would feel nothing even if he were stabbed in the back, and would not understand what had happened even after he lost all his blood and collapsed. If such sensitivity is highly developed, how-ever, he will not only feel a small thorn through his clothes, but the seams of his garments, too, and the stuff they are made of. Then unless he wears a "seamless divine garment," he will feel pricked all over and life will become quite unbearable. Naturally this does not apply to those who simply pose as hypersensitive.

Refined and sensitive feelings are obviously more ad-vanced than numbed obtuseness, but they must serve evolution. If they fail to do so, or are actually harmful, they are aberrations which will soon die out. If we com-pare these elegant gentlemen with their refined plea-sures and autumn ennui with the coarse fellows in rags who eat rough fare, it is quite clear which will survive. So as I drink my tea and look up at the autumn sky, I think it is just as well that I cannot appreciate good tea and have no autumn ennui.

September 30, 1933

PROHIBITION AND MANUFACTURE

I see from the paper that because so many pencils and fountain-pens are being imported, some districts have started prohibiting their use and are using brushes instead.

We need not argue pedantically that aeroplanes, guns, American cotton and American wheat are not Chinese products either. Let us just stick to pens.

We need not talk either about those famous men who write big characters and paint traditional paintings. Let us just stick to those who do practical work. For them, the brush is most inconvenient. They could do without the ink-stone and ink-slab and use liquid ink instead, but liquid ink is not made in China either. Furthermore, judging by my own experience, you cannot use liquid ink all the time for a brush, because after a few thousand words the brush becomes too clogged to write. If you use an ink-stone and grind your own ink, then spread out your paper and pick up your brush, suppose you are a student taking down lecture notes, your speed will be one-third less than with a pen. You will either have to stop taking notes, or ask the lecturer to go more slowly. In other words, one-third of your time will be wasted.

"Convenience" is not the same as laziness, but means that we can do more in the same amount of time. It means saving time and making a more effective use of our brief span of life: in other words, lengthening our life. When the ancients said, "The man is not grinding the ink, but the ink is grinding the man," they were lamenting the amount of time wasted in writing, and the fountain-pen was invented to make good this loss.

But it can exist only in places where they value time and human lives. As China is not such a place, it cannot be a Chinese product. China has records of imports and exports, but no record of the population. Parents expend endless material and energy to bring up a single child, yet boys and girls often disappear without arousing any comment. Of course fleeting time is even less important, and no doubt we should count ourselves lucky to be alive at all to wield a brush.

In Japan they used to use brushes too, just as in China. But in Japan now brushes have virtually gone out, and pencils or fountain-pens have taken their place, while there are even many copy-books for practice in using these pens. The reason is that this is more convenient and saves time. Are they not afraid of upsetting their trade balance then? No, they manufacture pens themselves, and even export them to China.

When a good thing is not a national product, China prohibits it, whereas Japan learns to manufacture it. This is where our two countries differ.

September 30, 1933

CIRCUS SHOWS

I like to watch "circus shows."

As they move from place to place, you find the same shows everywhere. Their essential stock-in-trade consists of two things: a black bear and a child.

The bear is so starved and thin, it has barely enough strength to move. Of course you cannot allow it to be strong, or it would get out of control. Half dead and alive as it is, its nose has still to be pierced with an iron ring to which a rope is attached, and by this it is dragged along to do its tricks. Sometimes it is fed with a scrap of bread soaked in water; but even so the spoon is held so high that the bear has to stand on its hind legs, and it must crane its neck and open its mouth for a long time before it can get this sop. Then the showman collects some money.

No one in China has ever told us where these bears come from. According to investigations made by Westerners, they are caught as cubs in the mountains; and big bears are no good, for once they are grown you cannot change their savage nature. Even small ones must be "trained," and the "training" consists of beating and starving, until finally they die of ill-treatment. I imagine this is true. While the bear is still alive and performing, we can see it is so shrivelled it no longer looks like a bear. Indeed in some places it is called a "dog-bear," showing the utter contempt in which it is held.

The child has a bad time of it too during the show. While the man tramples on his belly or twists his arms, he looks as if in agony or great trouble, or bearing too heavy a burden, and begs the audience to rescue him. Six coins, five coins, another four, three more. . . . Then the showman collects more money.

Of course the boy is trained too. His look of agony is only put on, for he is in league with the man. But this does not stop them making money.

The show starts in the afternoon when a gong is beaten, and goes on till evening when the spectators scatter, some of them having paid, some not.

When the show ends I walk away, thinking to myself: Of the two creatures out of which they make money, the first is ill-treated till it dies, when another small bear is found. When the other has grown up he looks for another small boy and cub, and puts on the same old show.

The whole business is so simple, if you think of it, that it seems completely futile. Still I keep on going to these shows. What else is there for me to see, gentlemen?

October 1, 1933

THINKING OF THE PAST

Recalling the end of the reign of Guang Xu*

I would like to say some good words about men who are gone, though I am not, I think, "hankering after dead bones."

By men who are gone I mean the "modern clique" at the end of the reign of Guang Xu, who were known at the beginning of the Republic as the "old modern clique." Convinced that they had learned their lesson after the 1894 defeat,** they wanted "reforms." Even middle-aged men in their thirties and forties started studying mathematics and chemistry, and tried to learn English and Japanese, not ashamed to let others hear them reading laboriously aloud with odd accents and odd expressions. Their aim was to study "foreign books," and they wanted to do so because that would help to make China rich and strong. Today on the old book-stalls you may still come across volumes from the "Rich and Strong Library," books which were all the rage at the time like the *Dictionary of Useful Terms* and *Basic English* today. Even Zhang Zhidong,*** who was brought up on *bagu* essays, tried to include all sorts of translated books in the *Handbook of Bibliography* which he asked Miao Quansun to write for him. This just shows the strength of the reformation movement.

But now the position has changed. There are some

---

* 1875-1908.
** China was defeated in the Sino-Japanese war.
*** A late Qing official who advocated studying Western science.

new young men, brought up quite differently from the
"old modern clique," who have never been contaminated
by *bagu* essays but come out of modern schools — they
are not experts in the Chinese classics either. Yet they
are learning the old hieroglyphic script, writing the classical verses on given rhymes, and advising others to read
Zhuang Zi and *Wen Xuan.* They make their own
hand-printed stationery, write the modern verse according to definite patterns, and, apart from their interest in
modern poetry, have exactly the same tastes as the literati
at the start of Guang Xu's reign. The only difference
is that they have no queues and sometimes wear Western
clothes.

Lately we have often heard the saying: "You cannot
put new wine in old bottles." Actually this is not so.
You can put new wine in old bottles and old wine in
new bottles. If you do not believe me, try changing
Chinese wine and brandy. The Chinese wine in brandy
bottles will still be Chinese wine. This simple experi-
ment shows that not only can old folk-tunes be fitted
with new words, but that in these modern youths there
may well lurk vestiges of conservatism and obscurantism.

Although the "old modern clique" did not know very
much, they had a goal: to make China rich and strong.
So they were firm and matter-of-fact. Though they had
odd accents and expressions when they spoke a foreign
language, they had a goal: to find the means to become
rich and strong. So they were serious and enthusiastic.
After the spread of anti-Manchu ideas, many of them
turned revolutionary, again because they wanted China
to be rich and strong and felt the first step was to oppose
Manchu rule.

The Manchu rule has long since been overthrown and
the May 4th Movement is also a thing of the past;
so today we have old hieroglyphics, *Zhuang Zi, Wen
Xuan*, old-fashioned stationery, and modern verse written
to definite patterns. For today we have a new aim: to

keep our footing in this world with our "ancient culture." If we can really do this, that will be unprecedented in the "struggle for existence."

October 1, 1933

THE QUINTESSENCE OF WORLDLY
WISDOM

It is certainly hard to live in this world. To "lack worldly wisdom" is not good, but neither is it good to have "too much worldly wisdom." Apparently "worldly wisdom" is like revolution. "A revolution is needed, but it should not be too radical." You need some worldly wisdom, but not too much.

My experience is that when a man is accused of having "too much worldly wisdom," he actually "lacks worldly wisdom."

Suppose I give the young advice like this:

"If you meet with social injustice, on no account rush forward to say what is right. Otherwise on your own head be it — you may actually be called a reactionary. If someone is wronged or slandered, even if you know he is a good man, on no account rush forward to explain or argue his case. Otherwise you may be called his relative or accused of taking bribes, while if he is a "she" you will be suspected of being her lover, and if he has any reputation you will be considered one of his hangers-on. Take myself, for example. When I wrote a preface for a collection of letters by a lady who was no relative, they said she was my cousin. When I introduced a few scientific theories of literature and art, they said I had accepted Russian roubles. In China today, kin and cash are all-important. Life has taught us this lesson. And therefore it is not strange if men are accustomed to it and think no one can dispense with such connections.

"Some men are not truly convinced of this, however, and merely say it for fun, to be amusing. If someone is sliced to pieces because of rumours, like Zheng Man at the end of the Ming Dynasty, it does not affect you in any way. It is not so important as telling a good story. If you start arguing, you will spoil the other fellow's fun, and it will be the worse for you in the end. I had such an experience myself over ten years ago, when I was a 'bureaucrat' in the Ministry of Education. I often heard my colleagues say that the students of a certain girls' school could be hired as prostitutes — they even gave details of the address and the number of the house. One day I happened to be passing that street, and as men always have a good memory for mischief, I remembered this and looked carefully at that particular house. But it consisted of a small plot of ground with a large well and a tumbledown shack, where a few men from Shandong sold water — it could have no other conceivable use. Accordingly, next time the subject came up, I said what I had seen. But to my surprise their smiles vanished, they left in a bad temper, and for two or three months after that no one talked to me. Not till later did I realize that I should not have spoiled their fun.

"So don't worry about right and wrong, straight and crooked; but try to agree with everyone. Of course, keeping silent is better still, and best of all is to give no sign on your face of what you are thinking in your heart. . . ."

This is the essence of how to get on in the world. If the Yellow River does not wet your feet and bombs do not fall beside you, you can be sure of plain sailing all your life. But I am afraid young people may not think this is good; and the middle-aged or elderly may think I am giving their children harmful advice. Too bad! The great pains I have taken have been wasted.

But to say that China today is the same as in the good old days of Tang and Yu also smacks of "worldly wisdom." Not counting what we see and hear for ourselves, just by reading the papers we can tell that there is much injustice in the world, and many people with grievances. But except on the rare occasions when a colleague, fellow provincial or clansman may remark what a shame it is, we would never hear the indignant protest of one who is not personally involved. It is very clear why all keep their mouths shut. Either they think the matter is none of their business, or they may not even think so at all. When your "worldly wisdom" is so deep that you are not conscious of having an abundance of it, you are genuinely "worldly-wise."

This is the essence of the essence of how to live in China.

And as for those who have read this advice of mine to the young and disagree with it, I have this answer. You think me foxy. But while my reasoning does reveal that I am foxy — and powerless too — it also reveals the darkness of society. To blame individuals is the safest thing; but if you blame society too, you must stand out and fight. Those who blame individuals for their "worldly wisdom" but will not blame the "world," show even greater "worldly wisdom." If they do this unconsciously, it is much more profound, approaching the very quintessence.

Once a thing is described, it has its limitations, and its quintessence is lost for good. So to talk of the "quintessence of worldly wisdom" is a contradiction in terms. The truth of the quintessence lies in deeds not words; yet just by saying "deeds not words" I have let slip the Truth again, and am further from the quintessence.

It suffices, with all good knowledge, to grasp its significance intuitively.

October 13, 1933

CHARGING

"Pushing" and "kicking" cause one or two casualties only. If you want more, you must "charge."

In its papers of October 13 there was a report from Guiyang of a joint demonstration held by the students of different schools to commemorate the September 18th Incident. The Commissioner of Education, Tan Xing-ge, lost his head and sent troops to occupy the street corners, ordering cars to charge at the students so that a tragedy ensued: two students were killed and over forty wounded. Most of them were from Zheng-yi Primary School, and their average age was ten.

I knew before that generals are often well versed in literature and, while "resting on their lances till dawn," may dispatch telegrams in the old euphuistic style; but now I realize that some of our civil officials have a profound grasp of military strategy too. General Tian Dan sent bulls with torches on their tails to charge the enemy,* but today we use cars instead, and this shows that we are in the twentieth century.

"Charging" is the most efficient method of warfare. How simple it is for a fleet of cars to charge straight ahead, crushing the enemy under their wheels! Charging is most awe-inspiring too. How heroic you feel when you start up and your machine hurtles forward like lightning or the wind, giving your foe no time to get out of the way! The armed police of other lands like to charge

* A general of the state of Qi during the Warring States Period, who defeated the invading Yan army.

372

with hoses, and the Russian tsar used Cossack cavalry — brave deeds, truly! In the foreign concessions of certain cities we can sometimes see tanks manned by foreign troops making the round of the streets — if you aren't on your best behaviour these things will charge you.

Though motor-cars are not ideal for a charge, luckily the enemy were primary school students. It is no use at all riding a jaded donkey on the battlefield, but it can easily canter through a meadow while the rider utters blood-curdling cries — though some people may think this a rather funny sight.

It is rather funny, come to think of it, for children of ten to start a revolt. But in China we have many infant prodigies, and it is quite common for them to start painting at one, write poems at two, go on the stage at seven, join the army at ten, and become a commissar in their early teens. Even a girl of seven or eight can be raped, yet her case is judged as if she were "on the threshold of womanhood."

Besides, if the opponent could resist the charge, that might prove rather awkward for the cars, and the charger might seem less heroic. So it is best to choose a weak opponent. Hooligans bully peasants, foreigners beat up Chinese, and commissioners of education charge primary school students — brave men, well able to defeat a foe!

"Standing up to a charge" used to strike me as empty talk, but now its truth has been proved, and it applies not only to grown-ups but even to children. The time has gone when the "slaughter of innocents" was a crime. I suppose it will not be long before we toss infants in the air and catch them on the tips of our spears for fun.

October 17, 1933

ON WOMEN'S LIBERATION

Confucius said, "Only women and low-class men are hard to keep. If allowed to approach you, they show no respect; if kept at a distance, they complain."* Here women and low-class men are lumped together, but there is no knowing whether this included his own mother or not. Although the later orthodox Confucians have always treated their mothers with a show of respect, those women who are mothers in China are still slighted by all men who are not their sons.

After the 1911 Revolution, in order to have her share of political power, the celebrated Miss Shen Peizhen** kicked over a guard at the entrance to parliament. Only I have a strong suspicion that the guard fell down himself, and that if one of us men had kicked him he would have kicked back several times. But this is one advantage of being a woman. Again, certain married ladies today can stand beside their plutocratic husbands to be photographed with them on docks or in conference halls; or before the launching of some steamship or aircraft they can step forward to smash a bottle of wine. (This may be the prerogative of unmarried ladies: the details are beyond me.) This is another advantage of being a woman. In addition, there are various new professions. Apart from women factory workers, whom the bosses like to employ because their pay is low and

---

* A quotation from the *Analects*.
** A native of Hangzhou who organized the Women's Northern Expeditionary Corps at the time of the 1911 Revolution, she later became an adviser to Yuan Shikai.

they do as they are told, in the case of others, although they are described as "flower vases" we often see the honourable announcement: "You are served by an all-female staff," and this no doubt is just on account of their sex. If men want to soar to such dizzy heights, to rely simply on being masculine will not do: they will have to turn into dogs at the very least.

These are the achievements since the May 4th Movement and the campaign for women's liberation. But we often hear the bitter lamentations of professional women and the gibes of critics at the New Women. By stepping out of their boudoirs into society, they have in fact supplied new material for general gossip and jokes at their expense.

This is because, although in society, women are still "kept" by others. If others "keep" you, you have to allow them to scold you or even insult you. We have seen how Confucius scolded, and know that was because he found women "hard" to "keep," neither keeping them "close" nor keeping them "at a distance" proving entirely satisfactory. This is the complaint of most male supremacists today. It is the affliction of most women too. Until the dividing line between "keeper" and "kept" is done away with, there can be no doing away with these complaints and afflictions.

In this still unreformed society, every single new fashion is just so much window-dressing. In point of fact nothing has really changed. If you take a small bird which has been caged and let it perch on a pole, its status appears to have changed; but actually it is still the plaything of men, at the beck and call of others. This is what is meant by the proverb: Accept a meal and accept orders. So before all women win the same economic rights as men, I regard all fine-sounding titles as empty talk. Of course, there are biological and psychological differences between men and women, as indeed there are between members of the same sex; but their status should be equal. Only after their status is equal shall we have real women and real men and do away with complaints and afflictions.

Before true liberation there will be fighting. I am not saying, however, that women should take up arms like men or suckle their infants with one breast only, leaving the other half of the responsibility to men. All I mean is that we should not rest content with the present temporary situation, but fight unceasingly for liberation in the realm of ideas, the economy and other fields. When society is liberated, we ourselves will be liberated too. But of course it is also necessary to fight against present-day fetters which are exclusively women's.

Never having made a study of women's problems, when constrained to express my opinion on the subject these few idle words are all I have to say.

October 21, 1933

FIRE

When Prometheus stole fire for mankind, he was sent to hell for breaking the laws of Heaven. But apparently when Sui Ren* procured fire from wood by friction he was not found guilty of theft or of destroying sacred private property — in those days trees still had no owners. Sui Ren has been forgotten too, however, and today no offerings are made to him — we find the Chinese sacrifice to the Fire God alone.

The Fire God simply starts fire: he has nothing to do with lamps. As he has his share in all fires, men make offerings to him in the hope that he will do less harm. But do you think he would receive any offerings if he did no harm?

Lighting lamps is too commonplace. Never since ancient times has a famous man won fame for lighting lamps, although five to six thousand years have passed since men learned how to make fire from Sui Ren. Starting a fire is a different proposition. The first emperor of Qin started one, to burn books, not men. Xiang Yu started another when he entered the Tongguan Pass and burned the Efang Palace, not private dwellings (? — further research is needed on this point). A Roman emperor started a fire to burn the common people; and the clergy of the orthodox church in the Middle Ages burned heretics like faggots, sometimes pouring oil over them. All these were heroes of their time, as Hitler is living evidence in this age. Of course offerings must be

---

* A legendary king, said to have discovered fire.

made to such heroes. Especially as this is the age of
evolution, and the Fire God goes from strength to strength
with each new generation.

Thus in parts where they have no electric light, ignor-
ing the fact that this year we should buy native products, all the common folk purchase a little foreign paraffin to light in the evening. But how paltry its dim
yellow rays look on the window paper! No, we cannot
have lamps like this! If we want light, we must ban
this "extravagant" paraffin. It should all be carried into
the fields and poured into tanks, to gurgle and spurt out
in one huge conflagration, burning everything for dozens
of miles around: the crops, the trees and the houses —
especially the straw shacks — till in a twinkling all is
whirling ashes. If this is not enough, there are incen-
diary bombs and sulphur bombs, which can be dropped
from the air and will burn for several days and nights,
like that great fire started in Shanghai on January 28.
Now that really was a great light.

Such is the power of the Fire God. But as a matter
of fact, he will not own up to this. They say that his
function is to protect humble folk; yet if a fire breaks
out, the humble folk are blamed or accused of committing arson in order to break in and steal.

Who knows? That is what famous incendiaries throughout the ages have said, not that men have always believed them.

As all we can see is that lighting lamps is commonplace
whereas starting fires is heroic, lighting lamps is forbidden while offerings are made to incendiaries. You may
have seen a circus where an ox able to plough the fields
is killed in order to feed a tiger — an example of the
"spirit of this age."

November 2, 1933